C000173556

An Illustrated History of the
WELSH HIGHLAND RAILWAY

An Illustrated History of the
WELSH HIGHLAND RAILWAY

Peter Johnson

OPC
Oxford Publishing Co

First published 2002

ISBN 0 86093 565 5

All rights reserved. No part of this book may be reproduced or transmitted in any form or by any means, electronic or mechanical, including photocopying, recording or by any information storage and retrieval system, without permission from the Publisher in writing.

© Peter Johnson 2002

Published by Oxford Publishing Co

an imprint of Ian Allan Publishing Ltd, Hersham, Surrey KT12 4RG

Ian Allan
60th ANNIVERSARY

Printed by Ian Allan Printing Ltd, Hersham, Surrey KT12 4RG

Code: 0208/B1

Front cover painting:
Rhyd Ddu in the summer of 1923, a union of two railways — *Russell* arrives from Dinas as *James Spooner* arrives from Porthmadog. *Original watercolour by David Perrin*

Back cover watercolou:
The WHR's ugly duckling, ex-War Department Baldwin 590, represented during the FR lease period.
Original watercolour by Jonathan Clay

Half title page:
A view that illustrates what appears to be an exceptionally busy time at Rhyd Ddu. *Author's collection*

Title page:
The road crossing at Portmadoc, although technically part of the FR, was one of the distinctive features of WHR operations. Festiniog Fairlie *Merddin Emrys* crosses, wreathed in steam. *Author's collection*

Above:
Beddgelert in 1923; *Russell* and NWNGR stock in original condition. The station bookstall is to the right. *Ian Allan Library*

Opposite:
Happy days; the same scene on 8 August 1935. The railway is on its last legs, the bookstall has gone but the excursionists are carefree. *H. F. Wheeler*

Contents

Introduction

THE construction of a new narrow gauge railway some 25 miles long in the 21st century is proving to be of great interest to public and railway enthusiasts alike. Its remarkable route, from the historic town of Caernarfon through some extremely varied scenery, via urban Waunfawr, with views of the highest mountain in Wales and the tourist honey pot of Beddgelert, not to mention the splendours of the towering Aberglaslyn Pass, using gradients as steep as 1 in 40 and curves as sharp as 198ft radius to bring it to the bustling harbour town of Porthmadog, has always caught the imagination. That this railway is narrow (2ft) gauge and a significant part of it routed through the Snowdonia National Park only adds to the excitement. The prospect of a link to the Festiniog Railway, with trains crossing the former Cambrian line to Pwllheli on the level and then the main road at Porthmadog, generates a further frisson. But this railway, the Welsh Highland, is no ordinary railway.

It was a child of the 1920s, but its origins go back to the earliest days of railways in Wales. The desire to link Porthmadog directly with Caernarfon by rail dates back more than 100 years and the wish to preserve and restore rails to the route more than 40. Throughout, its story is surely the most complicated of any railway.

Historically, the route was an amalgamation, completed in 1923, incorporating the North Wales Narrow Gauge Railways and the Portmadoc, Beddgelert & South Snowdon Railway. The former comprised a main line from Dinas, three miles from Caernarfon, to Rhyd Ddu, with a branch to Bryngwyn serving quarries in the Nantlle Valley. In 1920 this 12 miles of railway was all but moribund. The latter comprised part of the horse-worked Croesor Tramway from Porthmadog with some partially constructed sections of railway around Beddgelert abandoned since 1908.

These independent companies became very closely linked in the early years of the 20th century so here their story is combined and told sequentially, leading up to their absorption into the WHR in 1922. Like its predecessors, the WHR did not have a happy existence and proved to be a triumph of optimism over reality.

A proposal that the railway should be taken over by enthusiasts was first made before World War 2. Despite continuous effort since the 1960s, and in the face of opposition from many sources, it was only in 2000 that the first trains ran on part of the WHR trackbed. In the route's restoration, the former standard gauge trackbed between Dinas and Caernarfon, part of the Carnarvonshire Railway, itself incorporating part of the route of the Nantlle Railway, another horse-worked line, has been added. This fulfils another long-held ambition, to extend the narrow gauge into Caernarfon itself, rather than terminating three miles away.

So, at the time of writing, the revived railway is operating successfully between Caernarfon and Waunfawr, a distance of seven miles. Work is in hand on extending to Rhyd Ddu, although it now looks as though it will be 2003 before the revival of the North Wales Narrow Gauge Railways section is completed.

Thereafter, the hurdle of restoring rails between Rhyd Ddu and Porthmadog has to be overcome. The Snowdonia National Park Authority has already indicated that it will not permit another temporary terminus within the park's boundaries, for fear of generating additional traffic at Beddgelert, the obvious location for such a stop. Funding and constructing some 12 miles of railway with no hope of seeing any return on the investment before it is completed will be an enormous task, quite unlike any previously faced by UK heritage railways.

In the story of the WHR there are many strands, rarely straightforward, with a constant sense of *déjà vu*. It is a fascinating railway with an intriguing history and well deserves the attention it receives. That such attention will not diminish is quite clear.

Welsh Place Names

During most of the period covered by this book many Welsh place names were anglicised. Over the last 40 years or so the Welsh forms have been restored. The archaic forms are used here where most appropriate, including when quoting and in legal titles, the modern form being adopted otherwise. For clarification, the places concerned are:

Bettws Garmon = Betws Garmon
Bettws-y-coed = Betws-y-coed
Carnarvon/Caernarvon = Caernarfon
Portmadoc = Porthmadog
Quellyn = Cwellyn
Waenfawr = Waunfawr
Rhyd Ddu is used when referring to the station throughout, regardless of whether it was known as Snowdon or South Snowdon by the railway.

Abbreviations

FR	Festiniog/Ffestiniog Railway
LNWR	London & North Western Railway
LRC	Light Railway Commission/Light Railway Commissioners
LRO	Light Railway Order
MTRS	Moel Tryfan Rolling Stock Company Ltd
NWNGR	North Wales Narrow Gauge Railways
NWPT	North Wales Power & Traction Co
PBSLR	Portmadoc, Beddgelert & Snowdon Light Railway
PBSSR	Portmadoc, Beddgelert & South Snowdon Railway
PCBTR	Portmadoc, Croesor & Beddgelert Tram Railway Co
PRO	Public Record Office
SBLR	Snowdon & Bettws Light Railway
TWO	Transport & Works Order
WHR	Welsh Highland Railway
WHR(P)	Welsh Highland Railway (1964) Co/Welsh Highland Railway Ltd (Porthmadog)

Opposite:
Moel Tryfan at Dinas in North Wales Narrow Gauge Railways days, before continuous brakes were fitted in 1894. The function of the covered wagons alongside is not known. *National Library of Wales*

Acknowledgements

Being persuaded in 1995 to produce draft versions, eventually some 15 in all, of the then proposed WHR Transport & Works Order brought me much closer to the revival of the WHR than I ever thought likely. Similarly, the request to produce this, a second book on the railway, has brought me closer to its history still, especially in the light of discoveries made at the Public Record Office (PRO) in Kew and at the Gwynedd Archives in Caernarfon.

At the PRO I found much of interest in Treasury, Treasury Solicitor's, Board of Trade, Ministry of Transport, Ministry of Town & Country Planning, Ministry of Housing & Local Government and Welsh Office files, with material dating back to the 19th century shedding light on many aspects of the WHR's development and its demise. The availability of the PRO's index on the Internet saved some waiting time, but not much.

The Carnarvonshire County Council files, at Caernarfon, added enlightenment on the WHR's relationship with the local authorities and the attempts to find a way to wind it up.

A slightly tongue-in-cheek approach to the office of the Official Receiver, now part of the Insolvency Service, resulted in an invitation to examine some 30 files dealing with WHR matters since 1941. I am grateful to Mark Boyall of that office for his assistance.

The material viewed has allowed much of the WHR's story to be told by reference to original source material. The outcome has been a revelation on what was previously understood about many aspects of the railway's history. As time passes it has become quite clear, however, that some answers are still out there waiting to be discovered. The amount of material seen has also allowed me to avoid duplicating parts of my earlier book on the WHR, and to correct its identified errors. It has not eliminated the risk of errors or misunderstandings, however, and any that remain must be laid firmly at my door.

Against, it seems, all the odds a number of 'new' photographs have come to light and been made available for reproduction here. Thanks are due to: John Keylock and his friend David Allan, custodians of the largest-known collection of WHR-related historical photographs; both are long-standing supporters of attempts to revive the railway and without their assistance, compilation of this book would have been immeasurably more difficult. David Allan, who also supplied fine trackbed photographs of his own taking over many years, was a little surprised to find them being considered historic for the purposes of this book. The Railway Postcard Collectors' Club's Tony Harden, who kindly loaned cards from his own collection and allowed me first trawl through a substantial collection he had purchased just before the book was completed, provided much invaluable material.

Thanks also to Adrian Gray, the FR's archivist, and Wyn Hobson for supplying photographs, as did W. John Brown, whose father ran Beddgelert's Prince Llewelyn Hotel in the 1920s and 1930s and was a trade customer of the WHR; and Roger Kidner, founder of the Oakwood Press, who graciously gave approval for the use of some of his photographs.

My good friend Peter Jarvis guided me through the intricacies of the PRO's systems, and with his wife Su, was ever generous with hospitality. John Keylock also gave access to the 'Snowdon Ranger hoard' and other materials in his possession. John's enthusiasm for what he calls the 'silly railway in the Principality' is boundless, as is his willingness to share information with researchers. Welsh Highland Railway Ltd gave permission for the reproduction of the drawing of *Russell*. John Hopkins drew attention to the hitherto unknown NWNGR deviation from the deposited plans, and Derek Lystor discovered the Glanyrafon quarry records in Scotland.

Thanks are also due to David Perrin and Jonathan Clay for providing creative material for the cover and to John Sreeves for skilfully producing maps and plans at short notice.

Adrian Gray responded to the challenge of offering an opinion on the script just before Christmas, making a greatly appreciated contribution. Crown copyright is reserved for illustrations sourced from the PRO and the Ordnance Survey.

On the reconstruction, Roland Doyle and his staff, paid and volunteer, have always made me welcome and I thank them for the time taken to explain what was going on and for participating in the occasional photograph. Roland's assistant Jan Woods' ready offer of refreshments during visits to Dinas was/is always appreciated.

At this point I wish to pay tribute to two former editors of *Railway World* magazine, both regrettably no longer with us. Some 20 years ago Mike Harris, during his first incarnation with the magazine, not only commissioned and published the first article that I wrote for the general railway press but also submitted my first book proposal.

His successor, Handel Kardas, who was to become a good friend, later commissioned me to contribute a bi-monthly half-page narrow gauge railway news column to the magazine. It did not work out like that, of course, for we soon found that the narrow gauge world generated much more news than we forecast. Handel was a keen supporter of the WHR project and missed the opening to Waunfawr by only a few weeks, although he did manage to ride over the incomplete route on a works train.

It goes without saying that without the support of Mike and Handel my career in railway publishing would have been considerably diminished and I hereby acknowledge the valuable contribution they made to it.

Peter Johnson
Leicester
June 2002

— 1 —
Development of the Route
1863-1914

THE most significant strand of the Caernarfon-Porthmadog railway route was that built by the North Wales Narrow Gauge Railways (NWNGR). This was masterminded by Charles Easton Spooner, the Festiniog Railway's secretary and engineer from 1856 until 1887. His motivation was probably two-fold. He owned a slate quarry that came to be served by the Bryngwyn branch and was probably trying to maintain a narrow gauge monopoly on slate traffic in the face of competition from the LNWR. Or perhaps he was trying to create something out of nothing that would appear to be of such value to the LNWR that he would be bought out at a substantial price. The Euston-based company's acquisition of the Carnarvonshire Railway and its running powers into Portmadoc in 1870, and the later operation of 'The Welshman' express from Euston to Portmadoc via Afon Wen, could well have come about in response to Spooner's politicking.

Below:
One of the NWNGR's single Fairlies, *Moel Tryfan*, receives attention at Dinas. Attached to the locomotive's power bogie, just in front of the cylinder, is a funnel and a tube for sanding the rail. The train has no continuous brake. *National Library of Wales*

Parliament's response was severe. Proposals for eight railways were submitted, the objectives being:

- To link Portmadoc with Corwen, using part of the Croesor & Portmadoc Railway, and then via Beddgelert, Capel Curig and Bettws-y-coed (Nos 1-3).
  - A branch to the LNWR station at Bettws-y-coed (No 4).
  - A branch to Penmachno from Railway No 2 (No 5).
  - A branch from the LNWR (Carnarvonshire Railway) near Llanwnda to Bryngwyn (No 6).
- A branch from Railway No 6 to Rhyd Ddu (No 7).
- A branch from Pwllheli to Porthdinllaen (No 8).

Of these only Railways Nos 1, 6 and 7 gained approval, in 1872. Railway No 1 (truncated to Bettws-y-coed) was defined as the General Undertaking, and Railways Nos 6 and 7 as the Moel Tryfan Undertaking. The former was to be capitalised at £150,000, the latter at £66,000, both in £10 shares. An amount equal to a third of the capital was permitted to be borrowed on mortgage when all the capital had been subscribed and half of it paid up. Capital and revenue accounts were to be kept separately. The company incorporated by the Act was legally plural, The North Wales Narrow Gauge Railways Co, because there was, then, more

than one undertaking but the final 's' was often omitted on the company's own letterheads and even on the company's official seal.

The Act identified the promoters as Livingston Thompson (a director of the Festiniog Railway), Sir Llewelyn Turner, James Hewitt Oliver and Hugh Beaver Roberts, owner of the Croesor Tramway, to be encountered later. The gauge was defined as 'two feet'; it could be increased at any time, but not exceeding 4ft 8½in, subject to receiving Board of Trade approval.

The company started with the Moel Tryfan Undertaking. As three early directors and the company's engineer owned quarries in the Bryngwyn area nothing more need be said to explain this preference. First a contract was let for its construction, on 23 December 1872, then the company issued a prospectus and on 23 April 1873 it entered into an agreement with Roberts whereby he undertook to operate the railway for 21 years on lease. The NWNGR (Lease) Act 1873 confirmed this arrangement. Roberts was expected to cover the 6% debenture interest, the company's administrative expenses, 6% dividend on share capital and a proportion of any profits made additional to the total of those sums.

If this wasn't remarkable enough, Roberts was expected to have all locomotives (except shunting engines) constructed to Fairlie's patents, paying a specified royalty of £300 per engine. He was allocated £10,000 by the company for the purchase of locomotives and rolling stock. The stock was to be returned to the company on expiry of the lease, or on determination if sooner, to the full £10,000

Below:
For reasons as yet undetermined, the NWNGR was not built according to the deposited plans in the Plas-y-nant area. The plan shows significant differences beyond the limits of deviation.

value. That is, with no recognition being made of depreciation or wear and tear.

Construction was started in May 1873, with completion of both lines being anticipated within 12 months. There appears to have been a lack of communication between railway and contractor, with the contractor losing interest and slowing down work as payments from the company got into arrears, indicative of problems with fundraising, although the contractor did receive £40,000 of the contracted £56,000.

In 1874, work ceased and the contractor started to remove track materials he had bought. The company went to arbitration, unexpectedly losing. Unsettled by the delays, and likely taking time to ponder upon the wisdom of the contract he had signed, Roberts repudiated his lease. The company did not recognise his right to do so but pragmatically accepted that it was unable to deal with him from a position of strength.

Little more progress was made by the contractor, who succeeded with a further arbitration award against the company, and in August 1876 a new contractor was appointed. By an Act of 1876 the company abandoned its General Undertaking, presumably being unable to raise any capital for it, and gained approval for further funds raising an additional £40,000 in ordinary or preferential shares, or both, the company having declared that the Moel Tryfan Undertaking's capital, and authorised borrowing of £22,000, had all been spent.

As an aside, the General Undertaking's promotion had apparently prompted the advancement of the 2ft gauge Ruthin & Cerrig-y-drudion Railway to connect with the line between Bettws-y-coed and Corwen that had been rejected in the 1872 Act. This scheme gained Parliamentary approval in the 1876 session, just as the NWNGR abandoned the General Undertaking completely! Spooner was engaged as consultant engineer on an occasional basis but took no further part.

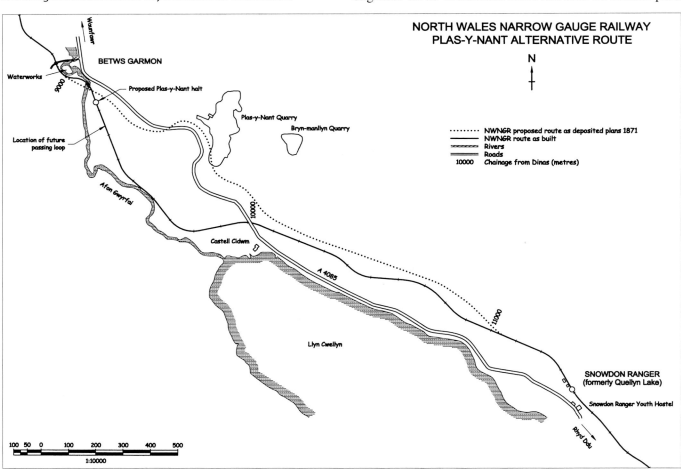

NORTH WALES NARROW GAUGE RAILWAY
PLAS-Y-NANT ALTERNATIVE ROUTE

N

BETWS GARMON

Waterworks

Proposed Plas-y-Nant halt

Location of future passing loop

Afon Gwyrfai

Plas-y-Nant Quarry

Bryn-manllyn Quarry

.... NWNGR proposed route as deposited plans 1871
——— NWNGR route as built
≈≈≈≈ Rivers
═══ Roads
10000 Chainage from Dinas (metres)

Castell Cidwm

A 4085

Llyn Cwellyn

SNOWDON RANGER
(formerly Quellyn Lake)

Snowdon Ranger Youth Hostel

Rhyd Ddu

100 50 0   100   200   300   400   500
1:10000

An extension from Cerrig-y-drudion to Bettws-y-coed was proposed in 1878, using the NWNGR's proposed route, when there was contact with the Tramways Corporation, then involved with the Croesor Tramway. Some 5½ miles of earthworks, not all within the limits of deviation, were constructed in 1879, but the company was without the skills and resources to complete its undertaking and it was abandoned by an Act of 1884.

The NWNGR's new contractor made good progress and the line to Bryngwyn was brought into use for goods and mineral traffic during 1877, and model by-laws deposited with the Board of Trade were signed by company secretary Joseph Oldham on 6 July. On the line to Rhyd Ddu the track had reached Quellyn Lake and was being used for goods services. Following inspections by the Board of Trade, both lines were approved for passenger traffic, but only to

Above:
A typical NWNGR train heading for Plas-y-nant and Rhyd Ddu. The NWNGR regularly ran its mixed trains with the goods wagons next to the locomotive, instead of the carriage(s); presumably doing so made shunting easier, but it failed to meet with the Board of Trade's approval. *WHR collection*

Below:
Looking towards Quellyn Lake and Dinas from near Rhyd Ddu. *Francis Frith*

Rhostryfan on the Bryngwyn branch, from 28 January 1878. Five months later, the main line was extended to Snowdon Ranger, a distance of nearly one mile further, and approval gained for passenger use. These definitions of main and branch lines were a reversal of those in the 1872 Act.

Fund-raising was clearly a problem for the NWNGR.

In 1879 it entered into an agreement with the Glanyrafon Quarry, near Rhyd Ddu, whereby the quarry's proprietors would subscribe for 80 £10 preference shares in exchange for certain rights. The money was to be paid in four monthly instalments from September 1879, provided that the last only became payable when the railway was completed and opened for goods and passenger traffic.

The initial objective of the contract was to complete the railway to a point where a junction could be made with the quarry's internal tramway, the target date being 31 January 1880. When the NWNGR was completed to Rhyd Ddu the quarry company would contribute half the cost, not exceeding £50, of any signalling required at their siding.

In return for the investment the NWNGR would stop one train in each direction at the siding daily, except Sunday, Christmas Day and Good Friday, and on prior notice having been given to the guard, for the benefit and convenience of the quarry owners, its agents and workmen; run workmen's trains, or suitable public trains, timed to arrive, from Dinas, at the quarry between 06.30 and 07.00 in summer and 07.00 and 07.30 in winter and to leave between 17.45 and 18.15,

provided the quarry guaranteed a minimum of 40 3rd class passengers travelling daily from Waenfawr and beyond. Workmen's tickets were to be made available at a single fare for the return journey.

The agreement, signed by John Owen and Edward Humphrey Owen for the quarry and James Cholmeley Russell (director) and R. H. Livesey (secretary) for the NWNGR, was valid for 21 years and subject to extension if the quarry's lease was renewed.

Despite this influx of capital it was to be 14 May 1881 before the line to Rhyd Ddu was opened. There is as yet no indication of an earlier goods service to Glanyrafon. A hand-written notice of 'rates for goods & mineral traffic between Dinas and undermentioned stations', signed by Livesey, was dated May 1881; stations were listed as Tryfan Junction, Rhostryfan, Bryngwyn, Waenfawr, Bettws Garmon, Snowdon and Rhyd Ddu; minerals could be despatched to 'top of incline', was inserted later. Packages could be sent to 'Moeltryfan (for slate quarries)'. The debentures issued under the terms of the agreement were issued on 20 February 1880 (80) and 12 October 1881 (5).

Right:
Dinas LNWR with a train bound for Afon Wen. The NWNGR station buildings are on the right, overlapping the boundary line between the two railways. The board on the left reads 'Change here for narrow gauge line'. At this point the Nantlle Railway had run to the right of the wall on the left of the picture.
Author's collection

Far right:
Dinas station.
Crown copyright

Below:
Moel Tryfan and train at Rhyd Ddu. The second carriage from the left is a six-wheeled Cleminson vehicle.
Author's collection

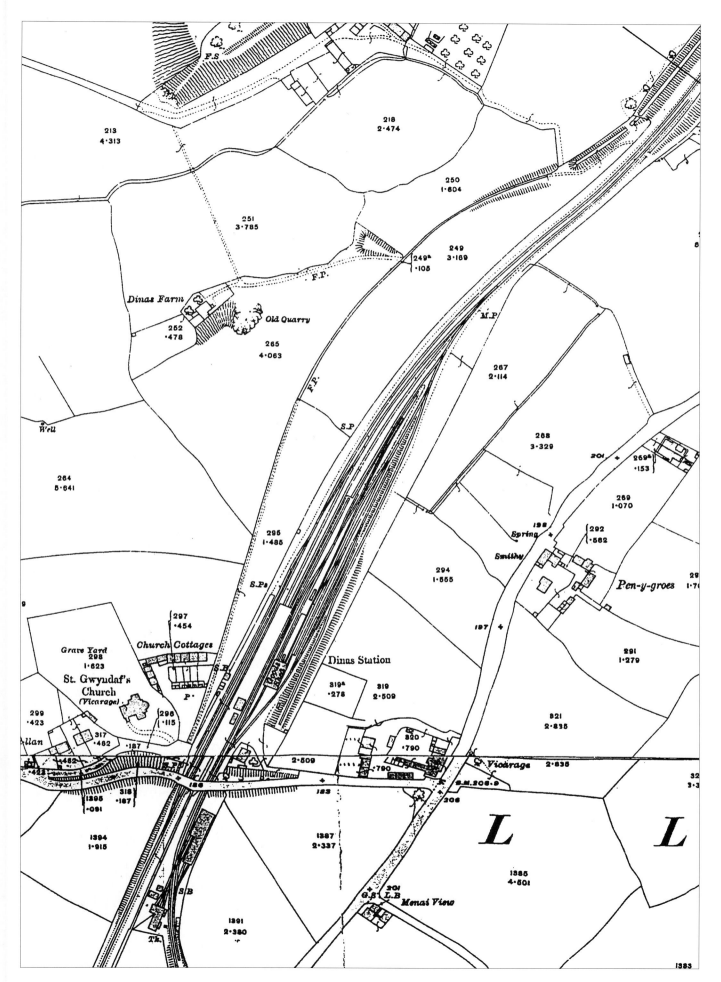

13

Station Plans

All drawings Crown Copyright

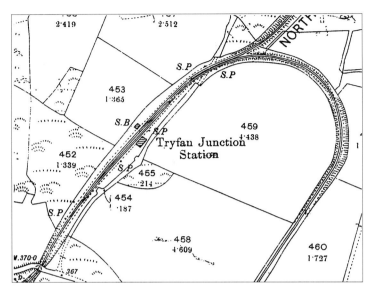

Tryfan Junction station

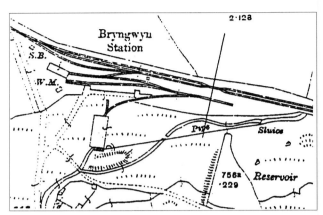

Bryngwyn station

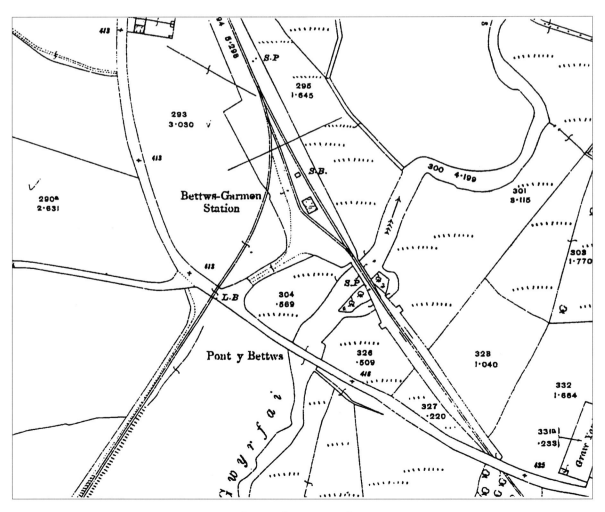

Bettws Garmon station

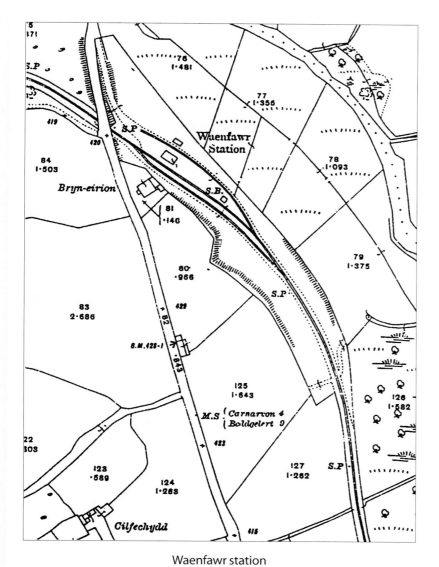

Waenfawr station

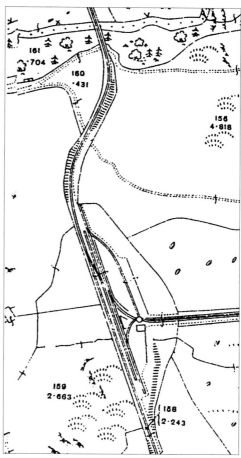

Glanyrafon sidings

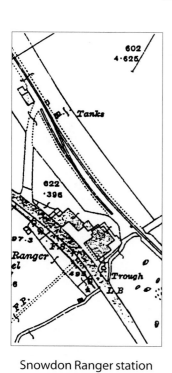

Snowdon Ranger station

Rhostryfan station

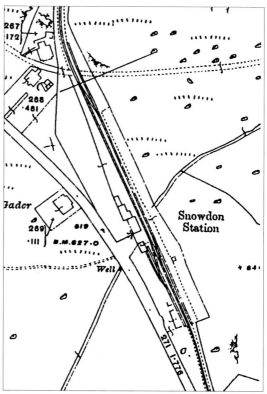

Rhyd Ddu station

Right:
Connecting services for Beddgelert seen at Rhyd Ddu. Note the stagecoach on the right. *Gwynedd Archives*

Right:
The section of the NWNGR seen here on 26 August 2001 was financed by the Glanyrafon Quarry, whose slate tips are seen above the trackbed. *Author*

Below:
At Rhyd Ddu, an exceptionally long train waits to return to Dinas. *Hudson's Series*

Above:
Snowdon Ranger at Rhyd Ddu, c1910. The Pickering brake carriage was one of two delivered in 1908. Presumably the box of Tate's cube sugar on the ground, left, was in transit.
Commercial postcard/A. J. Harden collection

Recent works on the trackbed in connection with its reopening have revealed a lack of drainage provision on parts of this section; surely an indication that funds were still in short supply during its building? The major structure on this part of the NWNGR, indeed the largest on the railway, was the bridge across the Afon Treweunydd ravine near the quarry, 8 miles from Dinas. Originally known as the Dingle Bridge but more recently as Glanyrafon Viaduct, despite not being a viaduct, it is a substantial iron structure. The span is nearly 100ft, some 50ft above the river, and the time and effort required for its erection would have been responsible for the final delay in completing the railway.

These works completed the NWNGR's Moel Tryfan Undertaking. Despite all its earlier, and later, ambitions nothing more was achieved by the railway. Route expansion occurred only after the NWNGR company had ceased to exist and the impetus had come from elsewhere.

At Llanwnda a joint station was established with the LNWR and named Dinas Junction, the LNWR's Llanwnda station continuing in use by that name. An agreement between the two companies on the use of sidings and location of facilities was completed on 16 March 1877. When times were good the main traffic was slate from the Bryngwyn Quarries bound for Caernarvon, although the additional cost of transhipment at Dinas Junction for the short onward journey to the port was incurred.

According to the company the railway climbed at 1 in 47 from Dinas to Tryfan Junction (2¼ miles), then ran through the Gwyrfai Valley, 'at comparatively easy gradients', to Waenfawr (4 miles) and Bettws Garmon (5 miles), then to Llyn Cwellyn where the line climbed at 1 in 76 to Snowdon (7¼ miles) and Glanyrafon Quarry siding (8¼ miles) before the gradients varied from 1 in 79 to 1 in 290, with curves of 3½ chains, for the final section to Rhyd Ddu (9½ miles), situated on the watershed separating the Gwyrfai Valley from the Glaslyn Valley, leading to Beddgelert and Portmadoc.

The Bryngwyn branch left the main line at Tryfan Junction and doubled back on itself before ascending at 1 in 41 to Rhostryfan (1 mile), and reaching Bryngwyn (2½ miles) on gradients of between 1 in 41 and 1 in 35. The railway owned and operated the incline which extended beyond Bryngwyn station, connecting it to the slate quarries' tramways.

As time passed, some NWNGR stations were renamed. Snowdon became Snowdon Ranger from July 1881 and Quellyn Lake from January 1893. Rhyd Ddu was renamed Snowdon from January 1893 and in WHR days became South Snowdon.

The railway published timetable guidebooks for tourists, making much of Rhyd Ddu's proximity to the summit of Snowdon. Other features promoted were 'Elephant Mountains', near Plas-y-nant, Quellyn Lake, Bettws Garmon Valley and Nant Mill waterfall.

Quite why Beddgelert, with a population of 1,423 in 1871 and only 3½ miles from Rhyd Ddu, and an obvious link with the General Undertaking, was never targeted at this stage is not known. As it was, the railway benefited from a mix of passenger, agricultural and mineral traffic, although, as will be seen, not in any substantial amount. Rhyd Ddu station's location by the start of the shortest walking route to Snowdon summit was to bring tourists to the line, and horse-drawn road vehicles provided the link to Beddgelert, the connections being included in the railway's timetable.

Despite Roberts having held his lease for only a year, and then some three years before any trains ran, his brief tenure still had an impact on the railway's future, for he had ordered locomotives and rolling stock. The company itself took over the orders for carriages and wagons, paying for them by instalments. Another solution was found for the locomotives, presumably because the company had insufficient resources to fund them directly.

The Moel Tryfan Rolling Stock Co Ltd (MTRS) was established in December 1878 to 'purchase . . . the locomotives . . . and rolling stock now in use by the NWNG Railways Co'; seven partners, including Russell, had capitalised it to the sum of £10,000. It appears that Russell had completed the purchase of at least the 1875-built locomotives and some other rolling stock, instead of Roberts, and had been hiring it to the company. He sold it to MTRS for £3,630. Russell was owed nearly £1,000 by the company in respect of hiring fees, and that debt was assigned to MTRS also. MTRS promptly sued for the arrears and succeeded in putting the company into receivership, with Russell appointed as receiver.

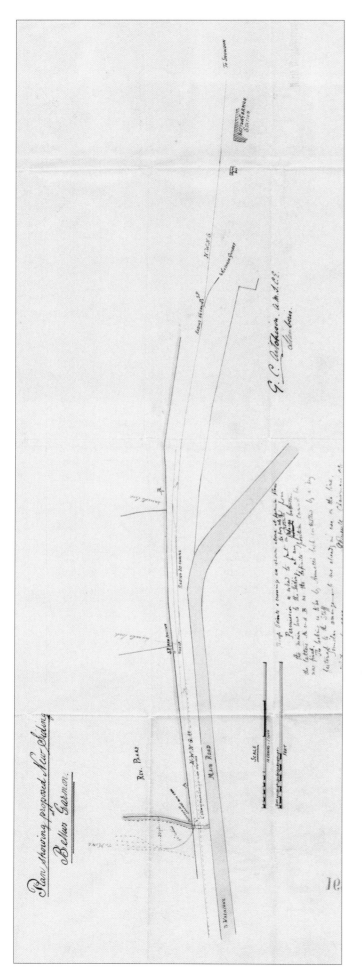

Russell was to influence the fortunes, or otherwise, of the NWNGR until his death in 1911. He became chairman in 1879.

Having got the railway operating, the financial position did not improve as it might have done, for the slate trade, on which so much depended, was in a state of depression. The loss of the main market at a time critical to a railway's performance will be encountered again before the end of this book.

In 1880, a debenture issue totalling £50,000 was approved to eliminate the company's debt and to acquire the locomotives and rolling stock from MTRS. MTRS was wound up in 1889 and dissolved in 1894 with £39,593 of the debentures to its credit. The railway remained in receivership.

Traffic was improved by 1882, when Russell was reporting increasing business in the carriage of slate, coal and lime. On the passenger side a decline in 3rd class passengers was accompanied by an increase in those travelling 1st and 2nd class. Extra trains ran on Saturdays, but the railway never ran on Sundays. The railway had a bad record for reportable incidents, both derailments and collisions. In two cases, in 1878 and 1901, staff members were killed.

Regardless of the indebtedness, the NWNGR was soon returning to Parliament, in 1885 obtaining the North Wales Narrow Gauge Railways (Extensions, &c) Act. This provided for a deviation avoiding the Bryngwyn incline and an extension from Dinas to Caernarvon. The need to work the slate traffic, the railway's main source of business, over the Bryngwyn incline was a hindrance; the railway and its customers would have benefited significantly had it been bypassed.

The Caernarvon extension was designed to avoid the break of gauge at Dinas; the line would have terminated opposite the castle, 'near the boat-house in the occupation of the Carnarvon Rowing Club'.

The use of Crown Lands at the incline summit was permitted by a 998-year lease, annual rental of £5 being payable — the Official Receiver was still paying this rent on behalf of the WHR, in receivership, until the FR acquired the assets in 1999. In recognition of the receiver's interest in the NWNGR these extensions were to be maintained distinctly from the Moel Tryfan Undertaking, and known as the Carnarvon and Bryngwyn Extensions Undertaking. This Undertaking was to be capitalised at £28,000, with powers to borrow further sums on mortgage.

Neither of these lines was built despite an extension of time being obtained by an Act of 1890. The Act also sanctioned the issuing of £10,000 in debentures. These would redeem £6,000 existing debentures and pay for continuous brakes, additional rolling stock, a telegraph/telephone system, turntables, additional buildings, sheds, signals and 'other matters and things for the permanent improvement of the Moel Tryfan Undertaking'. Installation of Westinghouse brakes was completed by 1894, at which time the last of eight new carriages funded by the 1890 debentures was delivered. There were never any turntables.

A passenger timetable for 1893 allowed 50 minutes between Dinas and Rhyd Ddu and 15 minutes from Tryfan Junction to Bryngwyn. Connections between the LNWR and the NWNGR were as short as one minute! At Tryfan Junction most trains had a connection for Bryngwyn. Fares were quoted from Dinas and Caernarvon. 'Amateur photographers' were solicited with the exhortation that they would 'be delighted with the views obtainable along this popular route to Snowdon and Beddgelert'.

Left:
There were several mineral lines connected to the NWNGR and WHR at different times. The Board of Trade received this plan when a line was built between Bettws Garmon and Treflan slate quarry in 1907. It was drawn by Aitchison and signed by him and Russell. *PRO*

Apart from its link with the LNWR at Dinas, the NWNGR operated in isolation, a situation that started to change from the 1890s as others began to take an interest in it. From this point most of what happened to affect the railway was as a result of the activities of outsiders.

The Portmadoc, Beddgelert & Rhyd Ddu Railway was first proposed to link the FR to the NWNGR in 1891, when an intention to promote an Act of Parliament was announced. Nothing happened until 1897, however, when a Light Railway Order (LRO) application was lodged by Richard Davies, Robert Isaacs and J. William Jones, Portmadoc businessmen. Their 1ft 11½in gauge, 11½-mile-long steam railway was estimated to cost £24,720.

The application was withdrawn due to objections by some county council members to proposals that the council should give financial support to the project, but two sets of plans were produced, the first with a route starting on the Gorseddau Railway formation opposite the Queen's Hotel at Portmadoc and running parallel to the Croesor Tramway before diverting to the abandoned formation of the standard gauge 1866 Beddgelert Railway. Reaching Beddgelert via a 280yd tunnel in the Aberglaslyn Pass and a river crossing lower than that later built at Bryn-y-felin, the route climbed to Rhyd Ddu via a series of reverse curves, including five of two chains (132ft) radius, on gradients as steep as 1 in 41. This route stayed to the east of Pitt's Head and dog-legged across the road to join the NWNGR at the south end of Rhyd Ddu station.

The second set of plans incorporated the Croesor Tramway into the route, starting at Portmadoc Harbour, with a spur serving the Queen's Hotel terminus, before heading off to Beddgelert from a point in the locality of the later Croesor Junction.

In May 1898 Davies, together with A. Bromurch and D. Morris, submitted an application for the Portmadoc, Beddgelert & Snowdon Light Railway (PBSLR). This railway used the Croesor route referred to above and was also estimated to cost £24,720. The promoters intended to use their LRO to gain powers to purchase the Croesor, then allegedly disused, but the application was rejected by the Light Railway Commissioners (LRC). They felt that they had no powers to authorise the sale and transfer of a railway operating under Parliamentary sanction.

The NWNGR then submitted, in November 1898, its own application for an extension to Beddgelert, terminating near the Royal Goat Hotel and with no intention of going further. From Rhyd Ddu the 4½-mile railway was level or rising slightly for nearly a mile but the remainder

Above:
Internal correspondence — Aitchison's memo allowed D. O. Jones at Dinas to keep his traffic revenue records up to date. *Author's collection*

Below:
An invoice form used for internal accounting in 1910. Notice that the cash breakdown includes gold currency. *Author's collection*

fell 426ft towards Beddgelert with a succession of tight curves, up to four chains radius, on gradients varying between 1 in 45 and 1 in 42. The proposed Beddgelert station site was criticised by the Ministry, being on less than 200ft of level ground at the foot of the incline and itself on a four-chain curve. Engineers James W. Szlumper and William W. Szlumper signed the estimate of expense totalling £11,496.

Charles Breese and William George, who were to participate in the WHR story some 20 years later, were somehow involved in the PBSLR scheme. In April 1899 they were party to an agreement reached with the NWNGR, whereby they agreed not to compete with the NWNGR scheme provided the latter raised the site of its proposed Beddgelert station by 5ft to facilitate a junction with any subsequent railway from Portmadoc, and granted running powers to Rhyd Ddu.

The LRC held an inquiry into the NWNGR scheme at Caernarvon on 16 December 1899, a Saturday. The Commissioners were told that the extension capital would be kept separate from that of the Moel Tryfan Undertaking and that the NWNGR would work the line for 60% of its revenue. As the NWNGR had been generating an income of £7 10s (£7.50) per mile per week, the extension ought to produce £1,700 annually on the same basis, 40% of which would pay 5-6% interest on its capital.

At the 1891 census Beddgelert's population had fallen to 672. It was presently rising, it was claimed, due to the existence of quarries and mines although copper mines had closed due to transport difficulties which it was hoped the railway would alleviate. Glanyrafon, the largest quarry in the locality, employed 500 men, 30 of them living in Beddgelert and who could be expected to use the railway daily.

The North Wales Narrow Gauge Railways (Beddgelert Light Railway Extension) Order was made on 3 August 1900. The Order specified that rails should weigh at least 41½lb per yard and that check rails should be used on curves of less than three chains radius. It was extremely detailed on the fixings to be used on flat-bottom rail.

Despite a special general meeting on 16 April 1901 to pass

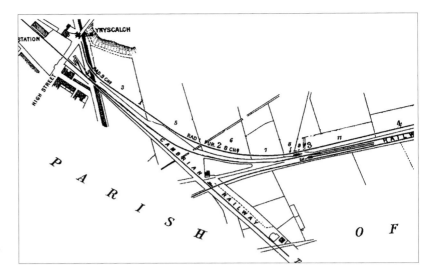

Above:
An extract from the Portmadoc, Beddgelert & Rhyd Ddu Railway's deposited plans. It shows the proposed terminus on the Gorseddau formation opposite the Queen's Hotel, later adopted by the PBSSR. *Author's collection*

the special resolutions necessary to bring the extension undertaking into effect, there is no clear evidence that any capital was raised for it or that any work was carried out. Pre-World War 1 construction to the south of Rhyd Ddu and around Pitt's Head is often attributed to the NWNGR, but is more likely to have been carried out under PBSSR auspices.

The next stage of developing the Portmadoc-Caernarvon route came about with creation of the Portmadoc, Beddgelert & South Snowdon Railway (PBSSR), authorised by Act of Parliament in 1901. The bill was sponsored by the North Wales & District Light Railway & Electric Power Syndicate Ltd, an organisation registered in 1900. The syndicate had applied for the Pwllheli & Nevin LRO in May 1900 (the application was withdrawn), and the Pwllheli, Nevin & Porth Dinlleyn LRO in November 1900 (the application was approved following a public inquiry, but was later withdrawn).

The PBSSR engineers were Bennett & Ward Thomas of Manchester and Alfred M. Fowler of Westminster. The solicitor was Evan R. Davies of Pwllheli, a name of some significance

Right:
Pont Aberglaslyn; the railway was tunnelled through the bluff in the middle of the picture. It was to preserve the view from the bridge that objections were made to the PBSSR's proposals, although it is difficult to see how any railway could have been seen through the trees. *FR Archives*

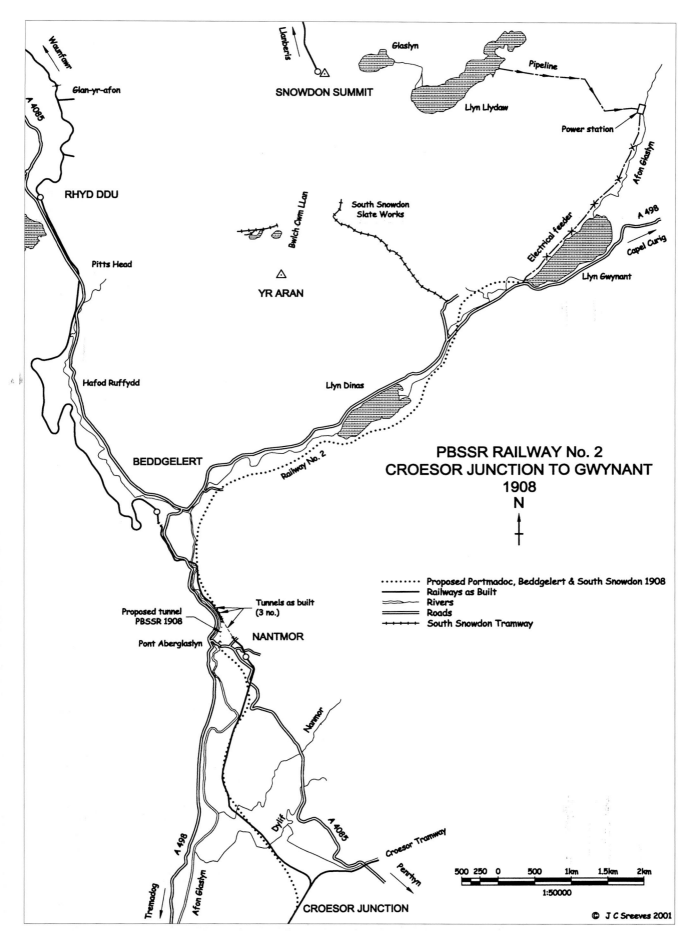

Above:
The PBSSR's proposed route between Croesor Junction and Llyn Gwynant.

Above:
Construction work in Aberglaslyn Pass, *c*1904.
The temporary bridge has rails for spoil removal.
John Pritchard/Gwynedd Archives

Far right:
Cwm Dyli power station, still generating on 16 April 2001.
It was the only one of the PBSSR's 1901 proposals to be completed.
Author

Below:
The lower incline to South Snowdon, Nant Gwynant, 6 May 2001.
The PBSSR would have passed in front of the buildings here,
terminating off the picture to the right. *Author*

later in this story. He remained involved with the PBSSR, on 24 February 1902 asking the FR's manager, J. S. Hughes, if the FR would use electricity for 'lighting or any other purpose' in order that the PBSSR could produce estimates of likely revenue — were there no revenue estimates before the Act was obtained? Hughes' response is unrecorded.

The estimates reveal an intention to build a line from Portmadoc to Borth-y-gest, an 1865 objective of the Croesor & Port Madoc Railway. However, the 1901 Act authorised only the following:

Purchase of the Portmadoc, Croesor & Beddgelert Tram Railway Co (PCBTR) for £10,000 within one year and the dissolution of the PCBTR; use of the Parliamentary section of the Croesor Tramway by passengers as well as

by goods and mineral traffic; construction of two railways, No 1, 5 furlongs 1 chain long, from Pen-y-mount, parallel to the standard gauge Cambrian siding, to a location on the former Gorseddau Railway, opposite the Queen's Hotel at Portmadoc, No 2, seven miles long, commencing at a junction with the PCBTR three miles from Portmadoc and terminating near Llyn Gwynant; the undertaking of agreements with any or either of the Cambrian, FR, NWNGR and the Snowdon Mountain Railways; the supply of electricity to Portmadoc, Criccieth and Beddgelert and the working of the railway by electricity.

Railway No 1 was estimated at £8,004, refurbishing the Croesor Tramway at £39,413 and Railway No 2 at £75,407, these prices including electrification. Capitalisation was set at £270,000 in 54,000 £5 shares, with a further £60,000 borrowing sanctioned, supplemented by an additional £30,000, in share subscriptions or loans, from four local authorities, to be repaid within 40 years.

Seven years were allowed for building the railways. Railway No 1 would have given the line a public face by the main road opposite the Queen's Hotel, near to the Cambrian Railways' station. Railway No 2 would have served the power station and South Snowdon quarry. There would have been exchange facilities with the FR and, according to the deposited plans, stations at Portmadoc, Pont Croesor, either end of the Aberglaslyn tunnel, Beddgelert, Llyn Dinas and Llyn Gwynant. The PBSSR was forbidden to tip debris or rubbish on the banks of, or into, the Glaslyn in the Aberglaslyn Pass without the sanction of the Lord Lieutenant. These requirements, with the extended tunnel referred to hereafter, were early examples of enforced environmental protection.

The power station was located at Cwm Dyli, separated from railway No 2's terminus by an overhead electrical feeder. It was to take water from Llyn Llydaw, a lake of about 100 acres at 1,400ft above sea level.

Objectors, including the National Trust, succeeded in extending the length of the Aberglaslyn tunnel from the 270yd of the deposited plans, to 700yd, to conceal the railway from observers at Pont Aberglaslyn, the promoters agreeing to the change, estimated to cost £3,000, without consulting its engineers to secure an unopposed reading in the House of Lords.

Having said that it was satisfied with the Bill in the Lords, the Trust, with the Commons Preservation Society, objected, contrary to normal procedure, to the third reading in the Commons. This time the objections were to the high-pressure water pipes and culverts in Cwm Dyli that would 'destroy two waterfalls in the cwm and disfigure it. The landscape of Llyn Llydaw will be permanently injured.' It seems that the Trust had concentrated its efforts on the rail section of the bill and had overlooked the power generation aspects of it. Others said that the population was too small to justify the scheme and that coal generation of electricity in Portmadoc would be better.

The PBSSR later claimed that it had organised its own Parliamentary whip to ensure the bill's success in the Commons! David Lloyd George spoke for the railway during the third reading, saying the Trust should have raised the objection in the Lords.

The Gorseddau Railway was at this time abandoned; from 1856/7 it had been a non-statutory 3ft gauge horse tramway, converted to 2ft gauge with Parliamentary powers obtained in 1872. Falling out of use in the 1880s, part of it survived at Portmadoc to give access to the Moel-y-gest Quarry and a stonemason's yard.

The Croesor Tramway was a 2ft gauge horse tramway built privately in 1864 to link quarries in the remote Croesor Valley with Portmadoc. The valley lies north of and parallel to the Vale of Ffestiniog. High and impossibly steep ground prevented rail links being established with the FR, on the opposite side of the Moelwyns.

The tramway's proprietor was Hugh Beaver Roberts, already encountered via his involvement with the NWNGR, a successful solicitor practising in Bangor. He had interests in several North Wales quarries; in the Croesor Valley he was also the landlord of several of them.

Wayleaves were used to secure the tramway's right of way where Roberts did not already own the land. Spooner was also involved, surveying the route in 1863. In the valley,

An engineering drawing showing detail of one of the retaining walls.
Dated 1906, this was countersigned by the National Trust's secretary. *PRO*

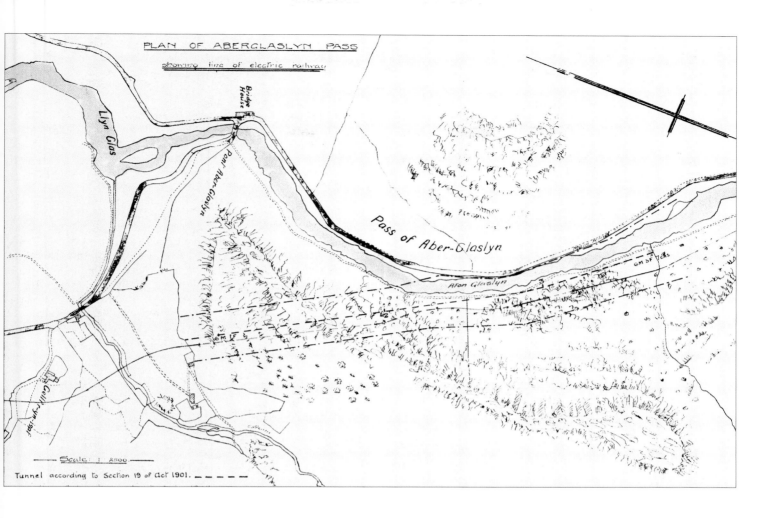

PLAN OF ABERGLASLYN PASS

showing line of electric railway

Scale 1:2500

Tunnel according to Section 19 of Oct 1901. — — — —

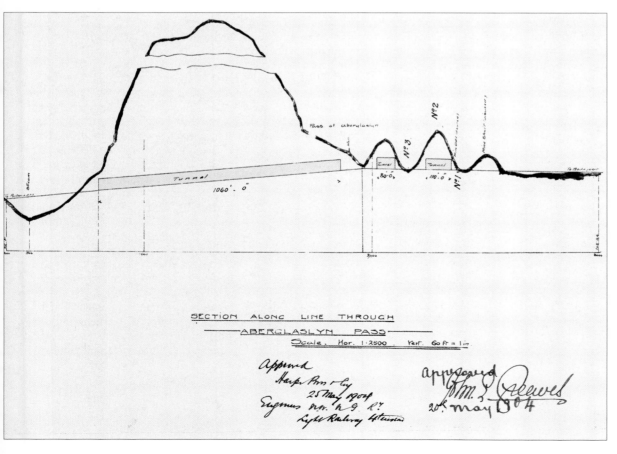

SECTION ALONG LINE THROUGH
ABERGLASLYN PASS
Scale. Hor. 1:2500. Vert. 60 ft = 1 in.

Above:
An engineer's plan showing the variation between the Aberglaslyn tunnel agreed by the 1901 Act and the tunnels as built. *PRO*

Left:
A 1904 section showing the alignment of the Aberglaslyn tunnels. The plan was signed by the Lord Lieutenant of Carnarvonshire and Harper Brothers & Co, the latter signing for the NWNGR Light Railway Extension. *PRO*

further private tramways and inclines made connections to the main line. At Portmadoc the tramway made use of the FR's tracks around the harbour.

The tramway's position had been regularised in 1865, with the passing of the Croesor & Portmadoc Railway Act. The Act incorporated the Croesor & Port Madoc Railway Co (CPR) with capital of £25,000. The 4½-mile tramway was vested in the company and authorised for passenger as well as mineral and goods traffic. Roberts was designated one of the original directors and allowed to be compensated by the company in respect of the tramway's construction. The extension to Borth-y-gest already referred to was also sanctioned.

The remaining 2½ miles of the 1864 tramway within the Croesor Valley, including two inclines, were not covered by the Act and remained under Roberts's control. The five directors held all the issued share capital. Another £8,000 capital was raised by mortgaging the undertaking in 1870; in 1868 Roberts had been saying, in a Board of Trade return, that it had proved impossible to raise funds by this mortgage!

In 1877, Spooner had tried, unsuccessfully, to persuade the FR to pay for a line to link up with the NWNGR's then proposed Rhyd Ddu terminus. This would have been achieved by taking over and re-laying part of the Croesor Tramway and by building a link line thence.

A second Act had been obtained in 1879, authorising a three-mile extension to Beddgelert, with £23,000 capital to pay for it. The company was allowed to enter into agreements with the Cambrian Railways and/or the FR for 'working, use, management and maintenance of their respective railways' and to change its name to The Portmadoc, Croesor, & Beddgelert Tram Railway Company (PCBTR). If the extension was maintained as a separate undertaking it was to be known as the PCBTR's Beddgelert Extension.

The inspiration for this Act had come from The Tramways Corporation Ltd, which promoted the Croesor and its Beddgelert extension as a railway that could match the Festiniog for traffic and dividends. The identities of the Corporation's backers are unknown; except for Roberts, who became secretary, the CPR directors ceased to be involved. Perhaps the Corporation had greater ambitions than Beddgelert, for it had been in contact with the Ruthin & Cerrig-y-drudion Railway's promoters. PCBTR shares were offered to the public shortly after the Act was obtained. Neither extension was carried out but the target of Beddgelert and sanction for Festiniog co-operation established a pattern for the future.

In 1882, the PCBTR had established a further link to the NWNGR when a second mortgage was obtained, this time from Russell, for £330; he was repaid by the PBSSR in 1901, by which time Roberts was the sole owner of the PCBTR.

The PBSSR's electricity was to be generated at a hydro power station located near Beddgelert, using water abstracted from Llyn Llydaw and Llyn Teyrn. Electricity could be supplied in bulk to any of the Cambrian, Festiniog, NWNGR, Snowdon Mountain Railways or 'any local authority, company or person authorised to supply electrical energy'; the Portmadoc and Criccieth Councils could buy the installations after 36 years had elapsed from the passing of the Act. The accounts of the electricity undertaking were to be kept separately from those of the railway.

The syndicate behind the PBSSR made its last LRO application in May 1903, seeking another Pwllheli, Nevin & Porth Dinlleyn Order. Although the application was provisionally approved, it was struck off in 1908 due to lack of response by the promoters. In the event none of the syndicate's railways were either built or completed, and only the power station was to be completed, remaining in service to the present day.

On 22 October 1903, NWPT minutes recorded payment of the £10,000 purchase price of the PCBTR, somewhat later than the 12 months allowed by the 1901 Act. Despite these changes in ownership the tramway continued as it always had done. The busiest section was between Portmadoc Harbour and Beddgelert Siding, including carriage of slate from the FR before the exchange yard was built at Minffordd in 1872, and afterwards when Minffordd was too busy.

The PBSSR became the subject of a takeover in 1903, with representatives of consulting engineers Harper Brothers & Co and electrical engineers Bruce Peebles Ltd driving the company. This changed its direction from being a railway company with generating powers to being a power generator with a railway, except to achieve that new Parliamentary powers were needed, the applications being made to Parliament's 1903/4 session.

The second PBSSR Act gained royal assent in 1904, at the same time as the North Wales Electric Power Act. The former authorised the construction of further railways, extending the NWNGR from Dinas into Caernarvon, agreements with the NWNGR, working the lines by electricity, additional time to build the 1901 railway and the transfer of the generating powers to the NWPT. Direct trains between Portmadoc and Nant Gwynant would not have been possible with this layout.

The only objector to the PBSSR was the LNWR, the objection of a main line railway company preventing the PBSSR from using the LRO procedures. The LNWR claimed that completion of the Portmadoc–Caernarvon narrow gauge route would bring it into competition with its own route and such competition was 'unnecessary and uncalled for, more especially as it will be established by means of piecemeal legislation', this last claim implying that the promoters had been underhand and had previously disguised their intentions.

Left:
A PBSSR remnant, alongside the WHR formation near Hafod Ruffydd in 1947.
WHR collection

The Croesor Tramway's crossing of Portmadoc High Street is clearly visible in this view. Also visible are the inner harbour, the Moelwyns and Cnicht. *Commercial postcard/Author's collection*

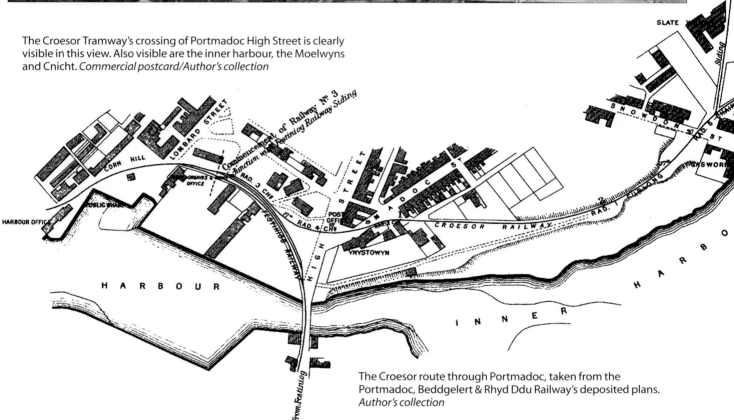

The Croesor route through Portmadoc, taken from the Portmadoc, Beddgelert & Rhyd Ddu Railway's deposited plans. *Author's collection*

Cross-examination in the House of Lords on 10 March 1904 identified other PBSSR backers, including Mr Pilkington of Pilkington Brothers Ltd, glass makers, of St Helens and Joseph Beecham, chemist, also of St Helens, a PBSSR director, both still household names. The PBSSR's chairman, James Ernest Rawlins had experience in power transmission in America, and another director, Percy Tarbutt, was a mining engineer with experience in South Africa. According to Rawlins, the PBSSR had £170,000 already subscribed, sufficient to complete the 1901 railway he said, although this money was more likely for the power station.

That said, there are no clues yet found to indicate what happened to this money. The NWPT had been registered on 30 July 1903, capitalised at £1 million, the Electric Power Act giving no indication that the company was to inherit any capital raised by the 1901 Act. Yet, as noted earlier, it was the

NWPT that paid for the Croesor Tramway. It also made the SBLR LRO application and was very likely responsible for the NWNGR's 1903 application, both referred to shortly, as it was submitted the same day, by the same legal team and with Harper Brothers as consulting engineers.

In 1903/4 the directors of the PBSSR and the NWPT were the same. Bruce Peebles began building the power station in 1905, with electricity generation starting the following year. Whilst the power business was very successful, it was capital intensive in its early days; it is hardly surprising that there turned out to be no spare cash to build narrow gauge railways, electric or otherwise.

In November 1903, the NWNGR had applied for an LRO to give it extra time to complete its Beddgelert extension, to link it to the PBSSR, to work the Moel Tryfan Undertaking as a light railway and by electricity, to sell any part of the Moel

Tryfan Undertaking to the PBSSR, to transfer the Beddgelert extension powers to the PBSSR, and for various capital purposes. By this stage NWNGR revenue was down to £6 per mile per week with costs of £5 per mile per week, producing a surplus of £600 per annum. It had carried 39,000 passengers and 28,496 tons of slate in 1902.

The proposed link with the PBSSR from Beddgelert was a bifurcated line two miles long in total, on gradients of 1 in 20 with spurs facing Nant Gwynant and Portmadoc, making two connections with the realigned PBSSR. The new line was to start a quarter mile short of the 1900 line's proposed Beddgelert terminus and pass through a tunnel 100yd long at the rear of the Royal Goat Hotel before crossing the Portmadoc road by a bridge to reach the Glaslyn meadows, crossed on embankment, and dividing; the two river crossings would have been 60ft and 80ft long.

An inquiry was held in Beddgelert on 2 February 1904, lasting two hours. The NWNGR had been unable to progress its 1900 extension due to lack of funds. The Portmadoc-facing spur was intended to supersede the PBSSR's 1901 route through the Aberglaslyn Pass, the engineers saying that the proposed long tunnel was impractical and dangerous and should be replaced by two shorter bores, due to the nature of the rock; a tunnel on the original centre line would have brought the railway over the river, with no means of support! Solicitor Randal Casson, appearing for the Tremadoc Estate and the Lord Lieutenant, said that he had drafted the 1901 amendment and agreed that it had been accepted by the PBSSR without due consideration, to get the bill before Parliament on the unopposed list.

Russell gave evidence that electric working would save the NWNGR £1,000 a year, even if there was no increase in business. Richard Davies, one of the 1897/8 promoters and now chairman of the county council attended the inquiry to support the application on behalf of the surveyor's committee. The secretary of the National Trust, Nigel Bond, said that the Trust was of the opinion that the pass was too narrow to accommodate the railway, the road and the river and that if it was found possible, the 1901 route should be adhered to. The NWNGR's solicitor, who also acted for the PBSSR/NWPT, said the NWPT had already entered into contracts for carrying out the proposed works, the contractors being ready to start work forthwith. Engineers Harper Brothers & Co and consulting engineers Douglas Fox & Partners signed the estimate of £10,291.

The modified route started what became a long-standing dispute with the owners of the Royal Goat Hotel Estate at Beddgelert. In this instance, agreement was reached, whereby the railway sold back some of the land purchased in 1903 whilst it bought additional land for the extension, both transactions taking place at the 1903 rate per acre. Amongst other conditions the railway agreed not to use any of the land as tea gardens or to build any other station within a mile of the hotel, except for a passenger platform on the eastern bank of the Glaslyn. The railway was to be built as far from Gelert's grave as permitted by the limit of deviation and the embankment across the Portmadoc road was to be planted with trees, shrubs or evergreens. The only access to the station was to be through the hotel's yard.

As the Order processing stretched into 1905 without the Order being made, the NWNGR's solicitors maintained pressure on the Board of Trade, asking when it was going to be confirmed, as their clients 'desired to proceed at once with the reconstruction' and were 'anxious to commence electrification'. Whilst the Order was made, its drafting was defective and did not include powers of abandonment for the former Beddgelert station site and the affected section of the PBSSR. Therefore, when the NWNGR (Light Railway) Order was made on 6 June 1905 it had only powers to work the existing lines as light railways, by electricity, to raise £12,000 '1905' debenture stock, of which £2,000 was to be allocated to the appointment of a receiver(!), and to be leased to the PBSSR. No extra time was given for the 1900 extension, although in August 1903 Aitchison had secured a 12-month extension from the Board of Trade. The LRC reported that the missing components would be the subject of a separate application by the PBSSR.

The NWPT also submitted an LRO application in November 1903, this in respect of the Snowdon & Bettws-y-coed Light Railway (SBLR), a 13¼-mile extension of the PBSSR. The steepest gradient would have been 1 in 19, with curves of up to six chains. An inquiry was held at Bettws-y-coed on 3 February 1904.

The scheme was promoted as part of a network of electric railways connecting Bettws-y-coed with Caernarvon and Portmadoc, the electricity to be provided by NWPT. It attracted considerable numbers of objections, with the National Trust and the Co-Op Holidays Association chief amongst them. There were letters published in national newspapers and a petition attracted 2,400 signatures, most of them from outside Wales.

Amongst many objections to the proposals there were criticisms of the Order, if made, being awarded to a limited company with the result that an agreement was reached that the Order would be made to the PBSSR, a statutory company. At this stage there were concerns that the PBSSR would be governed by two acts of Parliament and three LROs. The outcome was a suggestion that there should be a combination order to amalgamate the powers and to give it authority to operate the NWNGR additionally. It was proposed to deal with the deferred aspects of the NWNGR 1903 application at the same time. In these circumstances the SBLR application was held over by the Board of Trade.

Left:
Abandoned wagons on the non-statutory section of the Croesor Tramway, 22 August 1959.
D. Clayton/Author's collection

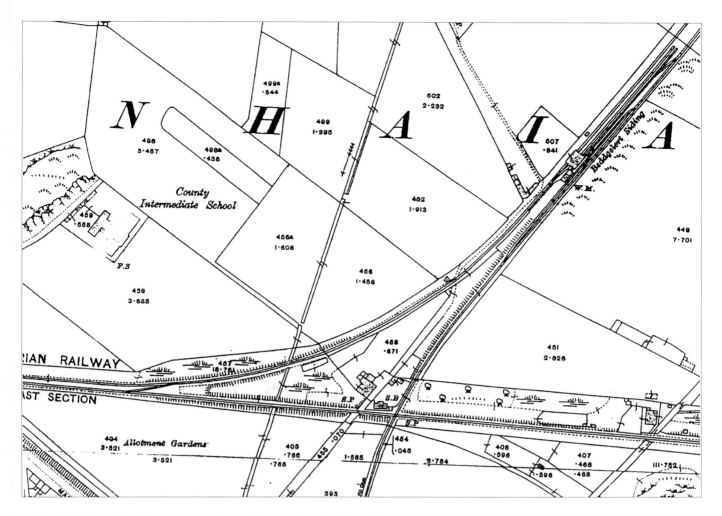

Above:
The Croesor Tramway's Beddgelert Siding interchange with the Cambrian Railways at Portmadoc. *Crown copyright*

The SBLR application seems to have triggered a simultaneous application from the Penmachno, Corwen & Bettws Light Railway Co. This 28-mile 2ft-gauge electric railway would, with the PBSSR and the SBLR, have completed the NWNGR's original general undertaking proposal along with its Penmachno branch. Its promoters, A. Carter and J. L. Owen were named in the application, were apparently independent of either the PBSSR or the NWPT. Following an inquiry held at Corwen on 28 July 1904 the LRC approved the Order but it was not confirmed by the Board of Trade and the application was struck off in 1910 because of lack of response from the promoters.

With the PBSSR/NWNGR powers now in place, the stage was set for an electric narrow gauge railway through Snowdonia, from Portmadoc to Caernarvon. As it was, there was no change at all in the position of the two operational railways and no obvious signs of action to implement the powers for new lines.

An agreement made between the NWNGR, the PBSSR and the NWPT 'containing the bases of working arrangements between the companies and the construction of railways' was approved by NWNGR shareholders at a special meeting held in November 1904. The PBSSR returned to the LRC that same month with an application to work its 1901 and 1904 lines as a light railway and to modify the 1901 route through the Aberglaslyn Pass. An inquiry was held in Caernarvon on Saturday, 15 April 1905.

There were some misconceptions about the purpose of the Order and inquiry, amongst which Ynyscynhaiarn (Portmadoc) and Deudraeth Councils asked that as the public had become accustomed to walking along the Croesor Tramway trackbed for more than 20 years the Commissioners should protect this 'right' in the Order. Not unnaturally, the Commissioners explained that this was beyond their remit!

Again, the National Trust objected to the modification of the tunnel, saying that it had been approved by Parliament and could be changed only by Parliament. It was generally felt that a shorter tunnel would bring the railway into view of those admiring the pass from Pont Aberglaslyn and spoil their enjoyment of it. It is difficult to appreciate this now, due to the considerable tree and rhododendron growth over the intervening period that has seriously reduced this perspective. As railway enthusiasts we would take the view that the appearance of a train would only enhance the scenery!

The National Trust could not say why its view should prevail over anyone else's and the LRC, in their report, did not think it was well founded, saying that even as modified, the railway would still be unseen from Pont Aberglaslyn. They recommended that the Order be made but the Board of Trade decided to hear further objections in London on 24 October 1905.

David Lloyd George had been involved again, during the processing of the SBLR application, when it was noted, on an internal briefing memo in the Board of Trade, that 'Mr Lloyd George himself visited the place, and saw the objectors.'

Whilst these applications were still pending the PBSSR made two further LRO applications in November 1905. The first was to resolve the outstanding extension at Beddgelert. In addition to transferring the 1900 powers, diverted at Beddgelert to suit a through railway, the application sought approval to connect to the PBSSR and to obtain extra time to build the 1900 extension. The NWNGR proposal to have a Nant Gwynant-facing connection to the PBSSR was abandoned, the connecting line being about three-quarters of a mile long, deviating from the 1900 line at Beddgelert to take the line behind the Royal Goat Hotel in tunnel and giving rise to the now famous abandoned road overbridge and abutments standing isolated in the field nearby. The county council was allowed to advance up to £2,000 by share subscription or loan. As the issue had already received a public airing at the 1904 inquiry the Order was processed without too much delay, being made on 24 October 1906 when it was signed by the President of the Board of Trade, David Lloyd George.

The second 1905 application was to amend the PBSSR's 1904 route at Caernarvon, abandoning the last quarter mile on the quayside and substituting a tramway half a mile long along St Helen's Road to the wharves alongside the castle. The estimated cost was £3,241 according to Harper Brothers, with £500 allowed for a station located beneath the castle walls. A public inquiry was held at Caernarvon on 30 January 1906.

The original terminus was to have been on the site of the disused de Winton foundry, de Winton & Co being in liquidation. The extension was needed to eliminate double handling of slate in transit to the wharves. There was some debate about the rate to be charged for freight carried over the extension, the railway wishing to charge more, on a pro rata basis, to allow for the expense of installing wagon turntables on the wharves. W. A. Darbishire, the Mayor of Caernarvon and owner of the Pen-yr-orsedd Quarry in the Nantlle Valley, said his quarry was being electrified and he was considering connecting it to the NWNGR at Bryngwyn. He told the inquiry that the LNWR charged 1s 7d (8p) per ton for carrying slate between Nantlle and Caernarvon but if the slate were being exported from Caernarvon by sea the rate was increased by 1s 1d (5½p). Aitchison, speaking for the PBSSR, said the rate by narrow gauge would still be less and breakages would be reduced. The LRC passed the Order to the Board of Trade for approval on 11 October 1906, but due a question arising over the interpretation of a clause on the application of capital it was 8 July 1908 before the PBSSR (Light Railway Extension at Caernarvon) Order was made.

Two days after the Beddgelert extension order had been made, 26 October 1906, there was further action on the SBLR and PBSSR applications, when the Board of Trade remitted them to the LRC for consolidation and for revision of the capital and borrowing powers of the PBSSR. By this time the PBSSR had raised £50,000 share capital for railway construction under its 1901 powers, but there was no sign of that £170,000 claimed in 1904. It now sought authorised share capital of £100,000 and borrowing of £100,000 in respect of Portmadoc–Rhyd Ddu and £90,000 plus £30,000 for the SBLR.

The Order was made on 7 July 1908. Its powers included bringing the 1901 and 1904 railways within the ambit of the Light Railways Act, giving until 24 October 1909 for the construction of the 1900 Beddgelert extension, authorising the SBLR and sanctioning the changes to the 1901 Aberglaslyn tunnel. The works in the pass were to be built according to plans countersigned by the county's Lord Lieutenant and the National Trust.

On the financial front the PBSSR's capital was reduced to £190,000 from £270,000, despite the additional expense of building the SBLR, because it no longer needed capital for the power station. The county council was allowed to advance £10,000.

The legal results of eight years' effort to connect Portmadoc with Rhyd Ddu, recognising that that was not always a priority, are shown in TABLE A. In railway terms it can be summarised as:

Act or Order	Route	Miles
1901 Act	Portmadoc–Beddgelert, including Croesor Tramway	11
1900 and 1906 Orders	Beddgelert to Rhyd Ddu NWNGR	5
1904 Act and 1908 Carnarvon Order	Dinas–Caernarvon	3

Whilst all this legal activity was in progress some construction work was carried out in 1905/6. Bruce Peebles & Co appears to have acted as main contractor, erecting at least one board to inform passers-by that it was acting for the 'North Wales Power & Electric Traction Co'. On 30 March 1905, the consulting engineers had told the Board of Trade that the priority was to complete the railway between Portmadoc and Caernarvon, with construction currently taking place to connect Portmadoc to the NWNGR. The latter was to be electrified 'at once', but the Bettws-y-coed extension 'does not form part of the present scheme' — in 1905 it had not been approved.

The overhead electrification was to be a twin-wire, three-phase, 600V ac system because it would be more cost effective than using dc. Ten 100kV substations were proposed, located at Beddgelert Siding, Croesor Junction, Beddgelert, Hafod Ruffydd, Rhyd Ddu, Bettws Garmon, Tryfan Junction, Bryngwyn, Dinas and Caernarvon. Two extra high-tension primary cables, one for the railway and the other supplying lighting power to Portmadoc and Criccieth, would pass through the Aberglaslyn tunnels in a protected trough.

Between Croesor Junction and the south end of the Aberglaslyn tunnels all ground works had been completed except for ballast, track and bridges. From the north end of the tunnels to the river crossing the formation was also complete. On the far side of Beddgelert the route to Rhyd Ddu was also substantially complete, although not all of it was located as shown on the deposited plans it might have been within the limits of deviation. This section was sufficiently complete for it to be used, without official sanction, to haul timber out of the Beddgelert Forest to Rhyd Ddu during World War 1.

Having funded the PBSSR since 1904 the NWPT was in financial difficulties by 1909, not necessarily cause and effect, and all work stopped. Bruce Peebles & Co, which had carried out the Beddgelert earthworks, was forced into voluntary liquidation. In 1915 it was reported that £102,668 had been spent on the PBSSR, including the purchase of the Croesor Tramway.

Prompted, no doubt, by the cessation of construction activities, the local authorities formed a joint investigative committee, the consequences of which are described in the next chapter.

Meanwhile, notwithstanding the effort to extend them, the existing railways continued in operation. The NWNGR's reputation for accidents continued on 31 July 1906 when the coal wagon attached to a mixed train approaching Rhyd Ddu ran away and collided with the locomotive of the following excursion train near Plas-y-nant, both trains being improperly in the same section. Seven passengers and the train crew reported injuries and the locomotive's trailing bogie derailed. Investigation revealed that it was not practice for the stationmaster at Rhyd Ddu to send 'train arrived' to Waenfawr, the NWNGR's rules only requiring it 'when there are "special reasons" for so doing'.

Setting aside any deficiencies in the rules, it may be surmised that, with Aitchison based at his Snowdon Mountain Railway office in Llanberis, the number and type of incidents indicate a lack of direct management supervision on the railway. It is equally possible that Aitchison had rather a *laissez faire* attitude towards safety. When proposals that rolling stock should be fitted with automatic couplings, to avoid the risk of staff being crushed when coupling up, were going through Parliament in 1899 he wrote to Hughes at the FR suggesting that they get together with other narrow gauge railways to gain an exemption.

The requirement to adopt by-laws to cover the handling of explosives developed into an ongoing correspondence with the Board of Trade, starting in 1904. Aitchison explained, on 8 December 1904, that all the railway's trains were mixed so he would propose carrying gunpowder in metallic cases placed in slate wagons attached to such trains. Further, he could not meet the requirement for a special vehicle because such a vehicle would not go up the (Bryngwyn) incline nor would it reach the 'places where the quarry companies require the powder delivered'. At the Board this generated a flurry of remarks, including: 'This company is *not* authorised to run all its trains as mixed trains,' and, 'Can you trace any papers . . . for the Festiniog Railway, probably in 1867?' The Home Office was consulted and, on 26 December, refused to allow any modification.

Aitchison responded by asking, on 10 January 1905, that if a wooden van or wagon that had its ironwork protected were designed which could get into the quarries, would it be acceptable? By return he was told that the by-laws in question applied only to explosives packed in metallic cases or cylinders, so he let the matter rest.

Twelve months later the Board of Trade was pursuing the matter again. On 17 January 1906 Aitchison replied: 'As the railway is about to be reconstructed and run in conjunction with another company which is being built, the company has decided to refuse to carry explosives until they had obtained suitable vans for the carrying of explosives. Under these circumstances I issued an Order to that effect, and at present the only explosives which we will deal with are those contained in such kinds of cylinders as will enable us to deal with it in the ordinary traffic'!

The frustrated Board of Trade returned to the Home Office for advice, to be told on 22 February 1906, 'In the circumstances there is no need to press the company to make by-laws at present, but as soon as reconstruction is completed the new company should be called upon to make by-laws.' Nothing more was heard on the subject.

Simultaneously the railway had been asked to adopt new model by-laws for ordinary traffic, some of the earlier by-laws having been superseded by the 1889 Regulation of Railways Act. This resulted in an exchange between Aitchison and the Board of Trade on the reason for the Moel Tryfan Undertaking appellation being added to the railway's name. The Board had unilaterally removed it and then sought an explanation! These by-laws were signed and sealed on 3 April 1906.

Despite all the plans for expansion, the NWNGR was in serious decline, not that it had ever achieved great success. It had only managed to keep going because the PBSSR funded the order for the locomotive *Russell* in 1906, although two years later it found sufficient funds for another single Fairlie.

In spite of appearances, operating costs were covered most years; indeed, the railway would not have gone on for so long in receivership had this not been the case. In 1913, a loss of £205 was incurred. The annual report informed shareholders that whilst excursion traffic was satisfactory, local traffic was very much decreased owing to competition from motor charabancs. The 226 1st class and 23,399 3rd class passengers generated revenue of £586; of them 163 1st and 13,438 3rd originated on the NWNGR. It may be assumed that most of the difference was accounted for by the way in which tickets were booked 'through' from other railways. They could be tourists, of course. The 1912

TABLE A

Act or Order	Date	Railway	Share capital	Borrowing authorised	Remarks
NWNGR (Beddgelert Light Railway Extension) Order	1900	From Rhyd Ddu terminus of existing NWNGR to Beddgelert	£13,800	£4,600	Powers transferred to PBSSR,1906, when capital and borrowing powers repealed.
PBSSR Act	1901	From Portmadoc to Beddgelert	£270,000	£60,000	Capital authorised included capital for power station scheme, reduced by 1908 Order.
PBSSR Act	1904	From Dinas terminus of existing NWNGR to Carnarvon	£24,000	£98,000	Borrowing powers of 1901 Act repealed, powers given to borrow not exceeding one third of capital authorised by 1901 and 1904 Acts repealed by 1908 Order, share capital repealed by 1908 Order.
PBSSR (Beddgelert Light Railway Extension)	1906	At Beddgelert, connecting railways authorised by 1900 Order and 1901 Act	£24,000	£8,000	Also transfer of powers of 1900 Order to PBSSR. Share capital and borrowing repealed by 1908 Order.
PBSSR (Light Railway Extension at Carnarvon) Order	1908	Deviation and extension at Carnarvon	None	None	
PBSSR (Light Railway) Order	1908	From Beddgelert connecting with railway authorised by 1901 Act to Bettws-y-coed	£190,000	£130,000	More than £100,000 share capital not to be raised until resolution on commencement of SBLR carried.

passenger figures, despite the statement, had actually been almost the same.

There had been, however, a big downturn over earlier years, when the railway consistently carried over 40,000 passengers annually. TABLE B shows the railway's passenger decline; it would be interesting to know what those 1st class passengers thought they were paying for, for they can't have received much in the way of comfort! The slate trade, said the 1913 report, continued in a state of depression, for some of the year the largest quarry sending traffic on the railway being closed down.

In 1914, a deficit of £387 was attributed to various causes. Owing to the outbreak of war all excursion bookings from other companies had been cancelled during August, 'thus the most profitable part of the passenger traffic for the year was lost'. Local traffic was further decreased; slate traffic was 'very much diminished', reduced by 20% on 1913, which itself had shrunk 22% on 1912. The Bryngwyn branch passenger service had not been operated since 1 January.

The 1915 deficit was £283, with all excursion traffic lost and local traffic further decreased. Slate was 60% down but iron ore, from Bettws Garmon, and timber, from Beddgelert, were satisfactory. In 1916, the results were judged to have been slightly better than in 1915, with a loss of £2 3s 8d (£2.18). Traffic in iron ore and timber was greatly increased. A report published in *Railway & Travel Monthly* in 1917 described the railway at this time; everything was run down and holes were seen in the panelling of carriages. The writer commented: 'A motor bus service along a road which follows the line bids fair to prove the proverbial "last straw".'

'Practically no passenger bookings' contributed to a loss of £166 in 1917. Slate trade was still further decreased owing to the 'stoppage of building'. The termination of loading facilities, the location of which is not known, had affected the iron ore traffic.

In 1918, the last year for which returns have been found, the deficit was £177. Aitchison reported that the traffic had been larger than for some years, mainly owing to the timber traffic. Expenses had increased due to higher wages being paid and 'repairs necessitated by the nature of the traffic'. No repairs to either locomotives or rolling stock had been recorded since 1915.

The Dolgarrog-based Aluminium Corporation obtained control of the NWNGR in 1920 by buying £36,100 face-value debentures for £6,219; in 1921 the corporation's managing director, Henry Joseph Jack, was appointed receiver. The debentures were nominally held by Aluminium Corporation director Sir John Henderson Stewart Bt.

By this time the WHR proposals were well in hand and it was obviously seen to improve the credibility of the scheme for the NWNGR to continue operating; the corporation paid Aitchison and Jack a total of £1,500 to keep it afloat. By 1922 the NWNGR had accrued interest outstanding of just over £50,000, full debenture interest not having been paid since 1878. Neither had the company been able to repay £1,749 to holders of Lloyd's' bonds and £3,487 in respect of unsecured debts, both sums due in 1888.

To purchase the undertaking the WHR allotted £8,500 in debentures and £34,540 in ordinary shares to the NWNGR debenture holders, ie Stewart. Stewart also received £1,500 of debentures in respect of the advance the corporation had made to the receiver. A further £5,460 in ordinary shares was allocated to the Lloyds' bond holders, to 1888 creditors and Stewart, in respect of interest due.

A return of £50,000 in certificates issued by a company that was, as will be seen, severely under-capitalised and which was never to make a profit, was hardly an outstanding result for some 50 years of effort. The ordinary shareholders got nothing.

Likewise, the PBSSR, in the guise of the Croesor Tramway, had little to show for its efforts. The results for its final years, when it was serving four quarries, are shown in the table below:

Year	Receipts £	Expenditure £
1912	458	390
1913	455	428
1914	397	466
1915	298	315
1916	197	292
1917	219	299
1918	225	285
1919	272	303
1920	404	455
1921	456	521

In 1913 it owned four wagons and operated 2,772 train miles, carrying 244 tons of merchandise, 467 tons of coal and 5,820 tons of other minerals (mainly slate). Hire of horses cost £153 and traffic expenses amounted to £52.

The PBSSR's returns for 1913-16 include a sum ranging from £1,656 to £1,936 each year payable to NWPT, and in 1913 £767 was paid to Aitchison in settlement of an action he had brought. No explanation has been found for these payments. Expenditure on 'lines not open' was shown as £37,382 in 1912, £37,422 in 1913, £37,423 in 1915 and £37,674 in 1916.

The Aluminium Corporation acquired a controlling interest in NWPT in 1918, which was still struggling financially, and thereby acquired the PBSSR.

Material sold 'in connection with line under construction' amounted to £374 in 1919; the same entry was £310 the year before, so perhaps it was a cumulative total. In all likelihood this represents materials acquired for railway construction being sold off; the FR bought 2,000 sleepers for £90 from the PBSSR in 1911.

In its final year of independent operation, before the WHR took over, the Croesor carried:

Slate	1,719 tons
Coal	282
Stone (roadmaking)	11
Lime	20
Timber	51
Flour (Sharp's Mill)	89
Miscellaneous	96

TABLE B

Year	Total 1st	Total 3rd	Originating 1st	Originating 3rd	Passenger revenue £	Freight revenue £
1912	174	23,419	109	13,802	582	1,568
1913	226	23,399	163	13,438	586	1,416
1914	130	14,229	95	8,912	336	1,184
1915	151	9,516	162	6,907	234	1,316
1916	75	4,013	74	3,146	104	1,863
1917		211			11	1,651
1918						2,148

—2—
The Creation of the Welsh Highland Railway
1914-22

WHILST the origins of the WHR as we understand it today date back to 1830, the endgame for the railway's creation started on 19 December 1914. That was when Evan R. Davies, Town Clerk of Pwllheli and Secretary of Education of Carnarvonshire County Council, a solicitor and friend of David Lloyd George, submitted an application for an LRO to unite the NWNGR with the PBSSR, the verbosely named Portmadoc, Beddgelert & South Snowdon Railway (Light Railway) and North Wales Narrow Gauge Railways (Light Railways) Revival and Transfer of Powers Order.

As implied, the application was to revive existing powers and to transfer them to a new, unnamed company. In submitting the application Davies was acting on behalf of the Portmadoc, Beddgelert & Carnarvon Light Railway Committee, the joint committee referred to in the previous chapter. Established in 1909, it represented Carnarvon County Council, Carnarvon Town Council, Carnarvon Harbour Trust, the Urban District Council of Ynyscynhaiarn (later renamed Portmadoc/Porthmadog) and the Rural District Councils of Gwyrfai and Glaslyn.

The local authorities required the joint committee to investigate the scope for developing the areas through which the railways ran, or would run, to the benefit of the community. At the time the NWNGR was dying on its feet and the PBSSR was operating the horse-drawn Croesor Tramway, with only some now-abandoned earthworks around Beddgelert to show for years of effort to link the two systems. Both were in receivership; the PBSSR had obtained powers to bring the route under its control and to complete it in 1908 but was not in a position to proceed. The committee's representative for Ynyscynhaiarn was solicitor William George, previously encountered and brother of David Lloyd George, later Prime Minister.

In 1911, the committee had been informed that NWPT was prepared to sell, for cash, the PBSSR, including railways finished and unfinished and all powers. To qualify for a Treasury grant the LNWR had provisionally agreed to construct, finish and work the line, but not to finance it! The NWNGR needed to agree to LNWR involvement but Russell would not give his consent; he died at the end of 1911.

The joint committee proposed that the authorities should take appropriate action to complete the rail link between Caernarvon and Portmadoc, bringing it under a single ownership/management, supporting the scheme by means of loans, hence the 1914 application. To meet the LRC's twice-yearly deadline for submission of applications, actually 'by November' and 'by May' so the 19 December application was late anyway, it was found necessary to submit it before the joint committee so members could obtain approval from their respective councils. The joint committee members therefore obtained a loan from the LC&M Bank and personally guaranteed the £50 fee payable for the LRO.

An application was also made to the Treasury for assistance under the terms of Section 5(1) of the Light Railways Act of 1896, which made funds available for the construction of light railways, provided, *inter alia*, that the Board of Agriculture certified the proposal would benefit agriculture or that the Board of Trade certified that it would improve communications under certain circumstances. A budget of £1 million was available for this purpose, specified in the Act, part of which could be advanced as a free grant, otherwise by loan. In their reading of the Light Railways Act the promoters were overtaken by events as the grant facility was removed in the 1921 Railways Act.

As the Light Railways Act funds could be applied only to new construction, Davies also made application to the Development Commission for an advance to support the acquisition and improvement of the existing lines. This turned out to be a fruitless application.

In comparison with other orders applicable to the route, or part of it, and the Order eventually made, the draft Order was relatively straightforward, having 27 sections. Unusually, the name of the company to be granted the new powers was not specified. The new company was to be granted permission to enter into agreements with either the LNWR or the Cambrian Railways regarding the construction, maintenance and management of the railway or the working and conveyance of traffic thereon as well as the usual commercial agreements. A leasing clause would have permitted leasing the railway to any other railway with which the company was authorised to enter into a working agreement.

An unsigned and undated document within Ministry of Transport files lodged at the PRO was apparently composed by the promoters in support of the 1914 application. It contains no more than a passing reference to the FR, which was involved more prominently by 1921, and in parts is too fulsome to be the product of a Whitehall civil servant! In a letter to the Board of Trade, dated 31 December 1914, Davies explained the basis for the grant applications by saying, *inter alia*, that he would 'at once prepare and submit . . . a statement setting forth the grounds upon which the application . . . is made' — the document could be that statement — and it was clearly the source of some of the evidence given at the 1921 public inquiry.

The document describes the background and objectives of the Order, pointing out that capital expenditure on the NWNGR had totalled £108,291, whilst that for the PBSSR was £102,668. The latter sum was broken down as follows: purchase of Croesor Tramway — £11,518 (contrary to the £10,000 permitted by the PBSSR's 1901 Act); purchase of land — £6,150; construction of railway — £73,000; and legal and engineering expenses — £12,000.

The parishes through which the completed railway was to pass were listed with acreages and population; the largest, by acreage, being Beddgelert at 26,060 and by population, Ynyscynhaiarn (Portmadoc), with 4,445. The smallest on both counts was Bettws Garmon — 2,723 acres with a population of 440.

Some 52 slate quarries and lead, copper, ochre and iron mines which had been active during the previous 50 years were listed by parish and name, along with the approximate number employed, totalling 3,500, not simultaneously. It was estimated that transport costs ranging from 3s 2d (16p) to

15s (75p) per ton could be reduced by three-quarters if a railway serving either Portmadoc or Caernarvon were available. Transport costs were said to have contributed to the failure of several undertakings and handicapped others. It was further anticipated that several properties could be developed given adequate transport facilities. The document further comments that with the coming of mains electricity to the district, from the NWPT's Nant Gwynant power station, the facility to establish manufacturing industries would be further advanced if transportation were improved.

Agriculture was also a significant activity in the district, with some 1,500 tenant farmers or smallholders active. Some land had gone over to pasture because transport costs were cheaper, presumably because the animals were herded to and from market.

The interests of tourism were not overlooked, attention being drawn to the attractiveness of the Rhyd Ddu path to the summit of Snowdon, the Aberglaslyn Pass and Beddgelert, as well as claiming that Rhyd Ddu 'is also regarded as one of the healthiest holiday resorts in Wales'! The tourist catchment area was forecast to include the North Wales coast as far as Rhyl or Prestatyn and the Cambrian coast as far as Aberystwyth, a pool of some half million tourists annually. The development of rail-based circular tours from the North Wales coast was proposed, using the proposed railway in conjunction with either the FR or the standard gauge Afon Wen line.

The owners of the NWNGR and the PBSSR had agreed to sell their undertakings for either £30,000 in cash or £10,000 in cash and £30,000 in shares in the new company, two-thirds for the NWNGR and one third for the PBSSR. The cost of completing the PBSSR was estimated to be £50,000, with a further £1,500 required for more land. Additionally, £5,000 was needed to refurbish the NWNGR and £3,500 for legal, engineering and contingent expenses, producing a conveniently rounded £100,000 total. Observe that there is no suggestion that the new railway should invest in any rolling stock; an estimate of expense dated 28 November 1914 had £5,000 for rolling stock but nothing for additional land or the legal, engineering and contingent expenses, so still producing a total of £100,000.

To finance the scheme the promoters sought a government grant of £30,000, a government loan (at 3½%) of £25,000 and loans from the local authorities totalling £15,500; with £30,000 to be issued in shares, the total came to £500 over the required amount.

Government rules for proportionate funding, that any advance should not exceed 50% of construction costs, led to the promoters seeking to have the £6,150 PBSSR land purchase and the £73,000 spent on PBSSR construction taken into consideration, claiming therefore a total expenditure of £130,650 on land and works. With a net cost of £100,000 for 25 miles of railway it was implied that the new Undertaking was a bargain.

The document concluded with the statement that the LNWR was prepared to work the railway on terms to be arranged and to provide such facilities that would 'minimise the inconvenience, delay and loss now experienced at Dinas Junction'.

The war brought an end to the application's progress and there was no further action on it until 1921. In March 1919, however, the news that the Aluminium Corporation had acquired control of the NWNGR resulted in two letters winging their way to the Board of Trade. (The news might have been premature, for according to Jones & Gwyn (see Bibliography) the transfer did not take place until April 1920.)

The first, from the Glaslyn Rural District Council, urged that the Board should use its influence to bring about completion of what it called the Portmadoc & Beddgelert Light Railway. The second, from Carnarvonshire County Council, sought the reimbursement of the £50 application fee. The bank had pressed for payment, with interest, and the council had paid it but was concerned that the arrangement might not meet with the district auditor's approval and that the committee members might have their guarantees invoked. The application for reimbursement was refused because the LRO application was considered to be current.

The application was reactivated, as stated, in 1921, most likely at the instigation of Jack and the Aluminium Corporation. By this time the Aluminium Corporation had the controlling interest in the PBSSR as well as the FR; Jack was a county councillor and had just become receiver of the NWNGR. A report commissioned from a consultant, Major G. C. Spring, submitted in the autumn of 1921 on the three operational railways, was clearly intended to inform the Corporation on their condition and future prospects.

Spring noted, *inter alia*, that passenger traffic on the NWNGR section would be improved if that originating from Caernarvon did not have to change trains at Dinas. He concluded by saying: 'The completion of the system, ie the connection of the three systems, Festiniog, Croesor branch, and North Wales Narrow Gauge, would doubtless open up a wonderful tourist route by rail through the heart of Snowdonia and would enable the proportionate cost of rolling stock maintenance to be lowered owing to the larger utilisation of the workshop facilities at Boston Lodge, but since the traffic over the incompleted portion would be seasonal passenger traffic only, it is unlikely that this traffic alone could provide a reasonable return on the cost of completion of the railway.' Unusually for a consultant he was not saying what the customer wanted to hear but his words proved to be prophetic.

The county council at this time was concerned about the state of the roads on the overbridges at Waenfawr, Bettws Garmon and Quellyn, which was the responsibility of the railway. In June 1921 the council wrote to the NWNGR's registered office, in Liverpool. Receiving no reply, it did the work for £31. On 15 June 1924 the NWNGR replied 'This company is not in a position to find either the men or the materials for the repair of these roads and moreover being in Chancery the Master of the Court refuses to allow any expenses except on the maintenance of the railway only. I would suggest that the county council repair these roads themselves.'

The Ministry of Transport reviewed the LRO application on 8 October 1921 and a public inquiry was set for Caernarvon on 18 October. At the inquiry it was revealed that the completed railway was to be called the Welsh Highland Railway (WHR); the origins of the name are not known but it was certainly much simpler than either of the alternatives on offer. By this time the cost of acquiring the PBSSR and the NWNGR had risen from £40,000 to £100,000, to be funded by issuing £10,000 in debentures and £90,000 in ordinary shares to the vendors. The cost of completing the railway was given as £128,000, including £43,000 for constructing the Dinas-Caernarvon line.

The only objector was the LNWR, protecting its monopoly in the area. The larger company was seeking to guarantee that it would retain any traffic 'arising at or destined to stations on the NWNGR and any other line connected thereto'. The WHR objected to the LNWR's proposed clause as it was in neither its nor the public's interest, pointing out that the LNWR had argued its case in both 1885 and 1904 but had not

Left:
Rhyd Ddu with a WHR train in 1922. *Moel Tryfan* is about to return to Dinas. *C. R. Clinker*

been able to secure such a clause. The greater debate, however, was regarding the usefulness, or otherwise, of the proposed narrow gauge line to Caernarvon, with both sides agreeing that it was unlikely to pay its way! In 1913, a record year the LNWR claimed, passenger traffic between the two stations had amounted to £323, whilst goods traffic, for an average year, in both directions totalled 14,000 tons, including 5,000 tons of slate. Only 250 tons of slate ex-Dinas were destined for the quay at Caernarvon, the proposed narrow gauge terminus. If slate and other goods were no longer to be transhipped at Dinas the LNWR claimed it would be sacrificing the 'considerable expense' of developing the facilities there, some 40 years earlier!

In presenting the case for the WHR, Jack was identified as managing director of the North Wales Power Company, chairman of the FR as well as having a controlling interest in it, receiver of the NWNGR and a director of the PBSSR. He told the commissioners that the chief advantage of bringing the railways together would be one of unified control and rolling stock, to reduce expenses. He did not foresee any difficulty in entering into a working agreement with the FR; in the circumstances it was rather odd that he should have been asked the question!

With Jack on the stand there was some confusion about the sum required to complete construction, between the £128,000 already quoted or the £132,000 Jack said it was. Jack said it would be financed as follows: £32,000 from government grant; £23,000 loaned from three local authorities; £10,000 from the promoters and the remaining £64,000 from the public. Either Jack or the minute taker was still £3,000 short of his target; this was most likely a further local authority contribution. He forecast that the WHR would be a good security for investment and that the railway would make a profit, saying that the FR had just carried more passengers than ever before, an increase of 92% and therefore demonstrating the demand from tourism for railways in scenic areas.

Earlier, when the inquiry chairman had asked how the development of road transport would affect the railway, he was told that with the 'enormous expenditure attached to road maintenance' the railway was the better alternative! Major Charles Breese, MP for Carnarvonshire and member of the county council, explained that before the war traffic was very heavy, it had increased after the war and further increased considerably during the previous two years, saying: 'The

traffic is too heavy for the roads and it is a danger to horse traffic.' He thought the position would be relieved by completion of the railway, summarising: 'I cannot conceive how it will be possible to widen and strengthen the roads to bear the additional traffic to anything corresponding to the cost of constructing the railway.' (Breese, with William George, also at the inquiry, had been involved in promoting the Portmadoc, Beddgelert & Rhyd Ddu Light Railway of the 1890s, see Chapter 1).

Supporting the railway scheme, the clerk of Gwyrfai Rural District, told how the rateable value of the district had declined by £20,000 to £18,642 since 1907 whilst the population had reduced from 29,000 in 1911 to 24,030.

Other witnesses gave evidence on how they thought the railway could improve mineral extraction businesses and tourism. At the close of the hearing the chairman declared that the commissioners had found in favour of the scheme except for Dinas-Caernarvon. This was, he said, because the application did not include powers for compulsory purchase for this section, notwithstanding some land at Caernarvon had previously been purchased from the Harbour Commissioners by the PBSSR.

Nevertheless, when the commissioners compiled their undated report in 1922 they revealed that the promoters had, as permitted by the LRO rules, applied to revive the Dinas–Caernarvon compulsory purchase powers, previously authorised by the 1904 Act. The commissioners made a site visit on 7 February, meeting landowners and occupiers, the result of which was a decision in favour of the Dinas–Caernarvon powers, although by the time of the report the commissioners had been notified that the promoters had decided not to proceed with this section for the time being.

Meanwhile, the promoters were trying to persuade the government that the WHR should benefit from various grants and loans permitted to light railways by statute. A high-powered delegation met officers of the Ministry of Transport, including two MPs and the LRC, in a House of Commons committee room on 8 November 1921. The delegation included five Welsh MPs, including those for Cardiganshire, Carmarthen, Neath and Pontypridd, the clerks to Deudraeth, Glaslyn, Gwyrfai and Beddgelert Councils, three of them named David Jones(!), as well as Davies and Jack.

During the course of the meeting Jack provided an insight into the involvement of the FR, saying: 'I would like to claim that this is an unusual application for an unusual district, and

Left:
A mobile coaling stage and temporary water tank were brought into use at Harbour station to facilitate refuelling through trains. *Merddin Emrys* was benefiting from these amenities in 1925, shortly before they were withdrawn.
R. W. Kidner/Author's collection

Right:
Moel Tryfan leaving Harbour station. Records reveal that the locomotive was regularly used on the FR, but no photographs of this activity have come to light. *Author's collection*

Below:
The remnant of the Gorseddau Railway left *in situ* to serve a slate mill, 1948.
Author's collection

Below right:
The WHR's other source of traffic in Portmadoc was the flour mill, seen here on the left in 1948. The loading canopy remains but the siding is overgrown. The mill continued as a source of FR traffic until that line closed in 1946.
Author's collection

Left:
Moel Tryfan at
Portmadoc New station.
Roye England/
Pendon Museum

Above:
After the GWR won its claim
for payment for the use of its
crossing in 1928 the WHR made
less use of it, establishing an
unapproved 'platform' by the
Beddgelert Siding. Here it is
equipped with a bench and
a small raised platform to aid
loading of small goods into the
brake van. The carriages are
Nos 26, 25 and 8.
WHR collection

Left:
Slate stacks at Beddgelert Siding.
The weighbridge is on the
extreme right.
Author's collection

I would like to set before you . . . that we have unfortunately been rather too innocent in our way of bringing the scheme forward. In the first place, there is no railway in existence worth speaking of, that is to say, there is no traffic, and the idea is to establish a railway, and when we first approached this scheme we saw that no railway could be a success unless it included the Festiniog Railway, so as to run from Festiniog to Carnarvon. Emphasis has been put on the fact today that we are asking for this money in connection with this small part of the railway, and it has been ignored completely that we have already found £40,000 in hard cash within the last few months to enable us to get the controlling interest in the Festiniog Railway.' 'Who?' interjected the chairman. 'The promoters of this scheme,' continued Jack. 'It could not be brought forward as a complete and unified scheme until the control in the Festiniog Railway could be acquired. That difficulty has stood in the way for the last 10 years.'

Some, if not all, of the £40,000 spent to acquire control of the FR probably came from the North Wales Power Co, which in 1923 transferred £25,000 ordinary stock in the FR to the Aluminium Corporation, for £500.

With no answer immediately forthcoming Davies and Breese were in Whitehall again on 19 December, seeking interviews with Treasury officials and announcing that they had just come from 10 Downing Street! Breese urged that the matter be dealt with quickly in order that he could take good news back to his constituents. Davies outlined the history of the scheme and the current financial status: the NWNGR and PBSSR had cost £270,000 and were to be purchased for £10,000 in debentures and £90,000 in ordinary shares. Completion would cost £75,000 and £10,000 had been spent already (by the Aluminium Corporation, to acquire the NWNGR debentures), 50% of the £85,000 therefore was being sought from government sources.

They were told that whilst the Treasury had not received details of the scheme from the Ministry of Transport, the government was interested in the scheme only from the standpoint of unemployment relief. For that reason the £10,000 already spent could not be supported, as doing so would not relieve unemployment. Davies said that 65%-70% of the expenditure would go on employment.

The meeting ended with Breese and Davies being told that the scheme was one that the Treasury might approve, on the recommendation of the Ministry of Transport, and subject to conditions.

Two days later Davies was back at the Treasury. The Ministry's submission had been received and it was agreed to see him to clarify some points in it; protocol actually should have prevented Davies from dealing directly with the Treasury, at least without Breese, the MP, present.

During the meeting Davies agreed that the most the government could be expected to contribute was £37,500. He prevaricated when asked what the £10,000 already expended had been spent on, answering only 'acquiring certain interests'. It was interpreted as being 'made up of sums required to buy out debenture holders in the old undertakings, and Mr Davies' fees for promotional expenses'. On leaving, Davies asked for the money to be made available as soon as possible in order that the work could be progressed. On being told that it would be a condition of grant that local funds

should be spent before calling on the government, Davies replied that it was not reasonable to expect the local subscribers to take the risk. This generated the telling response that if there were risks that local subscribers were unwilling to take, then the scheme was one to which the government ought not to be expected to contribute.

Whilst Davies and Breese were badgering the Treasury, the Ministry of Transport produced an analysis of the scheme, dated 20 December 1921. Signed by Cyril Hurcomb, who went on to become the first chairman of the British Transport Commission, this noted, *inter alia*, that no allowance had been made for rolling stock in the promoters' estimates as they were intending to use existing stock from the FR. The Ministry of Agriculture had assessed the project as desirable at a future date, whilst the Board of Trade had reviewed the scheme in 1920, and 'considered it reasonable to expect that the traffic, especially minerals, would increase, and they gave the scheme a priority . . . "urgent"'.

Further, the promoters expected the WHR to carry 250,000 tourists per annum, a figure reduced to 200,000 by the Ministry of Transport; given that in the 1920s the peak tourist season was very short, the month of August and part of September, it is difficult to see how the railway could have coped with such numbers with the restricted coaching stock at its disposal. Even when the FR, only half the length of the WHR, was carrying similar numbers in the 1970s, it needed more than 20 bogie coaches and a much longer season to do so.

In estimating freight traffic, however, the promoters seemed to err on the side of caution, producing an annual figure of 21,000 tons annually. The Treasury estimated 31,000 tons, based on the existing railways having carried 17,000 tons in 1920 and expecting completion of the PBSSR section to generate new business.

Hurcomb recommended the scheme as being suitable for assistance from unemployment relief funds. There were, he noted, 1,429 unemployed men in the district and the railway could give employment to over 500 for up to six months; unfortunately the fact that the unemployed were not navvies was overlooked!

The news the promoters desired was received in January 1922, when the Treasury wrote to Davies that the government would contribute a maximum of £37,500 to the WHR, subject to 11 conditions, including: the government's contribution was to be secured on debentures; any land required should normally be conveyed as a free gift or paid for in ordinary shares; guarantees were to be given that any excess of expenditure over £75,000 would be funded locally; government funding would become available only when expenditure of £20,000 from other sources was certified, when such expenditure would be matched; unskilled construction labour was to be obtained from the locality; the support was conditional on the LRO being made; debentures issued were not to exceed 50% of total capital; Dinas–Caernarvon was not to be undertaken without prior approval of the Minister of Transport, and no contribution from public funds was to be claimed for it.

A formal agreement to transfer control of the NWNGR and the PBSSR to the WHR, to be incorporated into the LRO, was made on 1 February. The Welsh Highland Railway (Light Railway) Order itself was made on 30 March 1922.

—3—

Completing the Portmadoc–Dinas Rail Link 1922-3

CONSIDERABLY more complex than the 1914 draft Order, the 1922 Order contained a preamble of four pages, 49 sections and two schedules. It defined the railway as: the railways respectively authorised to be acquired reconstructed or constructed as the case may be by the Act of 1901 and by the Act of 1904 as amended by the Carnarvon Order of 1908 and authorised by the Order of 1908 to be reconstructed or constructed as light railways under the Light Railways Act 1896 and the light railway authorised by the Carnarvon Order 1908 and the Moel Tryfan Undertaking and the light railway authorised by the Order of 1906 or as the case may be the works connected therewith or any part or parts of the above-mentioned railways or undertakings respectively: provided that the excepted railway as hereinafter defined is not included in the said expression 'the railway'.

Hence, a railway from Portmadoc Harbour to Caernarvon, except that there were no funds for the last three miles and no provision for a station in Portmadoc or a link to the FR. The excepted railway was the stub end of the PBSSR's 1901 line between Beddgelert and Llyn Gwynant and the 1908 line thence to Bettws-y-coed.

The Order incorporated a company to own and operate the railway, the Welsh Highland Railway (Light Railway) Company, with Davies, Jack and Sir John Henderson Stewart (owner of more than 75% of the NWNGR debentures and, since 25 January 1922, the NWPT's interest in the PBSSR) as its first directors; the investing authorities were also permitted to appoint a director to represent their interests. Several sections covered the raising of loans, and their repayment, by the investing authorities. The Carnarvon Harbour Trust, although a party in the draft Order and obviously a supporter of the railway was actually excluded from the Order because it was not a public authority as defined by the Light Railways Act and consequently did not require the authority of an LRO to invest in the railway.

Three years were allowed for the completion of any compulsory land purchases and five years, unless extended by application to the Minister of Transport, for construction, except that government funding would be withheld from any work not completed before 1 April 1923.

The company was empowered to enter into working agreements with the LNWR and the GWR and to lease the railway, or part of it, to any railway company with which it was permitted to enter into agreements. Interestingly, in the light of events, a clause in this section declared that 'any such lease shall imply a condition of re-entry if the lessees discontinue the working of the railway leased . . . for a space of three months . . .'

The WHR's civil engineering contract was let to Sir Robert McAlpine & Sons, a partnership, for a fixed price of £66,515 on 30 April 1922. Stewart and Jack signed for the railway and five members of the McAlpine family for the contractors; the original document, impressed with the WHR's seal, found its way into the archives at Caernarvon.

Under the contract the partnership was required to obtain any land required (clause 13), at its own expense, and to convey it to the railway, for which purpose £1,000 was allowed. This might have been a device to avoid the restrictions on using government money to purchase land. It applied around Beddgelert, where deviations were made from the PBSSR route; despite being included in the contract the railway did not, at this stage, have any authority for them.

The minimum radius on curves (clause 34) was to be 198ft and the maximum gradient 1 in 40, and 40lb rail in 33ft lengths was specified although 'second-hand or reject imperfect material will be accepted provided the engineers (Sir Douglas Fox & Co) are satisfied with the quality of the rails proposed'. All points were to have 1 in 12 turnouts.

The long tunnel in the Aberglaslyn Pass (clause 43) required completion, and working from both ends was required provided water did not require pumping, and the others needed opening out to the correct cross section where necessary.

Clause 56 required exposed steelwork to be given three coats of 'first class' paint, one before and two after completion; history shows that the contractors defaulted on this item.

Halts, passing places and stations (clause 59) were required at: 'about 3 miles' (from Rhyd Ddu) — halt with 40ft siding, shelter; Beddgelert — 300ft passing loop, 180ft siding, sidings to locomotive and goods sheds, waiting room/office, goods shed, locomotive shed, water tank; Nantmor — halt with 40ft siding, shelter; Croesor Junction — 300ft passing loop, 40ft siding; Pont Croesor — 40ft siding, waiting room; Portmadoc — 300ft passing loop, waiting room/office, water tank. Second-hand army huts or similar were permissible. All stations and halts were to have 'platforms' of 6in of rolled stone ballast or gravel 150ft x 10ft, except Beddgelert where 300ft x 15ft was specified.

Any transport required over the NWNGR section was chargeable at three-quarters of the usual rate. Use could be made of the Croesor section in connection with the execution of the works, provided any traffic offering was carried at the normal rate; when it was for WHR use, three-quarters of the usual rate became chargeable!

The schedule of prices and quantities divided the contract into three sections: refurbishing the NWNGR, including the Bryngwyn branch; construction between Rhyd Ddu and Croesor Junction, and repairs to the Croesor Tramway from the junction and Portmadoc. The latter was further divided into two parts: from the junction to Beddgelert Siding and thence to Portmadoc.

NWNGR section works were to cost £9,278. They included installing 5,000 new sleepers at £1,666, loosening existing ballast and laying 3in of top ballast at £3,510, replacing one turnout at Dinas and five at Bryngwyn at £20 each and renewing a diamond crossing at Dinas for £50. £1,000 was allowed for repair of rolling stock and £1,000 for fencing.

The new works were costed at £52,492. Trimming the Goat tunnel and the short Aberglaslyn tunnels was priced at 40s (£2) per cubic yard for an estimated 190cu yd. Excavating and trimming the long tunnel was only 30s (£1.50) per cubic yard for an estimated 2,100cu yd — quantity discount?

Diverting the road near Nantmor to pass under the railway, for which there was no approval at the time of the contract, was quoted at £500; a further £100 was the price for remetalling and steam-rolling the road. The three lattice girder bridges, crossing the Glaslyn at Bryn-y-felin and the Nantmor and Dylif river crossings, were quoted at £30 per ton erected complete: total £1,800.

Ten inches of ballast, including no more than 4in of bottom ballast, was to be laid; nine miles at £300 per mile; 17,000 sleepers were priced at £4,037 while 600 tons of rail and fittings were priced at £5,100. The line required 12 sets of points and six catch points, at £288, and £1,000 was allowed for the telephone system. Station buildings, water tanks and gates were to be to be supplied and installed at 'nett invoiced cash price plus 10 per cent'; £1,500 allowed with £2,500 allowed for fencing the trackbed.

The work to refurbish the Croesor Tramway to Portmadoc was estimated at £4,745. Of this the three miles from Croesor Junction to Beddgelert Siding was to be cleaned and weeded for £40 per mile and existing ballast was to be loosened and improved by the addition of 2in of top ballast for £638. A total of 500 new sleepers was required, together with three sets of points at Croesor Junction and one at Pont Croesor (Pond Croesor in the contract) and £1,000 was allowed for reconstructing Pont Croesor (eight 24ft spans) and £60 for the adjacent level crossing.

From Beddgelert Siding new rail was specified but half the sleepers and half the ballast were expected to be reusable; the inclusive cost, including the loop, was estimated at £1,311 while 400yd of slate sidings were to be relaid with 'light section rails' with ballasting and sleepers as required, for £300. Four turnouts were needed at the Beddgelert sidings and a further six turnouts and passing loops between that place and Portmadoc.

The deadlines set for completion were 22 July 1922 for Dinas-Beddgelert and Portmadoc-Nantmor, and 31 March 1923 for the remainder. This included a requirement to work at nights and on Sundays if necessary.

To deal with the diversions and some other matters an amendment LRO was applied for in July 1922, whilst preparations for reopening the NWNGR on 31 July, just a few days late, were in hand. Colonel J. W. Pringle inspected the line on 22 July and submitted his report three days later. He noted that the permanent way was generally in adequate condition for the class of traffic and a speed restriction of 15mph was proposed.

He reported that this part of the WHR would be operated in two sections: Dinas to Tryfan Junction and thence to Rhyd Ddu. Control would be by Wise's patent staff-and-ticket for the former and one-engine-in-steam (with staff) for the second. At Tryfan Junction a key on the Dinas-Tryfan Junction staff would lock the Bryngwyn branch points; passenger trains there would use the same track in each direction.

Pringle observed that some of the old sleepers were in a decayed condition and would require changing before too long. He noted that remnants of NWNGR signalling was still *in situ* and asked for it to be removed. The outlet of a new water tank at Quellyn Lake halt fouled an open carriage door and had to be moved. Subject to these and other minor works and clarification of some operating rules, he recommended: 'that approval be given to the working of passenger traffic on this Light Railway'.

The reopened railway was promoted as providing '10 miles of beautiful scenery' with streams, waterfalls, lakes and mountains to see and with observation cars provided. Four passenger trains daily were operated, with goods trains running as required. Gaumont News filmed the railway, for showing in over 500 cinemas, during the first week; regrettably the film has not survived.

Revenue for the week ending 5 August was £94; wages for 22 men amounted to £69 and a pro rata proportion of overheads to £22, leaving a small operating surplus of £3, considered a satisfactory result by Councillor Nee (see later), although by the end of the year a loss of £571 had been incurred. At that time Glaslyn and Deudraeth councils had made no arrangements to raise the finance required for their loans to the railway; Davies persuaded them to take action by allowing them to consult with the contractors on the use of local labour on outstanding work.

The second LRO application attracted much more attention than that for the first Order and, following a site visit the previous day, a public inquiry was held before the LRC in Portmadoc on 8 September the same year.

In addition to powers of deviation, and abandonment, around Beddgelert the promoters sought to limit the assessment of the railway to local rates for five years, requesting that the land occupied by the new railway, Rhyd Ddu to Croesor Junction, be assessed on the same basis as it had been before it had been acquired for the railway, that is as agricultural land. They had noticed that the 1921 Railways Act contained a provision to allow such relief where a light railway had been constructed with government assistance.

Naturally, it was the latter that excited the investing authorities and all were represented at the inquiry. William George was in attendance again, this time representing the Glaslyn Foundry, together with Mr R. Newell, owner of the slaughterhouse likely to be affected by the proposed FR station, and the Cwmcloch owners, affected by a deviation near Beddgelert, as well as Portmadoc UDC.

Others represented included the LNWR, Tourist Hotels Ltd (the Royal Goat Hotel, Beddgelert), Carnarvon Harbour Trust, the Tremadoc Estate, the National Union of Railwaymen, the Railway Clerks' Association and the North Wales Quarrymen's Association. Evan R. Davies, Cradoc Davies and Jack represented the promoters.

In its objection the county council sought primarily to rank the debentures authorised by the 1922 Order above any others that might be issued by the railway, except in respect of any issued to the authorities supporting the Dinas-Caernarvon extension that should rank equally with the first £85,000, and to reduce the period of rates relief from five years to two without any option for extension.

Davies opened the inquiry by commenting on the 'formidable array . . . of legal talent' present which was not at the previous inquiry. He said that he thought this indicated support for the scheme on its merits but with objections on detail.

He then said that a good deal of progress had been made between Rhyd Ddu and Portmadoc and explained that when the engineers reviewed the engineering details in March 'they found it might be possible to effect considerable improvement in the line of route below Beddgelert'. He justified the proposed route changes, saying that the PBSSR route, an embankment, from the road bridge near the Royal Goat Hotel to the Glaslyn, would be 'an interference with its natural beauty' that could be avoided by the route proposed.

Davies went on to say that the deviations below Rhyd Ddu were substantial but gave no explanation for them, commenting only that the landowners had no objections to them. The road diversion at Nantmor would, he said, replace a level crossing on a busy road with a bridge. The railway's engineers amplified the reasons for the diversions later.

On the matter of rates relief, Davies said the promoters had offered to meet the objection by having the relief withdrawn as soon as the railway was in a position to pay both the debenture interest and instalments on the investing authorities' advances. He said that in its early years the railway would have to pay interest on the debentures as well as one fifth of the local authorities' advance of £29,000. He thought rates

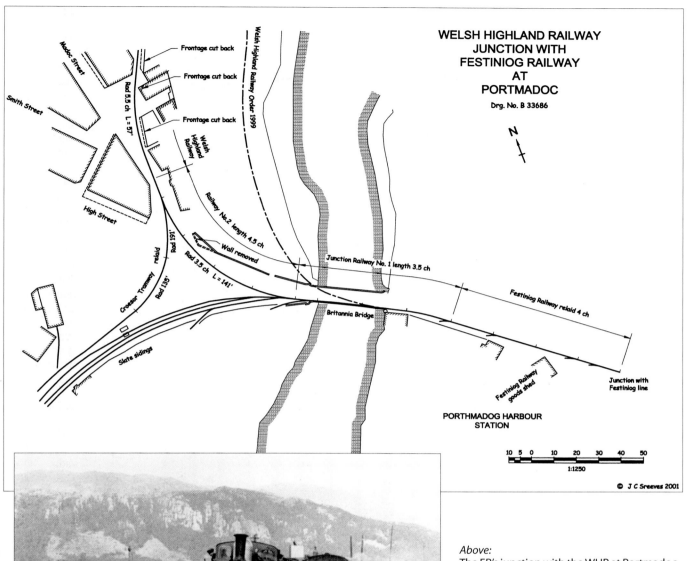

WELSH HIGHLAND RAILWAY
JUNCTION WITH
FESTINIOG RAILWAY
AT
PORTMADOC

Drg. No. B 33686

N

Madoc Street

Smith Street

High Street

Frontage cut back

Frontage cut back

Frontage cut back

Welsh Highland Railway Order 1999

Welsh Highland Railway

Railway No.2 length 4.5 ch

Wall removed

Rad 5.5 ch L = 57'

Rad 191'

Croesor Tramway relaid

Rad 3.5 ch L = 141'

Rad 135'

Slate sidings

Junction Railway No. 1 length 3.5 ch

Britannia Bridge

Festiniog Railway relaid 4 ch

Festiniog Railway goods shed

Junction with
Festiniog line

PORTHMADOG HARBOUR
STATION

10 5 0   10   20   30   40   50

1:1250

© J C Sreeves 2001

Above:
The FR's junction with the WHR at Portmadoc.

Left:
Portmadoc New station looking very new in 1923. The station building is to the left and the refreshment room, run by the Snowdon Mountain Railway, behind. The layouts for the workshops, running and exchange facilities suggested for the adjoining land (see pages 48/9) gave no indication as to how the difference in levels was to be accommodated.
Author's collection

payable could be in the order of £1,500, but no one really knew. In 1921 the FR had paid £1,630 in rates for a line half as long as the WHR was going to be — he thought WHR traffic would equal that on the FR! He observed that at present the authorities were getting virtually nothing from the railway, implying that they would be no worse off with the clause.

The objection of Tourist Hotels Ltd had some complexity, being based on a covenant entered into when Royal Goat Hotel land was sold to the PBSSR in 1905. Then the station access was to have been through the hotel yard, presumably the hotel hoping to attract additional business thereby. The promoters, noting an increase in road traffic in the intervening years and the unsuitability of the hotel yard as a route for charabancs, wished to build a new access from the Caernarvon side of the village, alongside what was then known as the Council School, as well as providing a better

access from the Portmadoc side, on the village side of the hotel, making it possible for charabancs to leave the station without having to turn. Davies said that the promoters would settle for a footpath from the Caernarvon side if they could not have a road but felt the commissioners were as empowered to overturn the covenant as Parliament was. In the event the commissioners were not required to make a decision on the matter for the parties agreed to negotiate further; the improved access was never made.

Davies examined Ralph Freeman, for Douglas Fox & Co, the railway's engineers, to bring out more information on the need for the diversions. Freeman explained that the PBSSR's route between the Royal Goat Hotel and the Glaslyn would have required some difficult work, with much of the land boggy, whilst the proposed route was shorter, required less earthwork and had easier gradients. Fox's plans reveal that

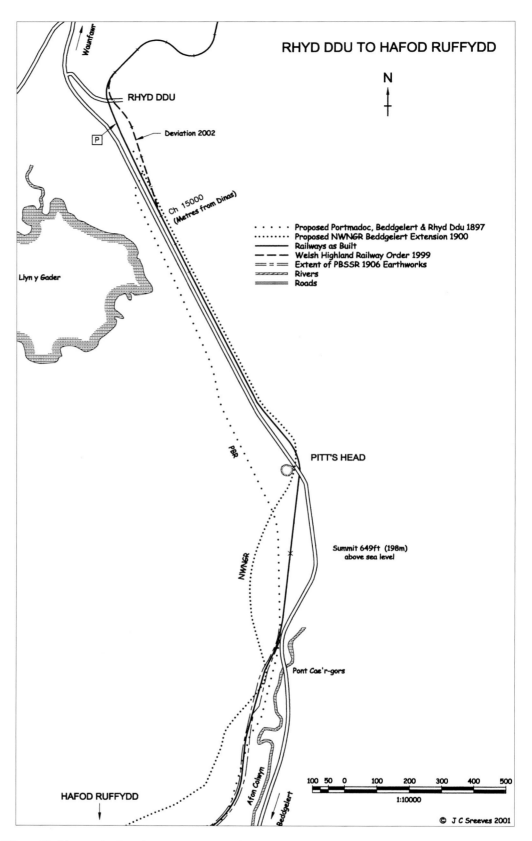

Right:
Rhyd Ddu to Hafod Ruffydd.

RHYD DDU TO HAFOD RUFFYDD

N

RHYD DDU

Deviation 2002

Ch 15000 (Metres from Dinas)

· · · · · Proposed Portmadoc, Beddgelert & Rhyd Ddu 1897
· · · · · · Proposed NWNGR Beddgelert Extension 1900
————— Railways as Built
— — — Welsh Highland Railway Order 1999
= = = Extent of PBSSR 1906 Earthworks
▨▨▨ Rivers
════ Roads

Llyn y Gader

PBR

PITT'S HEAD

NWNGR

Summit 649ft (198m)
above sea level

Pont Cae'r-gors

100 50 0   100   200   300   400   500
1:10000

HAFOD RUFFYDD

Afon Colwyn

Beddgelert

© J C Sreeves 2001

two other routes using the PBSSR road bridge and other river crossings had also been considered.

On the matter of the route between Rhyd Ddu and Beddgelert, Freeman said, the 1 in 28 gradients would require double-heading or split trains to deal with heavy loads; the proposed route would have 1 in 40 maximum gradients — here Freeman rather overstated his case, for only the short section, two chains long, connecting the station with the 1900 route at Tyn-y-coed was at 1 in 28; other changes to the route

were made to reduce the scale of earthworks needed. The modification near Nantmor avoided a level crossing on a sharp bend with limited visibility at the expense of providing a bridge.

Counsel for Gwyrfai RDC cross-examined Jack about the proposed clause dealing with debentures. Essentially, he said that as the authorities had to agree to the issue of further debentures he could not see what the problem was — the sticking point for the councils was the proviso 'which consent cannot be unreasonably withheld' which they saw as meaning they would have no say in the matter.

There were questions about the rates assessment, the councils saying that they had been told the railway would be responsible for increased rateable values in the area, and they would prefer the certainty of rates than the uncertainty of debenture interest. The councils were also concerned that their nominee on the WHR company board could not take his place until they had advanced £15,000 to the railway, as specified in the 1922 order; the railway agreed to the nominee taking up his post without the financial condition being met and this modification was incorporated into the new Order. Notwithstanding their objections, it was made clear that the authorities remained in support of the WHR development.

The maintenance of and the height of the proposed Nantmor road bridge came in for some comment also. The WHR wanted 14ft whilst the highway authority wanted the 16ft specified by the Railway Clauses Act of 1845 — there was some debate about whether a 'two-deck' charabanc would pass through a 14ft bridge without putting its top deck passengers at risk of decapitation. The county also wanted, for unspecified reasons, a span of 35ft instead of 25ft.

In their report of 16 September 1922 the commissioners approved the deviations without change, noting that the McAlpines were already at work on that between Rhyd Ddu and Beddgelert! The WHR lost on the question of the height of the Nantmor road bridge, but won on the matter of its span. On the issue of rateable assessment the railway got its clause, but restricted to two years and with no option to extend.

Whilst the Order was being processed, news of the Welsh Highland reached *The Times* in London, with the WHR forming the centrepiece of the Industrial Wales section of that paper's Trade Supplement published on 11 November 1922. Citing the railway as an imaginative enterprise, it called upon the newly formed LMSR and enlarged GWR to follow its example in improving access to Snowdonia.

The Order was made on 7 February 1923; it had cost £219 in legal fees to obtain. Deviation Railway No 1 started south of Hafod Ruffydd, 2 miles 2 furlongs from Rhyd Ddu, proceeding in a southeasterly direction and terminating north-easterly of Cwmcloch Isaf, 4 miles 1 furlong from Rhyd Ddu. Deviation Railway No 2 was 4 furlongs 7 chains long, starting by the Royal Goat Hotel tunnel, 4 miles 7 furlongs from Rhyd Ddu, and ending on the east bank of the Glaslyn east of Bryn-y-felin, crossing the river by a 75ft bridge. It required relocating some 300ft of the existing road, raising it over the railway on a new bridge. By these deviations the railway became 570yd longer.

The matter of connecting the WHR to the FR was left to the FR to resolve. This was probably because WHR funding was already severely constrained and the local authorities would have been most unhappy at the prospect of issuing further debentures. Whilst the FR was not flush with funds (share-holders had been told the undertaking was being carried on at a serious loss in 1921), it would perhaps find it easier to raise those necessary for the link line.

In addition to applying for powers to build the junction railways, the FR sought permission for a new station to replace Harbour station and locomotive facilities to replace Boston Lodge, alongside the WHR in Portmadoc, and at the same time, advantage was taken to apply for powers to operate the FR as a light railway. The route proposed was split into two for legal reasons, the first replacing part of the original line to the harbour by a new line over a widened Britannia Bridge, the second providing the actual link. The deposited plans for the Order left the detail of track layout and facilities vague but two proposed layouts were produced.

Projected facilities included a locomotive shed with capacity for nine locomotives, a turntable, exchange facilities for goods and locomotive coal with the Cambrian and a workshop.

Consulting engineers Douglas Fox & Partners' estimate for the works came out at £13,500 for 10 chains (222yd) of railway. The estimate included: legal and engineering expenses — £1,500, buildings — £3,000; alterations to bridge — £1,500; permanent way and resurfacing roads — £500; land/buildings acquisition — £1,000 and an allowance for contingencies of £1,000. The FR sought approval to borrow a further £20,000 in consequence, the difference being for working capital and current losses.

Strangely enough the estimate also included £5,000 for rolling stock. The amount is probably that for the same purpose previously 'lost' from the WHR estimates although Davies was to say, at the inquiry, that the FR's rolling stock was 'pretty old' and the directors thought 'it may be necessary to improve it'.

The LRO application was submitted at the same time as that for the second WHR Order and the inquiry was held on the same day. Those aspects of it relating to the FR solely will be left for another day. Regarding the link between the FR and the WHR, Davies said that the main purpose of the application was to make it possible for there to be a physical union between the two railways under joint direction.

Portmadoc UDC, represented by William George, had objected to the proposal, apparently failing to understand or remember, Davies reminded the inquiry, that the FR already had powers, that it made regular use of, to cross the Britannia Bridge and that the Croesor Tramway had statutory authority for its line to the harbour which had been upgraded, by statute, for passenger use by the PBSSR Act of 1901. The status of the road also caused some confusion as it still belonged to the Tremadoc Estate, owners of the Cob and successors to William Madocks, its builder, and not Portmadoc UDC as assumed.

The council proposed an alternative route through the garden of Ynys Tywyn but said it would accept the railway's scheme provided there were safeguards for public safety. In this respect it required a flagman to precede the trains and for the locomotives to be equipped with a bell. The council also hoped that the Croesor crossing would be done away with. When it was pointed out that such a move would require any goods traffic originating from the WHR and bound for the harbour to be double-shunted across the Britannia Bridge, William George responded that the goods could be taken to the FR for shunting!

On the matter of the station, Davies explained that it would be absurd to have two stations for 'these small undertakings' and as they were largely dependent on the GWR for passengers it would not be in the public interest to have the station a mile away from the GWR station. He expressed a wish for the GWR to stop some of its trains close to the proposed narrow gauge station to reduce the walking distance between the railways. The new station would be part of the FR undertaking and replace the existing station at the harbour. By the Order the FR would have running powers over the WHR as far as the GWR crossing.

When asked to speak 'generally' on the linking of the railways, Jack replied 'The original conception of the WHR was to enable the FR to be of greater service to the district, but it appeared to me when I first went into the figures that there were difficulties facing the railway that might have resulted in defeating the object altogether. A railway of 12½ miles could not possibly hope to prosper, but if 25 miles of railway were added to it, it would give such an average per passenger as to cover the expenditure, and one might therefore hope to

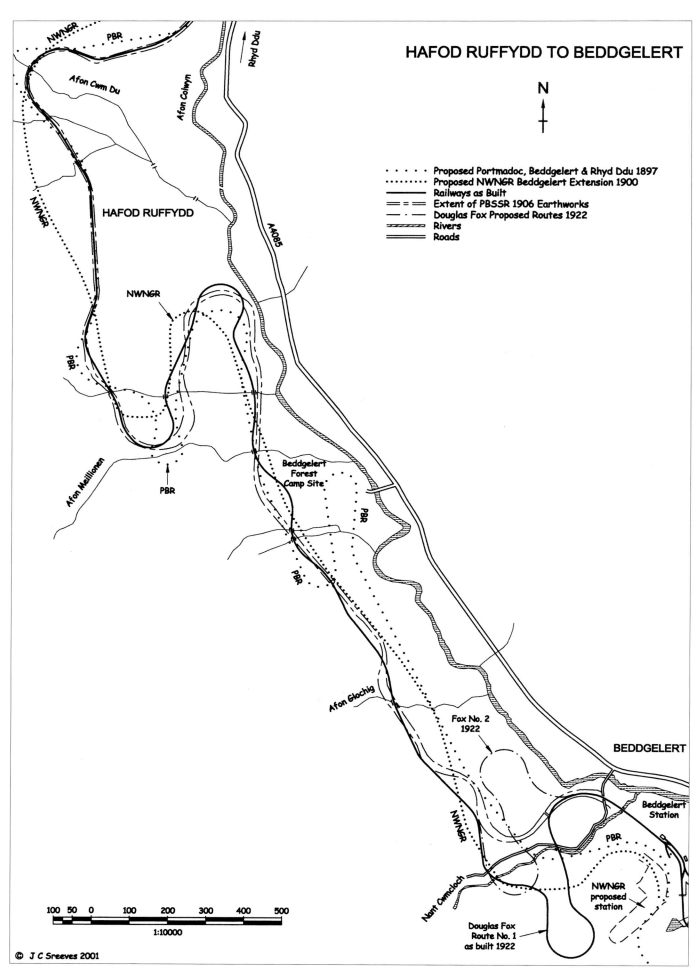

HAFOD RUFFYDD TO BEDDGELERT

N

· · · · · Proposed Portmadoc, Beddgelert & Rhyd Ddu 1897
· · · · · Proposed NWNGR Beddgelert Extension 1900
——— Railways as Built
≡≡≡ Extent of PBSSR 1906 Earthworks
—·—· Douglas Fox Proposed Routes 1922
░░░ Rivers
═══ Roads

Rhyd Ddu

Afon Cwm Du

Afon Colwyn

A4085

NWNGR

PBR

NWNGR

HAFOD RUFFYDD

PBR

NWNGR

Afon Meillionen

PBR

Beddgelert
Forest
Camp Site

PBR

PBR

Afon Glochig

Fox No. 2
1922

BEDDGELERT

Beddgelert
Station

NWNGR

PBR

Nant Cwmcloch

NWNGR
proposed
station

Douglas Fox
Route No. 1
as built 1922

100 50 0   100   200   300   400   500

1:10000

© J C Sreeves 2001

44

Above:
One of a series of publicity photographs taken in 1923, this one at Beddgelert, perhaps before the railway was opened; ironically all the stock visible belonged to the FR. With England 0-4-0STT *Little Giant* is brake/3rd composite No 2 (now No 10) and 1st/3rd composite No 17. On the left are a dual-braked four-wheel van and a coal wagon. *Author's collection*

Left:
Hafod Ruffydd to Beddgelert.

make it a success.' A somewhat different, and almost contradictory, response to the explanation he had previously given to the Treasury.

The Commissioners' report on the inquiry is undated; they generally approved the FR's application except for a general power of sale to any railway company or the WHR. The Commissioners said that if there were a proposal for such a sale they could deal with it. They further said that it would be useless to give the FR power to be sold to the WHR as the WHR was not authorised to enter into such a purchase and had no powers to raise the capital required. As the government had invested in the WHR its approval would be needed in any event. The Order was made on 30 January 1923.

The FR's ordinary shareholders, incidentally, were informed of these activities only on 17 February 1923, when Jack circulated his annual report. He told them what was in hand with regard to the LRO, working arrangements, through trains, the junction railways and the new station. He said the works were estimated to cost £6,000 and the company expected to issue not more than £10,000 of the £20,000 debenture stock authorised by the LRO. In the meantime the company expected to use the facilities of the National Provincial Bank. The McAlpines widened the Britannia Bridge and built the junction railways, accepting debenture stock for some or all of the work.

Following the WHR's agreement with the investing authorities, M. E. Nee, a Caernarvon solicitor and county councillor, was appointed a company director, provisionally, from 15 July 1922. On 25 April 1923 he submitted a progress report to the authorities.

In addition to commenting on the financial results of operating the NWNGR section, already quoted, Nee explained that each week he received reports detailing the number of men employed by the company, company progress, construction progress and the number of men employed on the contract. The latter ranged from 250 in July 1922 to 429 at the time of the report. Naturally, as the local unemployed did not include large numbers of navvies, the contract did little to relieve local unemployment as proposed; the WHR came in for some criticism in consequence but Nee makes no reference to it in his report.

He closed his report by adding that the WHR and the Snowdon Mountain Railway were producing a guidebook 'showing the beauty spots through which the line runs' and that copies would be distributed in 'America and the Colonies'. He concluded, with misplaced confidence, 'It is anticipated that in a few years' time the railway will be as popular as any mountain railway in Europe'!

It was in May 1923, nearly two months after the 31 March deadline, before the McAlpines completed the contract. On 22 May a special train notice was produced covering the programme for Lieutenant-Colonel Mount's inspection two days later. Starting from Bettws-y-coed by car, Mount travelled first to Waenfawr to inspect the loop there. Afterwards he joined a special train, consisting of FR Fairlies *Merddin Emrys* and *Livingston Thompson* and three bogie carriages, one of them possibly substituted by a trolley, at Beddgelert, with departure scheduled for 10.00. The purpose of the second locomotive was to test the bridges. Getting Jack's party to Portmadoc required two chauffeurs whose expenses were 7s (35p). *Merddin Emrys*, only, hauled the

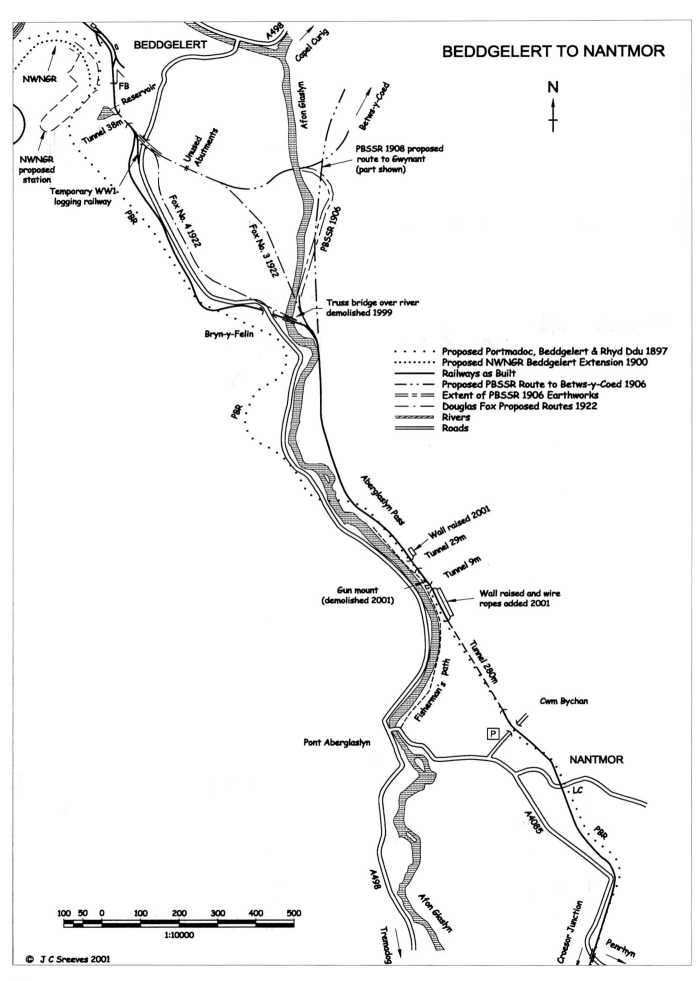

BEDDGELERT TO NANTMOR

N

BEDDGELERT

A498

Capel Curig

NWNGR

FB

Reservoir

Afon Glaslyn

Betws-y-Coed

Tunnel 38m

Unused Abutments

PBSSR 1908 proposed route to Gwynant (part shown)

NWNGR proposed station

Temporary WW1 logging railway

PBR

Fox No. 4 1922

Fox No. 3 1922

PBSSR 1906

Truss bridge over river demolished 1999

Bryn-y-Felin

Proposed Portmadoc, Beddgelert & Rhyd Ddu 1897
Proposed NWNGR Beddgelert Extension 1900
Railways as Built
Proposed PBSSR Route to Betws-y-Coed 1906
Extent of PBSSR 1906 Earthworks
Douglas Fox Proposed Routes 1922
Rivers
Roads

PBR

Aberglaslyn Pass

Wall raised 2001
Tunnel 29m

Tunnel 9m

Gun mount (demolished 2001)

Wall raised and wire ropes added 2001

Tunnel 280m

Fisherman's path

Cwm Bychan

P

Pont Aberglaslyn

NANTMOR

LC

A4085

PBR

A498

Afon Glaslyn

Tremadog

Croesor Junction

Penrhyn

100 50 0   100   200   300   400   500

1:10000

© J C Sreeves 2001

Above:
A 1920s winter train consisting of an England locomotive and Pickering brake composite carriage has just crosses into the Aberglaslyn Pass at Bryn-y-felin heading for Portmadoc.
C.A. Appleton/Author's collection

Left:
Beddgelert to Nantmor.

train returning Mount to Beddgelert. His report was submitted on 29 May.

Commencing at Rhyd Ddu, Mount recorded the locations of the intended stopping places, several more than specified in the contract, with facilities:

• Rhyd Ddu: existing 300ft loop reconditioned, new points and crossings laid; sidings at each end, existing station building.
• Pitt's Head (halt): 1 mile
• Hafod Ruffydd (halt): 2 miles, siding
• Beddgelert: 4⅝ miles, 320ft loop, trailing sidings at north end off both roads
• Nantmor (halt): 6¼ miles, siding
• Hafod-y-llyn (halt): 7⅛ miles, siding
• Ynys Ferlas (halt): 8⅛ miles, siding
• Croesor Junction: 8¾ miles
• Ynysfor (halt): 9 miles, siding
• Pont Croesor (halt): 10⅛ miles, 300ft siding
• Portreuddyn: 10⅞ miles, loop installed but not expected to be used
• Beddgelert Siding: 11¾ miles, 250ft goods loop
• Portmadoc (New): 12 miles, 150ft loop
• Corn Mill: 12⅛ miles, loop on east side, sidings on west, platform for use by goods traffic only
• Portmadoc (Old, FR): 12½ miles

Mount noted that with the exception of 1,000yd south of Rhyd Ddu, where existing track had been reconditioned and ballasted, the section to Croesor Junction had been laid with flat-bottom 40lb British Standard rail in 33ft lengths. The Croesor Tramway section to the GWR crossing was 'old' 41lb flat-bottom material and beyond, to the FR, new rail was used. Ballasting was incomplete on the new line, he observed, and forecast that some sleepers on the Croesor section, damaged by horses, would soon require replacement. Fencing was also incomplete, and causing problems with animals straying on to the track near the GWR crossing.

Working was to be by staff-and-ticket in two sections, dividing at Beddgelert. He had been told that there was no intention to work passenger trains between the two Portmadoc stations but instructed that a staff or a ticket must control any trains over that section. In the vicinity of the High Street the main line had to be protected from the harbour lines by locked stop blocks. Up was towards Portmadoc.

Mount observed that the highest embankment was near Nantmor (30ft) and the deepest cutting was on the Rhyd Ddu side of Beddgelert (42ft). The Goat Hotel tunnel and the long tunnel in the Aberglaslyn Pass were noted as being on 1 in 40 gradients. Some rock trimming was required and the long tunnel needed two further refuges, making nine in all.

The deflection of the Bryn-y-felin bridge was measured under the load of the two Fairlies and found to be 0.35in static, increasing to 0.42in at 15mph. Mount saw that this and the other similar bridges had not been painted and required an application of two coats. Pont Croesor, of a different construction, was similarly tested and gave the result of 0.35in static and 0.47in at 15mph.

At the GWR crossing he reported that during construction there had been 20 horse-drawn movements a day on the WHR, including Croesor slate traffic. A woman who had

Overleaf:
Suggested layouts for the FR station at Portmadoc authorised by the 1923 LRO.

47

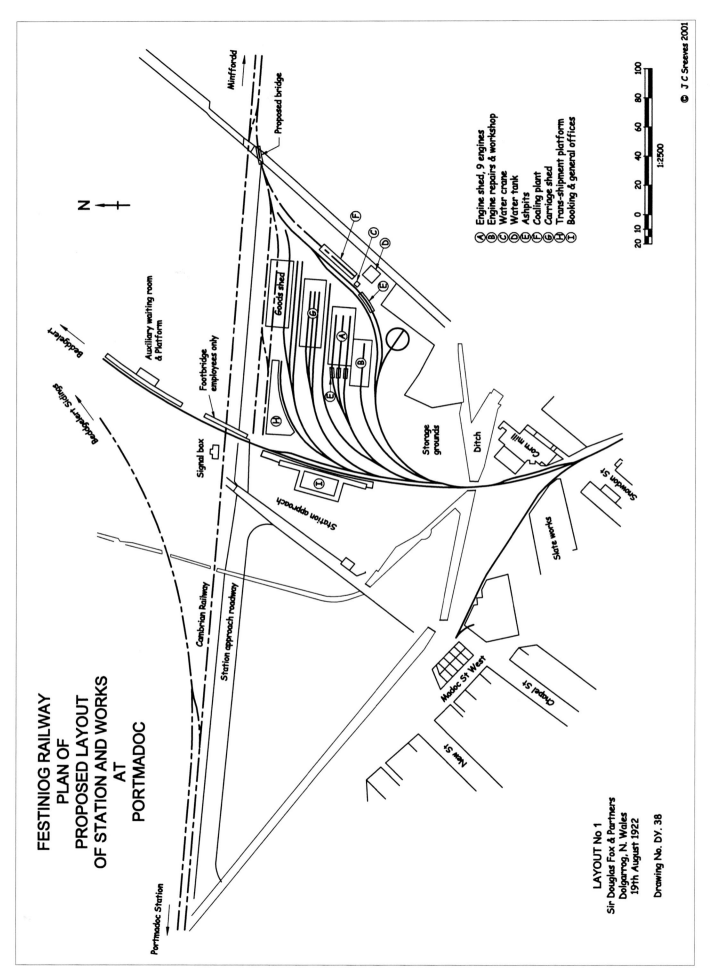

FESTINIOG RAILWAY
PLAN OF
PROPOSED LAYOUT
OF STATION AND WORKS
AT
PORTMADOC

N

Minffordd

Proposed bridge

Beddgelert

Beddgelert Sidings

Auxiliary waiting room & Platform

Footbridge employees only

Goods shed

Signal box

Station approach

Storage grounds

Ditch

Corn mill

Slate works

Snowdon St

Madoc St West

Chapel St

New St

Portmadoc Station

Cambrian Railway

Station approach roadway

Ⓐ Engine shed, 9 engines
Ⓑ Engine repairs & workshop
Ⓒ Water crane
Ⓓ Water tank
Ⓔ Ashpits
Ⓕ Coaling plant
Ⓖ Carriage shed
Ⓗ Trans-shipment platform
Ⓘ Booking & general offices

20 10 0   20   40   60   80   100
1:2500

Ⓒ J C Sreeves 2001

LAYOUT No 1
Sir Douglas Fox & Partners
Dolgarrog, N. Wales
19th August 1922

Drawing No. DY. 38

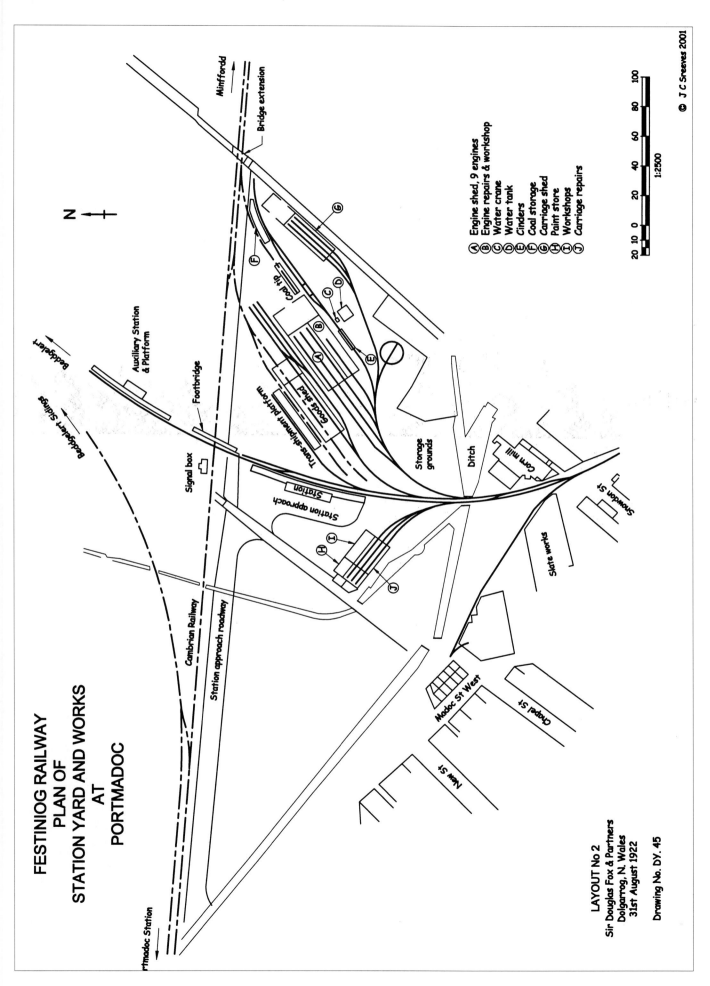

FESTINIOG RAILWAY
PLAN OF
STATION YARD AND WORKS
AT
PORTMADOC

N

Ⓐ Engine shed, 9 engines
Ⓑ Engine repairs & workshop
Ⓒ Water crane
Ⓓ Water tank
Ⓔ Cinders
Ⓕ Coal storage
Ⓖ Carriage shed
Ⓗ Paint store
Ⓘ Workshops
Ⓙ Carriage repairs

1:2500

20 10 0   20   40   60   80   100

© J C Sreeves 2001

Minffordd
Bridge extension
Coal tip
Ⓖ
Ⓕ
Ⓒ
Ⓓ
Ⓑ
Ⓐ
Ⓔ
Goods shed
Trans-shipment platform
Auxiliary Station & Platform
Footbridge
Signal box
Station
Station approach
Cambrian Railway
Station approach roadway
Beddgelert Sidings
Beddgelert
Portmadoc Station
Storage grounds
Ditch
Corn mill
Slate works
Snowdon St
Madoc St West
Chapel St
New St
Ⓗ
Ⓘ
Ⓙ

LAYOUT No 2
Sir Douglas Fox & Partners
Dolgarrog, N. Wales
31st August 1922

Drawing No. DY. 45

49

worked the crossing satisfactorily previously was being superseded by a porter signalman.

On the stations front, Mount noted that Rhyd Ddu was in a bad state of repair, with the floor falling in. At Beddgelert he required the distance between the loop lines to be increased from 8ft 6in centres to 13ft to improve sighting for passengers on down trains arriving there. Buildings had not been erected at Hafod Ruffydd, Ynysfor and Pont Croesor.

The maximum speed was to be generally 15mph. Exceptions were 10mph for trains descending the gradients on the 'S' bends between Rhyd Ddu and Beddgelert, Up trains traversing the Aberglaslyn tunnels and between Portmadoc New station and Madoc Street and 5mph through facing points, over public road crossings, in Madoc Street and on the Britannia Bridge. Mandatory stops were required before the trap points on either side of the GWR crossing, the level crossing over Portmadoc High Street in both directions and the fouling point of the connection at the FR station for up trains.

Subject to receipt of undertakings by the company on several outstanding matters, Mount recommended approval be given for the operation of passenger traffic for a temporary period of six months. He proposed that the WHR then be reinspected, together with the FR, to establish what, if any, additional requirements might be necessary.

The next day, 24 May, Mount inspected the works authorised by the FR's LRO, submitting his report on 1 June. Representatives of the company, the consulting engineers and the contractors had accompanied him; for the junction railways representatives of Portmadoc UDC and the town surveyor joined them.

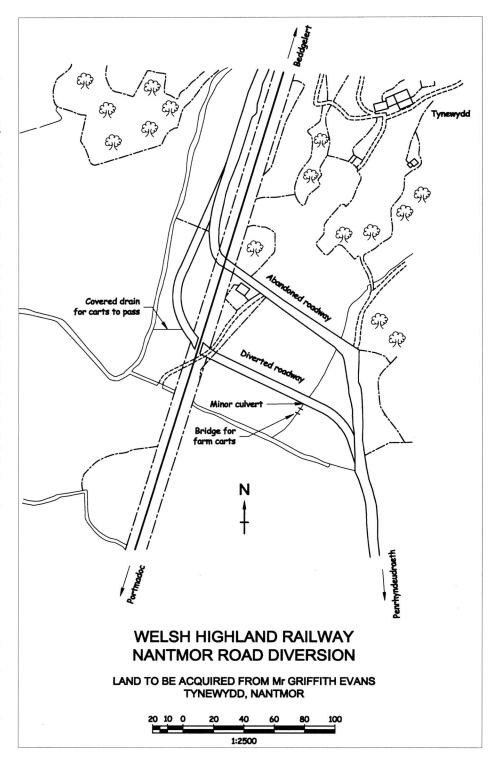

**WELSH HIGHLAND RAILWAY
NANTMOR ROAD DIVERSION**

**LAND TO BE ACQUIRED FROM Mr GRIFFITH EVANS
TYNEWYDD, NANTMOR**

1:2500

At the station, passenger facilities, waiting room, parcels and ticket offices and conveniences were contained within a 40ft x 12ft corrugated-iron building located below the embankment near the GWR crossing. A footpath connection to the GWR station had been made.

Inspecting the junction railways, he was unhappy with the timber surface provided between the rails, saying it was unsuitable and would not withstand heavy road traffic; tarmacadam should be used. He agreed with the council's concern over drainage on Britannia Bridge and recommended a kerb with gulleys be installed, having the effect of separating the railway from the road.

Mount approved the station and the junction railways for use by passenger traffic but would not recommend final

approval for the junction railways until he had been notified that a settlement had been reached with the town.

Mount's report on the loop at Waenfawr, referred to earlier, was submitted on 4 June. To break up the long section between Tryfan Junction and Rhyd Ddu the existing NWNGR loop had been fettled by replacing some of the worst sleepers; more would need replacing shortly, he forecast. With the station being permanently unmanned, guards would carry a key to gain access to the token instruments. He noted that the station building was in a poor state of repair. Use of the loop by passenger traffic was approved.

The Welsh Highland Railway was opened throughout on 1 June 1923.

— 4 —
The Welsh Highland Railway
1923-37

OPENED in a glow of optimism in 1923, the WHR was always going to struggle. Financed as it was from the public purse, costs had been pared to the bone. The £5,000 contained in the original estimates for rolling stock had gone. The newest locomotive available, *Russell*, had been built in 1906, the newest carriages, two, in 1907. The only shares issued were those used to acquire control of the NWNGR and the PBSSR so there was no working capital. In addition to covering its operating costs the railway had to produce profits of nearly £5,000 annually to cover the debenture interest, £4,238 14s (£4,238.70) and capital repayment, £580 to the local authorities. No indication has yet been found that any consideration was being given to repaying either the Ministry of Transport or the McAlpines! A loan account with the National Provincial & Union Bank was used to finance construction until the advances were made.

Full details of the company's capital account, of which the construction element eventually totalled £70,332, have come to light but despite raising some £75,000 from the local authorities and the Ministry of Transport there were insufficient funds to pay the McAlpines the £66,515 due for refurbishing and completing the railway. Therefore the McAlpine partnership loaned £10,000, secured by 5% debentures, to cover the deficiency; W. H. McAlpine was the nominated debenture holder. Other known capital expenditure was: Sir Douglas Fox & Co, 4%, £2,395, on the contract price, stamp duty £2,200 and parliamentary legal charges and expenses, to Evan Davies & Co, £1,267. Sundry construction expenses amounted to £729. The other debentures were issued as follows: Caernarvonshire CC — £15,000 (three instalments); Portmadoc UDC — £5,000 (three instalments); Gwyrfai RDC — £3,000 (two instalments); Glaslyn RDC — £3,000 (two instalments); Deudraeth RDC — £3,000 (two instalments); Ministry of Transport — £35,774 (six instalments); Branch Nominees (Sir John Henderson Stewart) — £10,000. The total, with the McAlpines' loan, came to £84,774. The interest payable on the debentures was intended to match that on the capital borrowed by the authorities to make the advances to the WHR.

On 1 March 1924 the WHR made an indenture with the local authorities covering the conditions attached to the issuance of the debentures; in July 1923 the county council had sought Counsel's opinion on the matter. The debentures were irredeemable in the sense that they were not redeemable on demand but the local authority advances were to be repaid over 50 years, starting from 1 January 1925, at a rate of £580 per annum. Interest for 1923 was paid from capital; the railway deducted duty from the interest but failed to pass it on; the Inland Revenue chased its dues of £363 in 1928, and it was still outstanding in 1933!

Two things become apparent from reading the correspondence about the local authority advances seen so far. First, not all the authorities were keen to invest in the WHR. They were happy for the railway to be built, but some needed persuasion to make their advances when due. Perhaps they felt pressurised into making a commitment in the first place. Certainly, the Glaslyn authority ultimately failed to meet its obligations, being divided between Gwyrfai and Lleyn in 1934, the former acquiring the WHR debentures; whether

Below:
One of the few photographs known to exist of a double Fairlie on the WHR outside Portmadoc, in this case a scene at Beddgelert water tower in 1923. *M. E. M. Lloyd/John Keylock collection*

Right:
The FR's *Prince* on the crossing that was to cause so much trouble with the GWR. *Author's collection*

Below:
A debenture certificate issued to Glaslyn RDC in 1924.

this was totally due to the burden of its advance to the WHR is unclear.

Secondly, there seems to have been an expectation on the railway's part that the advances were gifts and not repayable by it. In 1923 Davies wrote to the county council saying that he hoped the authorities would borrow the total sum advanced, repaying it over 50 years, covering both principal and interest, otherwise the WHR would repay the principal over 50 years. The 1896 Light Railways Act (Sect 3(1)(b)) allowed authorities to make advances, either by loan or as part of the share capital. Advances made against the issue of ordinary shares would not have been secured, but they would not have been repayable either.

Davies wrote, more than once, of temporary advances and permanent advances. By this he seemed to have meant that temporary advances would cover the construction period, then when all the bills were in the temporary advances would

be refinanced at a lower interest rate by the local authorities who would repay them out of rates income! Whatever Davies thought, and he had seemed quite clear about need for the repayments at the 1922 inquiry, the authorities would have none of it and made it quite clear that they expected to be repaid by the WHR.

The £10,000 debenture issue to Branch Nominees represented the acquisition of a controlling (£34,243) interest in the NWNGR debenture stock by the PBSSR in April 1921. The PBSSR obtained a loan of £10,000, guaranteed by Sir John Henderson Stewart, from the National Provincial Bank to pay for the debentures. When it appeared that the PBSSR was not empowered to hold debentures in another company the debt was transferred to Stewart personally, the bank holding the NWNGR debentures as security. Stewart promised to repay the loan in June 1922; in December the bank agreed to accept £9,950 in WHR debentures as security in substitution for the NWNGR debentures. Stewart died on 6 February 1923 and on 27 June 1924 the WHR took over responsibility for the loan. (By 1933 the bank was due £15,250 on the loan account and £4,798 debenture interest.)

To operate the railway the company contributed £60 a year to S. E. Tyrwhitt's salary as general manager. An employee of the GWR on loan, Tyrwhitt was also managing the FR and had been manager of the NWNGR for a short time. He left on 30 September 1923 and was replaced by John May who was given the title of Superintendent. May lasted for only a year and his replacement was E. H. R. Nicholls, also from the GWR, who was general manager/managing director; he stayed until 25 May 1925.

Tyrwhitt was to influence WHR events long after he had gone. He asked the GWR to carry out work on the mixed gauge crossing at Portmadoc, agreeing that the WHR would bear the cost. Having upgraded the facility and its

Right:
Russell at Beddgelert in 1923.
The line was newly opened
and the locomotive and
rolling stock unaltered.
Author's collection

staffing, the GWR decided to bill the WHR for the use of the crossing as well. Naturally the WHR board refused the GWR's claim but the matter arrived in court in 1928. Unfortunately, the 1861 Act empowering the Aberystwyth & Welch Coast Railway made no reference to the pre-existing Croesor Tramway, although it was shown on plans accompanying the conveyance, so the GWR relied on the Croesor and Portmadoc Railway Act of 1865, which described the narrow gauge line crossing the standard gauge, as evidence that the standard gauge was first on the scene. Writing to the county council in 1928 Col Stephens said Tyrwhitt 'must have been under a misapprehension'. Regrettably, from the WHR's perspective, the GWR's view prevailed.

Col Holman Fred Stephens, well known for his links with light, and impecunious, railways, had been appointed engineer of the WHR from 1 April 1923; his salary was £100 per annum plus expenses. In 1923, Moses Kellow, the Croesor Quarry's engineer and manager, was on a salary of £60 per annum to

Invoice 3	NORTH WALES NARROW GAUGE RAILWAY.						GUARD'S SIGNATURE.	

FROM _South Snowdon_ TO _Dinas_ STATION.

Departure _____ o'clock Train _____ 18 day of _June_ 191 24

Description.	Name.	Destination.	Weight. Tons. cwt. qrs. lbs.	Rate.	Paid on.	Paid.	To Pay.
Scrap Rails	T. Young & Son.	_Son_ T C 2 3 16 0 @ 6.	4 0 0 0	3/3			13 0

provide haulage for the remaining section of the Croesor Tramway, although he also invoiced £37, covering four months, for the same service! The following year he was paid only against invoice for this service, carrying 1,750 tons for £58 during the first six months.

To work the line the railway employed two three-man train crews, three two-man track gangs, a stationmaster and a clerk at Dinas, a carpenter and a loader, the latter paid on tonnage. These were full-time positions; station staff at Beddgelert and Rhyd Ddu were, presumably, seasonal. Naturally, the FR ran the new station at Portmadoc.

From the FR the WHR received proportional services of the managing director, Nicholls, and his assistant, Robert Evans, shorthand typist Miss E. Davies, storekeeper J. P. Roberts, clerk T. Davies, locomotive superintendent R. Williams, permanent way inspector G. L. Griffiths and Portmadoc stationmaster E. E. Jones.

Following a considerable publicity effort using advertising in the *Carnarvon Herald* and other print media along the

North Wales coast, 1923 proved to be the best year for the WHR, with services operating through the winter. Clearly it was intended to put on a good show to the public, for in 1923 the Snowdon Mountain Railway laid out gardens, perhaps at Dinas and Beddgelert, charging £6 13s 4d (£6.67) for the work.

To aid inter-working between the FR and the WHR the former NWNGR rolling stock was modified to suit the FR's loading gauge; in the case of *Russell* this proved a wasted effort. A compensation claim recorded on 30 September 1923 suggests that some passenger stock was returned to traffic sooner than desirable, with £3 16s (£3.80) being payable for 'damaged coats by paint in carriages'!

Initially there were four return passenger workings throughout, with short workings to/from Beddgelert. Single journey times varied between 140 minutes and 185 minutes between Dinas and Portmadoc and 145 minutes and 205 minutes in the reverse direction! With the first arrival at Dinas at 11.42 and at Portmadoc at 10.18 there was obviously no expectation that anyone should want to use the train to get to work but a service was continued, at a reduced level, after the tourists went home in September.

Tickets were to be examined and nipped at Portmadoc, Beddgelert and Dinas and collected at all stations and halts. This was important, not least because the GWR had been issuing free passes for the WHR (and the FR)! On 27 August

Below:
A series of press photographs was taken on the NWNGR section in 1923. Seen here at Waenfawr, the subject was an FR train consisting of two 'bowsider' carriages and a bogie brake van hauled by *Palmerston. Author's collection*

1923 instructions were issued that if any were found, their holders were to pay the appropriate fare.

The Bryngwyn goods service ran as required. It was scheduled to leave Dinas at 12.15, arriving back at 14.40, with an hour allowed for shunting at Bryngwyn. There was sufficient traffic to justify at least a daily service in the early years. A Croesor goods left Portmadoc at 07.50, returning thence at 09.10. In 1924, Porter Roberts was responsible for working this traffic, with the injunction that he 'work sharp to the time shown'.

In July 1923, Stephens persuaded the board to equip the WHR with a War Department surplus Baldwin 4-6-0PT, No 590, at a cost of £266. Its size restricted it to WHR operations. An armoured Simplex four-wheeled petrol locomotive, obtained from the same source by the FR at the same time, was used on the

Above:
A scene at Dinas, set up for the photographer in 1925. *Moel Tryfan* has been turned for the occasion. The sign reads 'Dinas Junction Change here for Snowdon & Beddgelert'. *Commercial postcard/WHR collection*

WHR for the Croesor slate traffic. Some of the six Hudson toastrack coaches acquired by the FR in 1923 were intended to be sold on to the WHR but no transfer was ever made; this did not inhibit their being used on the WHR, of course.

The company's own financial records are either lost or as yet undiscovered. However, Nicholls produced an itemised list of expenditure covering 1923 and the first nine months of 1924 for the investing authorities. The following items have been extracted, giving an insight in to railway operations.

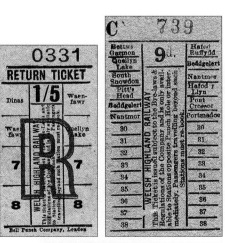

Under the heading of rolling stock maintenance in 1923, the FR retubed *Moel Tryfan*, the brass tubes costing £66 and asbestos 1s 11d (10p). Unspecified work on the locomotive was undertaken by J. L. Gordon for £47.

Also in 1923, the FR carried out repairs on *Russell*, with unspecified work costing £21, springs from Hunslet £6 and brass tubes £18, these charges being allocated to locomotive running expenses.

In 1924 *Moel Tryfan* received a new injector costing £24 and eight spiral springs costing £3 6s 8d (£3.33). Electric arc welding repairs to the locomotive's side frames cost £27. In the same year *Russell* was retyred at a cost of £47 and required three more springs, cost £1 10s (£1.50). Eight cast-iron wheels were obtained for carriage bogies (£21) and a further eight for a brake van (£21); four carriage axleboxes cost £4 and four sets of cast-iron letters for carriage sides £2 16s (£2.80). These sums were also charged to maintenance.

A sheep killed in April 1923 cost the railway £1 10s (£1.50) but R. Williams' sheep and lamb killed in August cost £3 5s (£3.25). Four sheep killed in 1924 cost £9 9s (£9.45). Damaged slates cost £27 8s 5d (£27.42) in 1923 but £39 0s 11d (£39.05) the following year. Portmadoc Flour Mills received 10s 6d (53p) for damaged flour in 1924.

Even at this early date, services did not always run as expected. On 18 September 1923, two carriages of the 10.53 from Portmadoc were derailed on the Bryn-y-felin bridge; the guilty vehicle was one of the six Hudson toastracks recently obtained by the FR. Adjacent saloon No 8 appeared to have derailed by one pair of wheels when the train stopped, for there were no signs of dragging by them. Perhaps it was another derailment that was responsible for Portmadoc paying 16s 8d (83p) out of petty cash for 'hire of cars to carry passengers owing to accident' on 31 January 1924. The incidents naturally resulted in delays to the train service.

Other delays cost the railway money: in 1923 the WHR paid the Saracen's Head hotel at Beddgelert £2 16s 8d (£2.84) for 'hire of car — lost connection' and in August 1924 the Sportsman in Portmadoc was paid £1 0s 3d (£1.01) for expenses incurred for the same reason. As time passed the railway's reputation for poor timekeeping was to become legendary.

In 1923, passenger revenue totalled £1,914, of which £23 was 1st class; in 1924 the figures were £1,698 and £20. Revenue from parcels was £99 and £77.

Particularly revealing, in the light of the railway's ultimate failure, are the entries under the 'travelling expenses account' heading. On 11 occasions in 1923, cars were hired, usually by the Aluminium Corporation, the cost being totally or partly

Welsh Highland Railway. TRAIN STAFF TICKET. TRAIN No._____ (UP) To the ENGINE DRIVER. You are authorised, after seeing the Train Staff coloured red for the Section, to proceed from **Beddgelert to Portmadoc** and the Train Staff will follow. Signature of person in charge .... Date.....................19 (over.)

borne by the WHR. On another four occasions, chauffeurs received expenses, also. Crossley Colley, the Aluminium Corporation's construction manager and later a WHR director, claimed 're-testing of Fordson tractor' on 27 April 1924 — this machine belonged to the Aluminium Corporation and was tried out on the FR, where it proved too light for the work. On two occasions in 1923 H. Thomas or W. J. West received 'Foden driver's expenses at Dinas', presumably the Aluminium Corporation's steam lorry. Intriguingly, on 6 June 1923 M. H. Williams had his rail fare paid to Portmadoc 're purchase of sand at Nantmor'.

Councillor Nee obviously spent some time looking after the investing authorities' interests, for he received £11 travelling expenses, not broken down, in 1923, which seems rather high considering he must have lived in, or near, Caernarvon! His only claim the following year was for less than £5, settled on 21 March.

Beddgelert seems, on the evidence of the Goods Received book preserved at the PRO, to have been established as a central handling centre for parcels traffic incoming to the WHR. The first entry, made on 12 June 1923, records a box shipped from Menai Bridge to the Royal Goat Hotel. The hotel received regular shipments of wet fish from Liverpool, too. A picture from Euston for 'Brown' at Beddgelert arrived on 16 June with the glass broken! Mr Till at Beddgelert received a box of live birds from Liverpool on 25 June. Beddgelert's bicycle dealer, Fred Clare, received regular shipments of cycle components and, on 29 June, a Raleigh cycle sign from Nottingham. Perhaps, to 21st century eyes, the most unusual item was a regular delivery of dry ice (solid carbon dioxide) from Llandudno to 'Griffiths' of Beddgelert.

Above:
Baldwin 590 on shed at Dinas. The locomotive was acquired in 1923 under Col Stephens's influence. *Paul Ingham collection*

Other stations receiving parcels via Beddgelert in the first few weeks were: Waenfawr (H. H. Roberts, parcel of wall-paper from Borough High Street, London, on 13 June); Rhos Tryfan ('Hughes', boots from Tottenham, on 15 June); South Snowdon (Miss Dyer, one bag, passengers' luggage in advance, from New Barnet, on 22 June); Bettws Garmon (Victoria Quarries, parcel from Camborne on 28 June); Bryngwyn (Amalgamated Slate Association, box from Sheffield on 4 July); Salem Halt (J. Roberts, parcel from Liverpool on 19 July); Tryfan Junction (William Owen (Plas) Bodaden, small box from Birmingham on 31 July) and Nantmor ('Hughes', a bag and leather trunk from Holyhead on 20 July).

In addition to its 'ordinary' passenger traffic the WHR man-aged to generate some business from party bookings and special workings. TABLE C gives an indication of the range covered.

The Congregationalists must have been hardy souls, for they certainly had a long day! Was it a coincidence that the Wesleyans had a festival in Portmadoc on the same day?

Initially, through trains to and from the FR bypassed Harbour station; the new Portmadoc station was intended to replace it after all. To facilitate engine working, a coaling stage, using an FR coal wagon, and a water tank were established outside the Harbour station goods shed. This failed to meet with everyone's approval and in August 1925 a complaint was received from the residents of Britannia Terrace concerning the nuisance of smoke from locomotives. Instructions were issued for engines to be coaled on the quay. Although the FR bought the land, the 'new' Boston Lodge was never developed; shortage of funds must have been the reason.

Tourist traffic in 1924 was badly affected by a wet summer. On 14 November, Nicholls, signing himself Managing Director, submitted a report to the directors with (requested) proposals for withdrawing the passenger service during the winter.

TABLE C

Date	Event	Arrangements	Comments
13.10.23	Minffordd band contest	Cheap half-day tickets on 12.18 and 15.00 from Beddgelert	Fare 1s 8d
1923 and 1924	Polytechnic excursions	Reserved carriages on 09.50 ex-Dinas, uncoupled at Beddgelert and added to 15.15 from there to Blaenau Ffestiniog	A programme of six weeks, 100 passengers each time, passengers rejoined train at Beddgelert or Nantmor
2.6.24	Congregational Festival, Caernarvon	Special train, depart Portmadoc at 06.50, connecting with LMS at Dinas at 09.44. Return by 20.25 ex-Dinas, arrive Portmadoc 22.35	2 June was a Monday
16.6.24	Rhyd Ddu Sunday School outing	Join 07.22 ex-Dinas at 08.18, to Minffordd; return by special train dep Portmadoc at 19.35	To Barmouth
6.6.25	Nantmor Sunday School outing	Empty stock dep Portmadoc at 09.00, arr Beddgelert at 09.40. Special dep Beddgelert 09.45 Nantmor 10.00. Return special dep Portmadoc 19.00, arr Beddgelert 19.47	To Barmouth

He observed that with average goods receipts of £82 per week since 22 September, when the winter timetable commenced, the railway would not be paying its way if it had to survive on its freight, even if the debenture interest were removed from the equation. Notwithstanding that, he proposed a daily goods between Dinas and Bryngwyn, and between Portmadoc and Croesor Junction, a twice-weekly service between Dinas and Beddgelert, and a once-weekly service between Portmadoc and Nantmor, but practically Beddgelert — there being no loop at Nantmor.

Such a service would require two engines in steam and two train crews but would reduce staffing by one station-master, two cleaners and six permanent way gangers, said Nicholls, reducing weekly operating costs to £156 from £210; these figures include £67 debenture interest, surely an indication of the burden placed on the WHR by its capital structure. Nicholls further noted that the Portmadoc operation was not a full week's (48 hours) work, suggesting that the men be deployed on the FR in between their WHR duties, for which service the FR would pay! The sum concerned was less than £4 per week.

Nicholls's report was implemented with effect from 15 December 1924. Despite his comments about the railway not paying its way with a goods service, revenue from this was considerably more than from passengers. The table below shows that during the first five years the revenue loss actually increased when the passenger service was more successful! It is notable, also, that the goods revenue showed very little change after 1922, when only the NWNGR section was operated.

Year	Passenger receipts	Goods receipts	Revenue loss
1922	£277	£3,790	£651
1923	2,462	3,635	1,573
1924	1,914	3,916	2,331
1925	1,089	3,987	742
1926	568	3,388	787

The WHR was not only available for the carriage of dead-stock, as a Traffic Office memo of 30 August 1926 reveals. Headed 'Foot & Mouth Disease', it informed staff that the borough of Conway had been declared an infected area and instructed that no animals, except dogs, were to be accepted for Conwy, Nant Conway, Dolwyddelan and Penmachno.

On 31 December 1924, the Ministry of Transport noted that the debenture interest had not been paid and advised the Treasury that it saw no benefit in exercising its right, because it had more than £10,000 in debentures, to appoint a receiver.

The winter service introduced on 21 September 1925 saw the Croesor shunt retimed to occur between 12.15 and 13.30. If the shunting was unfinished it was to be completed between the arrival of the 12.45 ex-Dinas, due Portmadoc (New) at 15.02, and the 17.10 departure to Beddgelert. Bryngwyn traffic was to be worked in a manner that ensured no overtime was incurred.

With traffic failing to improve, Jack accepted, or was forced to accept, responsibility and resigned from the WHR board in November 1925, terminating his involvement the following year. He was not replaced on the board and Davies became chairman.

Having approved the WHR for passenger traffic for a temporary six-month period in 1923, Lt Col Mount returned and reinspected the

Left:
WHR innovation — in 1928 one of the 'corridor' carriages was adapted to provide catering facilities, seen here in that year. The young couple were celebrating their engagement with a chaperoned holiday in Wales. *Keith Ladbury collection*

line on 6 October 1926. He saw that ballasting was still incomplete near Rhyd Ddu and Nantmor but subject to its being completed and some other minor works being carried out, he recommended that both the WHR between Rhyd Ddu and Portmadoc and the Festiniog's junction railways be approved for passenger traffic. He approved the works on Britannia Bridge as well, despite their not being done as he had recommended, and noted that the Croesor line to the harbour had been removed, eliminating the triangular layout.

Mount took the opportunity to inspect track alterations made at Croesor Junction, Beddgelert and Bettws Garmon. At the former a loop had been installed to the south of the junction, breaking up the long section between Beddgelert and Portmadoc. With train control by staff-and-ticket, the loop was unmanned. A cabin, actually a grounded former FR quarrymen's carriage, was provided in which was kept the staff box, tickets and a telephone. The Croesor line had been connected to the main line but following discussion with Col Stephens it was to be connected to the loop.

At Beddgelert, an 86ft coal siding had been connected to the loop at the south end of the station. A locked scotch had been provided to protect the running line but Mount required it to be replaced with an interlocked trap point.

The Bettws Garmon installation Mount inspected was a siding connection to the Dudley Park Granite Quarry. He required the single-blade trap point installed to be changed to a double-blade mechanism, and gave his approval to it.

By the time of Mount's delayed reinspection a winter service of one return train from Dinas was in operation. Running from 20 September, any slate wagons found at Croesor Junction were to be conveyed to Portmadoc, and accordingly, the train was designated mixed.

In 1927 Tourists Hotels Ltd, owner of the Royal Goat Hotel and in liquidation, partially succeeded in an action brought against the railway for breach of contract. In purchasing land from the company the WHR had entered into a covenant to provide an access road to land the hotel's company wished to sell as housing plots; the hotel company's liquidator claimed for loss of profit on 48 plots priced to sell at £5,450, £5,130 over the land's agricultural value, and for £1,000 for loss of patronage caused by the railway. An Order for £1,000 damages was made against the railway; perhaps the award could be interpreted as the railway winning the first claim but losing the second.

Tourist Hotels' liquidator had already been warned that a successful claim would result in the WHR being placed in liquidation. It can be no surprise, therefore, that when the investing authorities met on 12 February 1927, they resolved to take the necessary steps to appoint a receiver and

manager, recommending Col Stephens for the position. The claim, then £1,150, was still outstanding at the winding up in 1944.

Col Stephens was known for the brusque manner with which he communicated with staff, usually from his Tonbridge office. A softer side was revealed when he loaned £50 to cover the staff wages due on 3 March 1927. Occurring in the interval between the receivership application and his appointment as receiver from 4 March, the bank had indicated that it would not honour the railway's cheque. The

---

WELSH HIGHLAND RAILWAY.
WAY BILL.

.... day. Date 192

| OFFICE COLUMNS. The undernoted is a Copy and correct statement of Tickets, &c., supplied for which the Conductor is required to sign and account for together with— | | | | CONDUCTOR'S COLUMNS. Conductors are required to be careful to issue the Tickets in numerical order. Not to issue Thick Tickets that cannot be Punched, but to return them along with the Way Bill. The Punch, remaining Tickets, together with this Way Bill, must be returned in the Tin Box. | | |

Punch No....................... One Tin Box.

TICKETS— Quantity	Last Numbers	First Numbers	First Numbers Returned to Office	Quantity SOLD	FARES	AMOUNT £ s. d.
					1½d	
					3d	
					4d	
					6d	
					8d	
					9d	
					1/-	
					1/1	
					1/3	
					1/6	
					1/9	
					2/-	
					2/3	
					TOTAL.	

Remarks of Conductor regarding TICKETS, PUNCH, &c.

Less

NETT TOTALS.

PUNCH REGISTER.

Difference { OVER / UNDER

Cash Recv'd

Over

Under

Conductor's Signature

Errors must be Checked and Certified before the Conductor leaves the Office in the morning, otherwise they will not be credited.

N.B.—The Conductor will be held responsible for every Ticket issued to him, and any not sold or returned will be charged for as if sold.

KEEP THE TICKET BOX CUPBOARD ON THE TRAIN LOCKED.

The Punch, remaining Tickets, together with the Way Bill, must be returned in the Tin Box to the OFFICE.

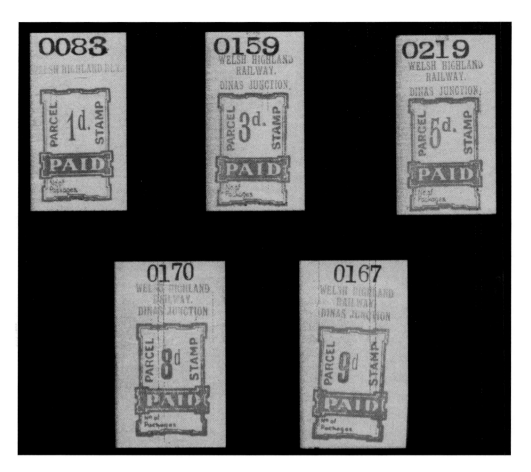

Right:
Stamps produced for the WHR's
parcel service; different values
are recorded as existing for Dinas
and South Snowdon (Rhyd Ddu).
Presumably the issue with no
station name was intended
for other locations.
John Keylock collection

matter came to light when the investing authorities angrily demanded an explanation for his claim for reimbursement.

Drivers' returns for the late 1920s/early 1930s give an insight into railway operations. On 16 March 1928, *Russell*, with driver William Hugh Williams in charge, worked 15 wagons loaded with coal and five with manure and a brake van from Dinas to Bryngwyn, taking 50 minutes for the journey; one wagonload of manure was left at Tryfan Junction and two at Rhostryfan. The crew, having spent 45 minutes working the incline and 20 minutes shunting, returned to Dinas with 17 wagons loaded with slate and the brake van, collecting an empty slate wagon from Tryfan Junction *en route*.

Driver Hugh Roberts and stoker Gwyn Roberts were in action with the Baldwin on 12 June 1930, with a Bryngwyn working of empty coaches, purpose unknown. Ten minutes were spent shunting at Rhos Tryfan and at Bryngwyn, 45 minutes working the incline. Arriving at Dinas at 12.20 the rest of the day was spent lifting *Moel Tryfan* to adjust its springs.

On 12 May 1931, the same team worked a goods train, load unspecified, hauled by *Moel Tryfan*, to Rhostryfan, then to Beddgelert before returning to Dinas. The 29-mile journey took 4 hours 20 minutes including 50 minutes shunting at Rhostryfan and Beddgelert. Two days later they spent the day, from 08.30 until 16.00, cleaning *Russell*, the Baldwin and *Moel Tryfan*.

Some idea of the state of the railway may be gained from the directors' returns that have survived for 1929. Data from specimen weeks, not entirely random, is shown in TABLE D.

Traffic staff included a guard; during this year the others were based at Dinas; in 1928 a member of traffic staff had been based at Beddgelert, at least until September. Slate carried via Portmadoc probably represents Croesor production. 36 goods miles might represent three trips to Bryngwyn and a trip to Croesor Junction; the drivers booked five miles to the former.

The week ending 1 June represents the year's peak for slate carriage and that ending 17 August the peak for passenger carriage, 403 of those passengers being booked via Dinas. The financial consequences of these weeks are shown in TABLE E.

It is notable that, except in August, the goods traffic was much more productive in terms of mileage operated than the

TABLE D

Date	Traffic staff	Loco staff	PW staff	Coal used	Passengers carried	Goods carried (tons)	Slate carried - Dinas (tons)	Slate carried - Portmadoc (tons)	Passenger mileage	Goods mileage	Shunting mileage
12.1	3	2	5	36cwt	-	47	81	67	84	36	46
20.4	3	2	4	51cwt	4	71	89	51	114	36	47
1.6	3	2	4	50cwt	27	60	197	79	132	45	49
17.8	3	2	4	80cwt	483	64	139	59	220	36	49
7.12	2	2	2	30cwt	2	37	45	41	100	27	30

W. H. R. Up Trains.

Dist (M.C.)	Station		1 Pass	2 Mixed Pass and Goods	3 Sh Eng Goods and Slates	4 Pass	5 Sh Eng Goods and Slates S.X.	6 Pass	7 Pass	8 Sh Eng and Slates S.X.	9 Sh. Eng Goods and Slates S X	10 Pass	11 Goods and Mineral	12 Pass	13 Pass
	aDinas Junction	dpt	A.M. ...	A.M. 7 22	A.M. ...	A.M. 9 50	A.M. 11 0	A.M. ...	P.M. ...	P.M. ...	P.M. 2 15	P.M. 1 5	P.M. 2 30	P.M. 5 25	P.M. 8 0
2 0	aTryfan Jct.	arr	...	7 31	...	9 59	11 15	...	...	...	2 30	1 15	2 39	5 35	8 10
	,,	dpt	...	7 34	...	10 3	11 19	...	...	...	2 34	1 18	2 42	5 38	8 13
	Bryngwyn	arr	...	...	...	...	11 45	...	...	...	3 0	...	...	...	...
3 60	aWaenfawr	arr	...	7 42	...	10 11						1 26	2 50	5 46	8 21
	,,	dpt	...	7 46	...	10 15						1X39	2 55	5 50	8 25
4 40	Bettws Garmon	,,	...	7A51	...	10A20						1A44	A	5A55	8A30
	Salem	,,	...	A	...	A						A	A	A	A
7 20	Quellyn Lake	arr	...	8 5	...	10 33						1 57	3 14	6 8	8 43
	,,	dpt	...	8 8	...	10 37						2 1	3 18	6 12	8 47
9 20	aS. Snowdon	arr	...	8 17	...	10 46						2 10	3 30	6 22	8 57
	,,	dpt	...	8 19	...	10X59						2 14	3X45	6X42	9 2
10 24	Pitt's Head	,,	...	A	...	A						A	A	A	A
11 20	Hafod Ruffydd	,,	...	A	...	A						A	A	A	A
13 25	aBeddgelert	arr	...	8 44	...	11 24						2 40	4 10	7 7	9 30
	,,	dpt	8 30	8 47	...	...		11 30	12x18			3 X 0	4X15	7 10	9X38
15 43	Nantmor	,,	8 42	8 59	...	...		11 42	12 30			3 12	4 27	7 22	9½50
16 25	Hafodyllyn	,,	A	A	...	...		A	A			A	A	A	A
17 25	Hafod Garregog	,,	A	A	...	...		A	A			A	A	A	A
17 77	Croesor Junct	,,	...	...	10 30	...		...	...	12 55		...	...	...	...
18 27	Ynysfor	,,	8 58	9A15	...	...		11A58	12A46			3A28	A	7A38	10A 6
19 27	Pont Croesor	,,	9 A4	9A21	...	...		12A 4	12A52			3A34	A	7A44	10A12
21 22	aPortmadoc	arr	9 15	9 31	11 10	...		12 15	1 3	1 40		3 45	5 5	7 55	10 23
	,,	dpt										3 55			10 25
	,, F.Ry.	arr										3 59			10 30

Vertical notes: col 1 "From Nov 1st"; col 3 "Runs during October only / During October"; col 5 "From 1st Nov"; col 6 "Runs from 1st Nov. (Saturdays excepted)"; col 7 "Runs during October and on Saturdays only after"; col 8 "From 1st Nov"; col 9 "During October only"; col 13 "Starts from Nov. 1st / Saturdays only".

W. H. Rly. Down Trains.

Dist (M.C.)	Station		14 Pass	15 Sh. Eng and Slates S.X.	16 Mixed Pass and Goods	17 Sh Engine and Slates S.X.	18 Sh Eng Goods and Slates X	19 Pass	20 Pass	21 Sh. En. Goods and Slates	22 Pass	23 Pass
	aPortmadoc (F. R.)	dpt	A.M. ...	A.M. ...	A.M. 9 25	P.M. ...	P.M. ...	A.M. ...	P.M. 1 55	P.M. ...	P.M. 5 0	P.M. 8 25
	Portmadoc	arr	...	...	9 30	...	...	...	2 0	...	5 5	8 20
	Do	dpt	7 30	10 0	9 35	12 25	...	11 25	2 10	...	5 15	8 35
1 75	Pont Croesor	,,	7A41		9A46	...	...	11A36	2A21	...	5A26	8A46
2 75	Ynysfor	,,	7A47		6A52	...	...	11A42	2A27	...	5A32	8A52
3 25	Croesor Junct	arr	...	10 20	9 55	12 45	...	...	...	...	...	...
	Do	dpt	...	...	9 56	...	...	...	...	...	...	...
3 77	Hafod Garregog	dpt	A		A		...	A	A	...	A	A
4 77	Hafod y Llyn	,,	A		A		...	A	A	...	A	A
5 59	Nantmor	,,	8 3		10 8		...	11 58	2 43	...	5 48	9 8
7 77	aBeddgelert	arr	8 15		10 20		...	12 10	2 55	...	6 0	9 20
	Do	dpt			10 24		...	12X25	3 X 5	...	6 5	9X39
10 2	Hafod Ruffydd	,,	...		A		...	A	A	...	A	A
10 78	Pitts Head	,,	...		A		...	A	A	...	A	A
12 2	aSouth Snowdon	arr	...		10 54		...	12 55	3 35	...	6 35	10 13
	Do	dpt	...		10x56		...	1 0	3X40	...	6X39	10 13
14 2	Quellyn Lake	,,	...		11 A8		...	1A13	3A53	...	6A52	10A26
	Salem	,,	...		A		...	A	A	...	7A 3	10A39
16 62	Bettws Garmon	,,	...		11A19		...	1A26	4A 6	...	7A 3	10A39
17 42	aWaenfawr	arr	...		11 24		S. X.	1 31	4 12	S.X.	7 8	10 45
	Do	dpt	...		11 27		...	1X35	4 16	...	7 12	10 49
	Bryngwyn	dpt	...		...		1 0	...	4 15	...	...	...
19 22	aTryfan Junction	arr	...		11 35		1 25	1 43	4 24	4 40	7 20	10 57
	Do	dpt	...		11 38		1 29	...	4 27	4 44	7 23	11 0
21 22	aDinas	arr	...		11 47		1 40	1 55	4 36	4 55	7 32	11 10

Distance measured from Portmadoc (New Station). Vertical notes: col 15 "From Novr. 1st / During October"; col 17 "From 1st Nov."; col 18 "From 1st Nov."; col 19 "Daily during October, Saturdays only after"; col 21 "During October only / S.X."; col 23 "On Saturday only".

Above and left:
This working timetable from 1923 might have been a draft, for it seems rather intensive and would have been expensive to operate given the late finishes.
PRO

TABLE E

Date	Passenger revenue	Goods revenue	Loaders	Croesor haulage	Wages	Profit/(loss)	Revenue (year to date)	Profit/(loss) (year to date)
12.1	11s 11d	£17 17s 2d	£5 18s 5d	£5 2s	£25 7s 2d	(£26 18s 2d)	£59 9s 10d	(£53 1s 8d)
20.4	4s 6d	£10 12s 6d	£6 1s 7d	£4 1s	£21 19s 10d	(£7 2s 1d)	£598 6s 11d	(£396 15s 3d)
1.6	£1 8s 5d	£13 3s 5d	£11 3s	£6	£24 6s 11d	(£2 7s 2d)	£821 6s 9d	£468 6s
17.8	£49 17s 3d	£14 12s 8d	£8 17s 5d	£4 13s	£24 18s 3d	£37 7s 10d	£1,437 15s 3d	(£375 19s 2d)
7.12	2s	£7 18s 6d	£3 15s 10d	£3 13s 6d	£17 12s	£23 3s 6d	£2,101 19s 3d	(£483 11s 2d)

passenger traffic. In the winter the railway would have been better off offering passengers the fare to use the bus!

The slate loaders at Dinas were self-employed on piece-work for the slate they transhipped. In November 1930, D. O. Jones, the factotum at Dinas, was in correspondence with Col Stephens over their situation. There were normally two men working as a team but to deal with 20 wagons a day, 200 tons a week, another pair was needed, paid for by the regular loaders, even if there was insufficient work to keep them fully occupied. If the work fell away and they were laid off they could expect no dole, for they were outside the remit of the Employment Insurance Act.

On 16 December 1930, the investing authorities decided to approach the LMS and the GWR to see if either company would take over and operate the WHR. Neither would, but each indicated a willingness to work it on a cost basis. A net loss of £218 was made during the year. Nothing done for the railway had worked out — £1,200 deposited against the Caernarvon extension and invested in government stocks was worth only £700 in 1931 when Stephens was in correspondence with the county council about getting it released to the revenue account.

The investing authorities then set up an advisory committee to investigate the means by which railway operating costs could be reduced, reporting on 17 January 1931. On the Croesor section, Moses Kellow was contracted to provide haulage at 1s 6d (7½p) per ton; whilst both Rhosydd and Park & Croesor quarries were closed due to a depression in trade, it was hoped that Rhosydd would reopen. In that event it was suggested that the WHR arrange its own haulage as 'we have reason to believe some of the neighbouring farmers would undertake the work at 1s (5p) per ton'.

It was suggested that operations be restricted to the NWNGR section temporarily, permitting staffing to be reduced to (Dinas) agent, driver, fireman and ganger, until

Above:
There is little available about the people who actually ran the WHR. Where they do appear in photographs it is usually as unknown incidentals. Here, right, is Goronwy Roberts. With family members already working for the WHR, he joined as a stoker (fireman) and became a driver in the 1930s. He probably drove all the locomotives but preferred *Russell* and was the last to drive it when the railway closed. Afterwards he joined the LMS. He was reunited with *Russell* when it was restored. Regrettably, the identity of the others in the picture and its purpose are unknown. *WHR Heritage*

Below:
A pocket version of the summer 1925 timetable. *PRO*

TIME TABLES—From July 13th to Sept. 19th, 1925.

DOWN TRAINS (Weekdays only)

		a.m.	a.m.	p.m.	p.m.	p.m.	p.m.	p.m.	p.m.	p.m.			
Duffws	dep.	9 25	11 15	12 25	12 55		4 25	6 5		7 15			
BlaenauFestiniog(G.W.R.)	,,	9 26	11 16	12 26	12 56		4 26	6 6		7 16			
BlaenauFestiniog(L.M.S.)	,,	9 28	11 18	12 28	12 57		4 28	6 8		7 17			
Tanygrisiau	,,	9 34	11 24	12 35	1 4		4 35	6 14		7 22			
Ddualit	,,			s	s		s	s					
Tanybwlch	,,	9 54	11 48	12 57	1 26		4 57	6 40		7 41			
Penrhyndeudraeth	,,	10 15	12 9	1 18	1 47		5 18	7 1		7 58			
Minfford (for G.W.R.)	arr.	10 21	12 15	1 24	1 53		5 24	7 7		8 3			
,,	dep.	10 23	12 18	1 25	1 54		5 25	7 9		8 6			
Portmadoc (Old Station)	arr.	10 33	12 28	1 35	2 6		5 35	7 19		8 15			
,,	dep.	11 5	12 32		2 10	3 55							
Portmadoc (for G.W.R.)	arr.	11 10	12 37		2 15	3 55			7 10				
,,	dep.	11 20	12 45		2 25	4 0			7s19				
Pont Croesor	,,	11s29	12s54		2s34	4s 9			7s19				
Ynysfor	,,	11s3	12s59		2s38	4s14			7s24				
Hafod Garregog	,,	s	s		s	s			s				
Hafod-y-Llyn	,,	s	s		s	s			s				
Nantmor	,,	11s58	1 17		2 55	4 33			7 43				
Beddgelert	arr.	12 10	1 30		3 10	4 45			7 55				
,,	dep.	12 20			3 20	4 50							
Hafod Ruffydd	,,	s			s	s							
Pitts Head	,,	s			s	s							
South Snowdon	arr.	12 50			3 50	5 20							
,,	dep.	1 5			3 55	5 27							
Quellyn Lake	,,	1 18			4 8	5 38							
Plas-y-Nant	,,	s			s	s							
Salem	,,	s			s	s							
Bettws Garmon	,,	1 31			4 21	5 51							
Waenfawr	,,	1 40			4 30	6 0							
Tryfan Junc.	,,	1 51			4 41	6 11							
Dinas Junc.(forL.M.S.R.)	arr.	2 0			4 50	6 20							

Saturdays Excepted. · *Runs Saturdays only.* · *Runs Thursdays & Saturdays only.* · *Runs Fridays only.*

UP TRAINS (Weekdays only)

		a.m.	a.m.	a.m.	a.m.	p.m	p.m.	p.m.	p.m.	p.m.	p.m.		
DinasJunc.(forL.M.S.R.)	dep.			9 50	12 0				4 30				
Tryfan Junc.	,,			10 3	12 13				4 43				
Waenfawr	,,			10 15	12 25				4 55				
Bettws Garmon	,,			10 20	12 30				5 0				
Salem	,,			s	s				s				
Plas-y-Nant	,,			s	s				s				
Quellyn Lake	,,			10 37	12 47				5 17				
South Snowdon	arr.			10 45	12 55				5 24				
,,	dep.			10 50	1 0				5 35				
Pitts Head	,,			s	s				s				
Hafod Ruffydd	,,			s	s				s				
Beddgelert	arr.			11 15	1 25				6 0				
,,	dep.			11 20	1 35	2 20			6 5	8 5			
Nantmor	,,			11 31	1 46	2 31			6 16	8 16			
Hafod-y-Llyn	,,			s	s	s			s	s			
Hafod Garregog	,,			s	s	s			s	s			
Ynysfor	,,			11s51	2s 2	2s47			6s32	8 32			
Pont Croesor	,,			11s57	2s 8	2s53			6s38	8 38			
Portmadoc (for G.W.R.)	arr.			12 9	2 20	3 5			6 50	8 50			
,,	dep.			12 13	2 23	3 8			6 55	8 55			
,, (Old Station)	,,	5 15	8 0	11 0			2 35		4 10	5 55		7 55	
Minffordd (for G.W.R.)	arr.	5 25	8 10	11 10			2 45		4 20	6 5		8 5	
,,	dep.	5 26	8 12	11 15			2 47		4 22	6 10		8 10	
Penrhyndeudraeth	,,	5 33	8 19	11 22			2 52		4 29	6 16		8 17	
Tanybwlch	,,	5 57	8 42	11 46			3 16		4 58	6 39		8 41	
Ddualit	,,	s	s				s		s	s		s	
Tanygrisiau	,,	6 19	9 3	12 8			3 38		5 20	6 59		9 4	
BlaenauFertiniog (LMS)	arr.	6 25	9 9	12 14			3 44		5 26	7 5		9 10	
BlaenauFestiniog(G.W.R.)	,,	6 27	9 10	12 16			3 45		5 28	7 6		9 11	
Duffws (G.W.R.)	,,	6 28	9 11	12 17			3 46		5 29	7 7		9 12	

Saturdays Excepted. · *Runs Fridays only.* · *Runs Thursdays & Saturdays only.*

31 March. The positions of delivery agent and checker, at Portmadoc, and audit accountant could be abolished, the latter function to be carried out by the receiver. On the commercial front, the transhipment charge should be reduced to 8d (3p) per ton, the average for the district.

The extent of any reaction to these proposals is not known. In March the advisory committee recommended that the railway should reopen for tourists in July, operating in conjunction with the FR and the main line railways; that one of the locomotives be 'put in proper working order' for the passenger traffic; that fresh sleepers be laid where required and that buildings should be repaired where necessary. These proposals were adopted by the investing authorities. On 17 March Col Stephens was reported to be unable to undertake his duties so the authorities resolved that his accountant, J. A. Iggulden be appointed in his stead.

Col Stephens died on 23 October 1931, the settlement of his affairs with the railway being protracted and not resolved until 1944; in 1933 it was established that his estate was due £691, including arrears of salary. Caernarvon accountant Richard Thomas Griffith took over from Iggulden as receiver; he was also clerk to Gwyrfai Rural District Council, one of the investing authorities.

On 23 March 1932, Iggulden wrote to the county council that there were insufficient funds for the railway to renew its third party insurance policy at £35. By return, the council offered to advance the £35 but by then Iggulden had a coal bill, £12, and the locomotive boiler renewal premium, £6, to pay. Stephens's associate, W. H. Austen, became his successor as engineer and locomotive superintendent.

The passenger service was restricted to the holiday season of July, August and September. In 1932 it just covered its costs, with 3,232 passengers generating £228. The figures for 1933, 6,445 passenger generating £484, were almost double. Such a restricted service wasn't always convenient for the railway, either. On 27 June 1932, an engineman took a locomotive from Dinas to Boston Lodge, returning thence by bus; fare 1s 6d (8p), and on 30 July, driver Roberts took one of *Moel Tryfan's* steam pipes to Boston Lodge, again at a cost of 1s 6d (8p) train fare according to the records. Might he have travelled via the LMS? Operationally, the railway ended 1933 £30 to the good but it was not enough. After consultation with the investing authorities the railway's closure was announced to take effect from 1 January 1934.

Continuous attempts were made, including approaches to the Ministry of Transport, to encourage the quarries to send their output via the WHR. On 19 January 1934, the county council held a meeting with O. W. Owen, the manager of the Caernarvonshire Crown Slate Quarries Company, operators of Cilgwyn, Braich, Moel Tryfan and Alexandra quarries since 2 August 1932. Cilgwyn output could be diverted to Penygroes by road with considerable savings in both time and cost. The railway was the most cost-effective means of shipment from Moel Tryfan and the company expected to link the Alexandra Quarry, not then in production, to Moel Tryfan by road and then send its output by WHR also.

No. M 3189

LMS

LONDON MIDLAND AND SCOTTISH RAILWAY

Excursions to the Welsh Highland Railway

EVERY WEEK-DAY, Day Excursion Tickets
WILL BE ISSUED TO

SOUTH SNOWDON, BEDDGELERT, NANTMOR AND PORTMADOC,
(For Aberglaslyn)

Welsh Highland Railway.

(Via Menai Bridge, Carnarvon and Dinas Junction)

FROM JULY 13 UNTIL SEPTEMBER 19, 1925,
AS SHEWN BELOW

FROM	Times of Starting.	THIRD CLASS RETURN FARE—TO			
		South Snowdon.	Beddgelert.	Nantmor for Aberglaslyn.	Portmadoc.
	a.m.	s. d.	s. d.	s. d.	s. d.
Holyhead	7 25	5 10	6 9	7 3	8 3
Valley	7 33	5 5	5 9	6 10	7 10
Rhosneigr	7 42	4 10	5 9	6 3	7 3
Ty Croes	7 49	4 3	5 7	6 1	7 1
Bodorgan	7 58	4 4	5 3	5 9	6 9
Gaerwen	8 46	3 6	4 5	4 11	5 11
Llanfair	8 51	3 1	4 0	4 6	5 6
Dinas Junction ...arr.	9 38				

		RETURN ARRANGEMENTS.	
	a.m.		
Dinas Junction ......dep.	9 50		p.m.
South Snowdon ......arr.	10 45	Portmadoc (New)	3 50
„ „ ......dep.	10 50	Nantmor (for Aberglaslyn)	4 33
Beddgelert ....arr.	11 15	Beddgelert	4 50
„ .... dep.	11 20	South Snowdon	5 27
Nantmor ....dep.	11.31	Dinas Junction ......arr.	6 20
(for Aberglaslyn)		Dinas Junction ......dep.	6 28
Portmadoc ....arr.	12 9		

Children under 3 years of age free ; 3 and under 12 half-fares.   No Luggage allowed.

CONDITIONS OF ISSUE OF EXCURSION TICKETS.
EXCURSION TICKETS are NOT transferable and will be available only to and from the stations named upon them, and by the trains, and on the dates specified on the announcements. The Company give notice that tickets for Excursions are issued at a reduced rate, and subject to the condition that the Company shall not be liable for any loss, damage, injury or delay to passengers, arising from any cause whatsoever. Day and Half-day Excursion tickets will not be extended, nor will any allowance be made on return portions not used.

All information regarding Excursion Trains on the London Midland and Scottish Railway may be obtained on application to Divisional Passenger Commercial Superintendent, Victoria Station, Manchester.

July, 1925.   (XM 34615/C)

H. G. BURGESS,
General Manager.

McCorquodale & Co., Ltd, Printers, London and Newton.—722

Unfortunately, the slate industry was set for another of its periodic depressions.

Responding to a good 1933 season on its own line, the FR decided to try to run the WHR directly. In May 1934 Evan R. Davies told the Ministry of Transport he believed the line could be made to pay if worked in conjunction with the FR 'by a management experienced in the working of light railways of this nature'. He said he looked to a considerable development of tourist traffic, and that he would be disappointed if in the course of a few years the receipts were not at least doubled!

A 42-year lease was brought into effect from 1 July. The FR was to pay £1 for the first half year, at which point it could back out. For the following 13 years the rent would be 10% of the gross income, reflecting intended expenditure to bring the railway up to scratch. For the next 7½ years the rent was to be 10% of the gross plus 5% of any gross income exceeding £2,000. Thereafter the rent was to be reviewed.

The Ministry had been keen to press for what it felt were better terms but felt Davies 'clearly knows the strength of his position and appears to have secured the support of the local authorities'. In the short term the deal might not benefit the stockholders but it afforded 'the best prospect of keeping the line open and thus of securing in some measure the objects for which it was built, so that the money spent on it . . . may not be entirely wasted'. It was realised that, if the line closed, there was no prospect that the realisation of assets would provide anything for the stockholders.

Had WHR traffic picked up as expected the lease might have been a reasonable deal, although it was still unlikely to earn enough to pay the debenture interest. The lease detailed all the WHR's assets, including two broken clocks at Beddgelert! It excluded the land acquired by the PBSSR at Caernarvon. For the FR it was a disaster, committing it to pay rent even if the WHR made no operating profit. With hindsight there should have been a further opportunity for the FR to withdraw from it, but that would have required a rent review that Davies was anxious to avoid, saying it was only proper that the FR should have the opportunity of profiting from its investment in the WHR. Regrettably, Davies died before the year's end, and his co-directors may have failed to realise that they had the option of abandoning the WHR at the end of it.

In August 1934, *The Railway Magazine* published a reader's suggestion that the WHR should be taken over by a 'railway enthusiast with means' for a negligible sum and popularised, like the Ravenglass & Eskdale Railway, with miniature stock and scale locomotives; the first published suggestion that the WHR's focus should be changed radically.

Despite the lease and reopening, 1934 was not a good year for the WHR. Stephens's executors issued a summons for the monies due to the estate. By October the bank account was overdrawn and the bank told the receiver, Griffith, that it held him personally responsible for the shortfall. Not unnaturally he thought this was unfair and offered to settle by instalments. On the railway the FR repainted the locomotives and carriages, the latter appearing in different bright colours. It also offered a special through fare from Dinas to Blaenau Ffestiniog, on different trains either side of the GWR at Portmadoc. It failed, however, to outdo road competition offering more spectacular routes over the Llanberis Pass and similar roads.

In February 1935, Austen submitted a report on WHR repairs and renewals to the FR's Robert Evans. The state of the Bryngwyn branch, including the incline, was deplorable; he said it was a surprise that stock stayed on the road and that there had not been serious derailments. At least 1,000 sleepers

Attach to September 1925 bills

WELSH HIGHLAND AND FESTINIOG RAILWAYS

NOTICE
Train Alterations
From May 24th to July 10th, 1926

WELSH HIGHLAND RAILWAY.

The Train times shown on the Time Table dated September, 1925, will be altered, and the service will be as under :—

DOWN TRAINS.

				a.m.	p.m.	p.m.
Portmadoc (New) for G. W. Rly.			dep.	11 20	2 14	5 16
Pont Croesor			,,	11A35	2A23	5 25
Ynysfor	..	.. ..	,,	11A40	2A28	5 30
Hafod Garregog	..	.. ..	,,	A	A	A
Hafod-y-Llyn ..	..	.. ..	,,	A	A	A
Nantmor	..	.. ..	,,	11 59	2 46	5 49
Beddgelert	..	..	arr.	12 11	2 58	6 1
,,		..	dep.	..	3 1	6 5
Hafod Ryffydd	..	..	,,	..	A	A
Pitts Head	..	..	,,	..	A	A
South Snowdon	..	..	arr.	..	3 31	6 35
,,		..	dep.	..	3 34	6 38
Quellyn Lake ..	..	..	,,	..	3 47	6 51
Plas-y-Nant ..	..	..	,,	..	A	A
Salem	..	.. ..	,,	..	A	A
Bettws Garmon	..	..	,,	..	3 58	7 3
Waenfawr	..	..	,,	..	4 6	7 11
Tryfan Junction	..	.. ..	,,	..	4 16	7 21
Dinas Junc. for L.M. & S. Rly.			arr.	..	4 25	7 30

UP TRAINS

				p.m.	p.m.	p.m.
Dinas Junc. for L.M. & S. Rly.			dep.	..	12 55	4 40
Tryfan Junction	..	.. ..	,,	..	1 8	4 53
Waenfawr	..	..	,,	..	1 22	5 5
Bettws Garmon	..	..	,,	..	1 27	5 10
Salem	..	.. ..	,,	..	A	A
Plas-y-Nant ..	..	..	,,	..	A	A
Quellyn Lake ..	..	..	,,	..	1 44	5 27
South Snowdon	..	..	arr.	..	1 52	5 35
,,		..	dep.	..	2 0	5 38
Pitts Head	..	..	,,	..	A	A
Hafod Ryffydd	..	..	,,	..	A	A
Beddgelert	..	..	arr.	..	2 25	6 3
,,		..	dep.	12 20	3 0	6 10
Nantmor	..	..	,,	12 31	3A12	6 22
Hafod-y-Llyn ..	..	..	,,	A	A	A
Hafod Garregog	..	..	,,	A	A	A
Ynysfor	..	..	,,	12 47	3 28	6 38
Pont Croesor ..	..	..	,,	12 53	3 34	6 44
Portmadoc for G.W.Rly.	..		arr.	1 5	3 46	6 56

See September Time Tables for connections at Portmadoc G.W.Rly. and Dinas L.M. & S.Rly.

" A "—Stops if required.

FESTINIOG RAILWAY.

The Train Services shown on September, 1925, Time Table will remain in operation until July 10th, with the exception that every Thursday and Saturday, the 12.55 p.m. Train from DUFFWS **WILL LEAVE AT 1.20 p.m.** to provide for a Half-Day Trip to PORTMADOC and INTERMEDIATE STATIONS returning by **SPECIAL TRAIN** leaving **PORTMADOC** at 8.15 p.m. for DUFFWS, calling at ALL STATIONS.

On **THURSDAY** and **SATURDAYS CHEAP HALF-DAY TICKETS** will be issued on the 1.20 p.m. train ex DUFFWS from DUFFWS, BLAENAU FFESTINIOG and TANYGRISIAU to PENRHYNDEUDRAETH and PORTMADOC.

THIRD CLASS RETURN FARE, ADULTS 1/3d., CHILDREN under 12 years of age 8d.

SUPPORT THE LOCAL LINES

PORTMADOC,   H. F. STEPHENS,
May, 1926.   *Managing Director.*

DAVID ALLEN AND SONS, LTD.—HCM ALLEN.

Above:
This 1926 summer timetable was published as a modification to the reduced service operated previously. *WHR Heritage*

Right:
By 1929 the service had been reduced to a single working in each direction on three days a week. If this timetable was operated as shown it required two trains and two crews, the trains crossing at Portmadoc New; there were no return options for passengers from Portmadoc. *PRO*

were needed to bring it up to fair condition. Elsewhere, 1,500 sleepers were needed as well as attention to fencing.

He considered the Baldwin to be in satisfactory condition but *Russell* required a new smokebox and other work at a cost

FESTINIOG
AND WELSH HIGHLAND RAILWAYS

RUNNING THROUGH THE

WONDERLAND OF WALES

AND CONNECTING THE

NORTH WALES COAST AND CARDIGAN BAY

Travel across Country away from the dusty and crowded roads, seeing beautiful scenery not visible from the highways on Home-made Steel, instead of on imported rubber, by Home-produced coal instead of by imported oil, and

SUPPORT THE LOCAL LINES

TIME TABLES—From May 20th, 1929, and until further notice

DOWN TRAINS (Weekdays only)

		a.m.	p.m. SO	p.m. SX	p.m.	p.m. SO	p.m.	p.m. SX	p.m. SO	p.m.
Duffws	dep.	9 17	12 20	12 36		1 30		4 25	4 55	
Blaenau Festiniog (G.W.R.)	"	9 18	12 21	12 37		1 31		4 26	4 56	
Blaenau Festiniog (L.M.S.)	"	9 20	12 23	12 39		1 33		4 28	4 58	
Tangrisiau	"	9A25	12 30	12A44		1A38		4A33	5A 3	
Dduallt	"	A	A	A		A		A	A	
Tanybwlch	"	9 45	12 51	1 5		1 59		4 54	5 24	
Penrhyndeudraeth	"	10A 7	1 11	1A27		2A20		5A15	5A45	
Minffordd (for G.W.R.) arr.		10 12	1 17	1 32		2 25		5 21	5 50	
" (") dep.		10 15	1 19	1 34		2 27		5 23	5 52	
Boston Lodge Halt	"	A	A	A		A		A	A	
Portmadoc (Old Station) arr.		10 25	1 29	1 44		2 37		5 33	6 2	
" dep.		..	..	..	1 47					
Portmadoc (for G.W.R.) arr.		..	..	..	1 51					
" dep.		..	..	..	2 46					
Pont Croesor	"	..	..	..	2A55					
Ynysfor	"	..	..	..	3A 0					
Croesor Junc.	"	..	..	..	A					
Hafod Garregog	"	..	..	..	A					
Hafod-y-Llyn	"	..	..	..	A					
Nantmor	"	..	..	..	3A18					
Beddgelert	arr.	..	..	..	3 30					
" dep.		..	..	..	4 41					
Hafod Ruffydd	"	..	..	..	A					
Pitts Head	"	..	..	..	A					
South Snowdon	"	..	..	..	5 10					
" dep.		..	..	..	5 18					
Quellyn Lake	"	..	..	..	5A20					
Plas-y-Nant	"	..	..	..	A					
Salem	"	..	..	..	5A37					
Bettws Garmon	"	..	..	..	5 45					
Waenfawr	"	..	..	..	5 55					
Tryfan Junc.	"	..	..	..	A					
Dinas Junc. (for L.M.S.R.) arr.		..	..	..	6 4					

Mondays, Wednesdays and Fridays only

UP TRAINS (Weekdays only)

		a.m.	a.m.	a.m.	a.m.	a.m.	p.m.	p.m. SX	p.m. SO	p.m.
Dinas Junc. (for L.M.S.R.) dep.		..	..	..	..	12 30				
Tryfan Junc.	"	..	..	..	..	12 43				
Waenfawr	"	..	..	..	..	12 55				
Bettws Garmon	"	..	..	..	..	1A 0				
Salem	"	..	..	..	..	A				
Plas-y-Nant	"	..	..	..	..	A				
Quellyn Lake	"	..	..	..	..	1A15				
South Snowdon arr.		..	..	..	..	1 23				
" dep.		..	..	..	..	1 26				
Pitts Head	"	..	..	..	..	A				
Hafod Ruffydd	"	..	..	..	..	A				
Beddgelert arr.		..	..	..	..	1 50				
" dep.		..	..	..	..	1 55				
Nantmor	"	..	..	..	..	2 6				
Hafod-y-Llyn	"	..	..	..	..	A				
Hafod Garregog	"	..	..	..	..	A				
Croesor Junc.	"	..	..	..	..	A				
Ynysfor	"	..	..	..	..	2 22				
Pont Croesor	"	..	..	..	..	2 27				
Portmadoc (for G.W.R.) arr.		..	..	..	..	2 36				
" dep.		..	..	..	..	2 45				
Portmadoc (Old Station) arr.		..	..	..	..	2 49				
" dep.		5 15	..	8 0	11 5			2 30	3 30	
Boston Lodge Halt	"	A	..	A	A			A	A	
Minffordd (for G.W.R.) arr.		5 25	..	8 10	11 15			3 0	3 40	
" (") dep.		5 26	..	8 12	11 22			3 2	3 42	
Penrhyndeudraeth	"	5 33	..	8A17	11A27			3A 7	3A47	
Tanybwlch	"	5 57	..	..	..			A	A	
Dduallt	"	A	..	A	A			A	A	
Tangrisiau	"	6 19	..	9 A 0	12A10			3A50	4A50	
Blaenau Festiniog (L.M.S.) arr.		6 25	..	9 5	12 15			3 55	4 35	
Blaenau Festiniog (G.W.R.)	"	6 27	..	9 7	12 17			3 57	4 37	
Duffws	"	6 28	..	9 8	12 18			3 58	4 39	

Mondays, Wednesdays & Fridays only

CIRCULAR TOUR TICKETS and DAY RETURN TICKETS

issued via these Railways at Special Excursion Fares between nearly all Stations in North Wales on the L.M.S. and G.W. Railways. Full Particulars at the Stations.

THIRD CLASS HOLIDAY CONTRACT TICKETS

over these Two Railways issued on application.

One WEEK	15/-
Two Weeks	25/-

A fully licensed BUFFET CAR runs on the 12.30 p.m. train from Dinas Junction to Portmadoc, and on the 2.36 p.m. train from Portmadoc to Dinas Junction.

The distance from South Snowdon Station to the summit of Snowdon is 2½ miles. The ascent takes approximately 1½ hours, and the descent 1 hour.

Nearly Fifty Miles of Narrow Gauge Railway running through beautiful scenery, and giving comfortable access to views unobtainable by any other means.

First and Third Class Coaches on all Trains.

NOTES.

A.—Stops if required.

B.—On Saturdays, arrives Llandudno 6.18 p.m.

S.—Saturdays only from Pwllheli.

SX.—Saturdays excepted.

SO.—Saturdays only.

LONDON, MIDLAND and SCOTTISH RAILWAY
Connections at Dinas Junction

		p.m.	p.m.
Dinas Junc.	dep.	5 16	7 34
Afonwen	arr.	5 58	8 20
Pwllheli	"	6 15	8 50

		p.m.	p.m.
Dinas Junc.	dep.	4 44	6 31
Caernarvon	arr.	4 54	6 40
Bangor	"	5 20	7 5
Llandudno	"	6B 3	8 44
Colwyn Bay	"	6 5	9 10
Rhyl	"	6 25	9 39

		a.m.
Rhyl	dep.	10 45
Colwyn Bay	"	11 2
Llandudno	"	11 0
Bangor	"	11 50
Caernarvon	"	12 15
Dinas Junc.	arr.	12 24

		a.m.
Pwllheli	dep.	10 25
Afonwen	"	11 5
Dinas Junc.	arr.	11 52

Connections at Blaenau Festiniog

		a.m.	a.m. SO	a.m. SX	a.m.	a.m. SX	a.m. SO	p.m.	p.m.
Chester	dep.	6 5	9 2	9 2	10 3	1 55	1 55		
Rhyl	"	7 0	9 45	10 0	10 45	2 39	2 39		
Colwyn Bay	"	7 30	10 3	10 18	11 2	2 57	2 57		
Llandudno	"	7 35	10 15	10 15	12 5	2 40	2 40		
Llanrwst and Trefriw	"	8 19	10 59	10 59	12 44	4 20	3 38		
Bettwsycoed	"	8 33	11 10	11 10	1 0	4 30	3 52		
Blaenau Festiniog	arr.	9 6	11 44	11 44	1 28	5 3	4 25		

		a.m.	a.m.	a.m.	a.m.	p.m.	p.m.	p.m. SX	p.m. SO	p.m.
Blaenau Festiniog	dep.	7 35	9 45		12 8	1 45	4 30	4 40	5 40	
Bettwsycoed	arr.	8 6	10 15		12	2 11	5 1	5 10	6 10	
Llanrwst and Trefriw	"	8 19	10 26		1 2	2 21	5 22	5 22	6 25	
Llandudno	"	8 57	11 19		1 45	3 3	6 3	6 18	7 24	
Colwyn Bay	"	9 12	11 46		2 10	3 0	6 5	6 5	7 31	
Rhyl	"	9 33	12 9		2 35	3 20	6 25	6 25	8 3	
Chester	"	9 52	1 31		3 17	4 10	7 7	7 7	9 0	

GREAT WESTERN RAILWAY
Connections at Portmadoc and Minffordd

		a.m.	a.m.	p.m.	p.m.	p.m.	p.m.	p.m.
Barmouth	dep.	7 40	9 34	12 15	2 38	4 10	5 36	
Harlech	"	8 6	10 0	12 42	3 7	4 38	6 4	
Minffordd	"	8 24	10 17	12 59	3 22	4 57	6 20	
" dep.		8 25	10 18	1 0	3 23	4 58	6 21	
Portmadoc	arr.	8 30	10 22	1 5	3 27	5 2	6 25	
" dep.		9 20	10 26	1 10	3 30	5 5	6 30	
Criccieth	arr.	9 31	10 36	1 21	3 40	5 16	6 40	
Afonwen	"	9 40	10 45	1 30	3 48	5 25	6 49	
Pwllheli	"	9 55	11 0	1 45	4 5	5 43	7 5	

		a.m.	p.m.	p.m.	p.m.	p.m.	p.m.
Pwllheli	dep.	6 5	10 35	1 0	1S25	5 5	5 10
Afonwen	"	6 20	10 51	1 15	1 40	4 16	5 30
Criccieth	"	6 29	10 58	1 22	1 48	4 22	5 37
Portmadoc	arr.	6 39	11 10	1 33	2 0	4 33	5 50
" dep.		6 44	11 15	1 36		4 37	6 0
Minffordd	arr.	6 48	11 19	1 40		4 41	6 4
" dep.		6 49	11 20	1 41		4 42	6 5
Harlech	arr.	7 5	11 37	1 59		5 3	6 32
Barmouth	"	7 29	12 3	2 27		5 32	6 57

Connections at Blaenau Festiniog

		a.m.	a.m.	a.m.	p.m.
Llangollen	dep.				
Bala	"	6 45	9 20	11 50	
Trawsfynydd	"	8 5	9 55	12 28	3 15
Blaenau Festiniog	arr.	8 35	10 26	12 57	3 56

		a.m.	a.m.	p.m. SO	p.m. SX	p.m. SO	p.m.
Blaenau Festiniog	dep.	7 35	9 30	12 20	2 20	4 25	5 45	7 10
Trawsfynydd	arr.	8 3	9 58	12 58	2 47	4 52	6 25	7 35
Bala	"	8 39	10 34		3 25		7 4	8 13
Llangollen	"	9 42	12 23		4 55		9 25	

TIMES OF OTHER COMPANIES' TRAINS ARE SHOWN FOR CONVENIENCE OF PASSENGERS AND ARE NOT GUARANTEED

The Company give notice that they do not undertake that the trains will start or arrive at the time specified on the Time Tables, nor will they be accountable for any loss, inconvenience, or injury which may arise from delays or detentions, but every endeavour will be made to ensure punctuality as far as practicable. Passengers booking at intermediate Stations can only do so conditionally upon there being room in the train.

Portmadoc, April, 1929.　　　SUPPORT THE LOCAL LINES.　　　H. F. STEPHENS, Managing Director.

WELSH HIGHLAND RAILWAY

Runs from
Caernarvon Bay
to
Cardigan Bay.

Sea to Sea.

Vales, Lakes,
Alpine Villages and
Splendid Mountain
Scenery.

22 Miles
through a
Riot of Splendour

TIME TABLE—JULY 9th to SEPTEMBER 29th, 1934. WEEKDAYS ONLY.

From Dinas.

L.M.S. connections	A.M.	P.M.	P.M.
Rhyl - dep.	9c25	1c12	3 41
Colwyn Bay	9·45	1c33	4 5
Llandudno	9·40	1c35	4 0
Bangor	10 40	2 15	5 5
Caernarvon	10 56	2 31	5 23
G.W.R. connections			
Pwllheli	10 15	1s35	4 0
Criccieth	10 17	1s35	3 37
Afonwen	10 40	2s 0	4 16
W.H. Railway			
Dinas - dep.	11 25	2 50	6s15
South Snowdon	12 15	3 40	6s55
Beddgelert - arr.	12 45	4 5	7s25
dep.	12 55 (2 25)	4 55	7 30
Aberglaslyn	1 6 (2 36)	5 6	7 41
Portmadoc - arr.	1 30 (3 0)	5 30	8 5
F. Railway - dep.	3 20	5 55	—
G.W.R. Afonwen	3 26	6 5	8 15
do. Barmouth	4 37	5 47	8 38

From Portmadoc.

G.W.R. connections				
Barmouth - dep.	9 39	12 15	2 37	5 18
Pwllheli	9 5	12 55	3 15	5 15
Criccieth	9 24	1 14	3 37	5 36
Festiniog Ry. arr.	-	12 40	3 10	5 30
W.H.R.				
Portmadoc dep.	10 45	1 40	4 0	6 20
Aberglaslyn	11 9	2 4	4 24	6 44
Beddgelert - arr.	11 20	2 15	4 35	6 55
do. - dep.	1 15	4 50	8 0	
South Snowdon	1 45	5 20	8 25	
Dinas - arr.	2 30	6 5	9 10	
L.M.S. DEPART FOR Caernarvon	2p42	6 23	9 24	
DEPART FOR Afonwen	2 40	7 25	-	

C MONDAYS to FRIDAYS ONLY. FOR SATURDAY TIMES SEE L.M.S. TIME-TABLES. D ON SATURDAYS PASSENGERS TRAVEL FROM DINAS TO CAERNARVON BY CROSVILLE, PAYING SUPPLEMENTARY FARE ON BUS.

S SATS. EXCEPTED. B WEDS. and THURS. ONLY.

PASS OF ABERGLASLYN.

SPECIAL EXCURSION FARES.

	S.	R.
Dinas to Sth. Snowdon	1/-	1 6
„ Beddgelert	1 6	2/-
„ Aberglaslyn	1/9	2/3
„ Portmadoc	2/-	2/6

	S.	R.
Beddgelert to Aberglaslyn	3d.	4d.
„ Portmadoc	9d.	1/3
„ Sth. Snowdon	6d.	9d.

Observation Car Seats 6d. Extra.

L.M.S. and G.W.R. Holiday Contract Ticket Holders can get link-up tickets over W.H. Railway at Portmadoc, Afonwen and Dinas.

SPECIAL EXCURSION BOOKINGS
are available from L.M.S. and G.W.R. Stations to South Snowdon, Beddgelert, Aberglaslyn and Portmadoc (or Dinas.)

SPECIAL TICKETS FOR FIVE VALLEY CIRCULAR TOUR
are issued from L.M.S. Stations via Dinas or Blaenau Festiniog, over Welsh Highland and Blaenau Festiniog Railways embracing Conway, Lledr, Maentwrog, Glaslyn and Gwyrfai Valleys, also

CIRCULAR TOUR from G.W.R. Stations via Portmadoc over Welsh Highland Railway to Dinas thence by L.M.S. to Afonwen, and to destination or vice-versa.

HIKERS TOUR TICKET also available to South Snowdon, whence to ascend Snowdon afoot, returning from Summit by Snowdon Mountain Railway to Llanberis.

For details of all Excursions and Tours see Bills at L.M.S. and G.W.R. Stations, or from Festiniog Railway, Portmadoc.

The Company give notice that they do not undertake that the trains will start or arrive at the times specified on the Time Tables, nor will they be accountable for any loss, inconvenience or injury which may arise from delays or detentions, but every endeavour will be made to ensure punctuality as far as practicable. Passengers booking at intermediate stations can only do so conditionally upon there being room in the train.

The Welsh Highland Railway is operated by Festiniog Railway.

PORTMADOC, June 1934.

R. EVANS, Traffic Manager.

---

of about £65. *Moel Tryfan* was in really poor condition, though, and needed a heavy overhaul. Austen identified frame repairs, cylinder boring, piston renewal, retubing and stay replacement amongst work needed, at a cost, including labour, of between £250 and £300. However, he said that with the availability of the Baldwin, and if *Russell* was repaired, then attention to *Moel Tryfan* could be deferred.

So far as the carriages were concerned an expenditure of £25 would make them fit for the season's operation. The state of the wagon fleet was a different story, for he thought many of them were beyond repair, and recommended spending £150 to bring 30 of them up to serviceable condition. Whether *Russell* received its new smokebox has not been

determined but the locomotive did remain in service. Certainly *Moel Tryfan*, partially dismantled in Boston Lodge, never worked again.

In 1936, FR shareholders were told that expenditure for the previous year included '£100 rent payable under the terms of the lease of the WHR undertaking. The traffic . . . did not come up to expectations and the directors are hopeful that the rent, or some part of it, will be waived.'

On 31 December 1936, W. Cradoc Davies, then FR company chairman, met the investing authorities. The FR had run the WHR for 2½ years and wanted to be released from the lease. He said the track was in poor condition when the FR took it over and needed a 'substantial sum of money' spending on it;

Above:
When the FR took its lease on the WHR in 1934 the locomotives and carriages were repainted, as represented by this photograph of *Russell* at Dinas. *Paul Ingham collection*

Left:
The timetable produced by the FR for use after it obtained the lease in 1934. *Author's collection*

1934 produced a loss of £506. Moel Tryfan Quarry stopped using the railway in 1935, one train a week having sufficed for coal and groceries traffic, covering its cost. Receipts for 1935 were £1,001, producing a loss of £596 including the 10% rent. At 30 September 1936, when the seasonal passenger service ended, revenue had been £1,033, against costs of £1,283. A weekly goods train run after that period had to be taken into account, a proportion of overheads and the 10% rent added, too. The WHR faced strong bus competition and took twice as long to make the journey.

The FR made a loss of £105 in 1935, after allowing for the WHR's 10%; without it, both lines would have cleared their expenses. From March 1936, the Blaenau Ffestiniog quarry-men were on strike for nine weeks, during which the FR continued operating to clear stocks from the quarries; at the end of the year the FR was £1,000 worse off than it was the previous year. Most FR passengers were from the North Wales coast, travelling via the Conwy Valley, a fair percentage travelling through to Dinas; very few joined the WHR from the LMS at Dinas. The LMS had an interest in Crosville Motor Services and encouraged its passengers to take the bus at Blaenau Ffestiniog — the FR objected to this and traffic picked up. The WHR lost FR passengers to the buses at Port-madoc, despite the railway's best efforts. The situation would be worse in 1937 because Crosville had erected additional stands alongside the platform at Blaenau Ffestiniog.

By the time of this submission the last passenger train had already run, on 26 September 1936; on 14 May 1937 the FR resolved to suspend all traffic from 1 June. During the lease period passenger trains had been restricted to the tourist season of July, August and September each year, whilst goods trains ran as required.

The creation of the WHR can be attributed to two men, Evan R. Davies and Henry Joseph Jack. Davies had an involvement with 2ft gauge railways in Caernarvonshire from at least 1901 until his death in 1934. He submitted the 1914 LRO application, was a director of the company and was behind the FR's lease in 1934. As a friend of David Lloyd George he had access to those crucial Whitehall contacts.

Jack had been working at the Aluminium Corporation's Dolgarrog plant since 1909 but appears not to have become interested in narrow gauge railways until after 1918, when that company acquired control of the PBSSR; he had been designated one of the Conway Valley Light Railway's first directors in 1913. In 1920, he was responsible for his company acquiring control of the NWNGR, becoming its receiver. From this it may be inferred that Jack was behind the revival of the 1914 LRO application in 1921 and the acquisition of the FR. Being remembered for his strong personality and as chairman of the county council, he was very likely responsible for persuading the smaller councils to support the WHR. Perhaps it was Jack who invented the 'Welsh Highland' soubriquet for the railway.

What were their motives? Jack was a successful businessman and he probably believed the WHR could be successful too; had it been *really* successful it would have been electrified and a big NWPT customer. Davies said it would open up the locality to tourism and improve access; for him success would have been increased local authority revenues and employment. They succeeded in getting the railway built without any private funding beyond that of the Aluminium Corporation to acquire the NWNGR debentures, and the 'missing' £10,000 put up by W. H. McAlpine. The two were friends, but their big weakness was in not noticing that the world was changing.

THROUGH
THE ABERGLASLYN PASS
From Nantmor to
Bryn-y-felin

Above:
The Baldwin arrives at Nantmor station from Beddgelert.
The photographer has obviously been set up for such a long time
that most of those present have forgotten about him.
The child's toy locomotive is lettered 'LMS'.
Commercial postcard/A. J. Harden collection

Left:
The newly completed embankment preceding the long tunnel
at Aberglaslyn in 1923. *WHR collection*

Below:
A view through the short tunnel at Aberglaslyn in later years.
R. W. Kidner/Author's collection

Right:
Looking back down the Pass, towards Portmadoc from the train, in 1936. *S. W. Baker*

Below:
A train approaches Bryn-y-felin in 1925. An FR four-wheeled carriage brings up the rear. *Photomatic/Author's collection*

Left:
Palmerston climbs away from the Bryn-y-felin bridge in the 1930s. *William Norman Brown/ Author's collection*

Left:
Russell at the Nant Gwynant end of
the Pass, probably in the early 1930s.
J.E.Cull/Author's collection

Right:
Bryn-y-felin bridge, seen from the train.
R.W.Kidner/WHR collection

Below:
Moel Tryfan at Bryn-y-felin in 1923; the
locomotive is unmodified. The PBSSR
formation towards Nant Gwynant is still
prominent along the river bank.
J.Valentine/WHR collection

Above:
An unusual view of Beddgelert station, mid 1920s. The bookstall opened in 1923 had not lasted this long. The goods shed, on the right, was occasionally used to lodge a locomotive overnight. Two coal wagons are in the coal merchant's siding on the left. In an area beyond the station now obscured by trees, the route of one of the WHR's reverse curves may be seen. *WGR collection*

Below:
Another view of *Little Giant* on the same occasion as the photograph reproduced on page 45. *Author's collection*

Beddgelert

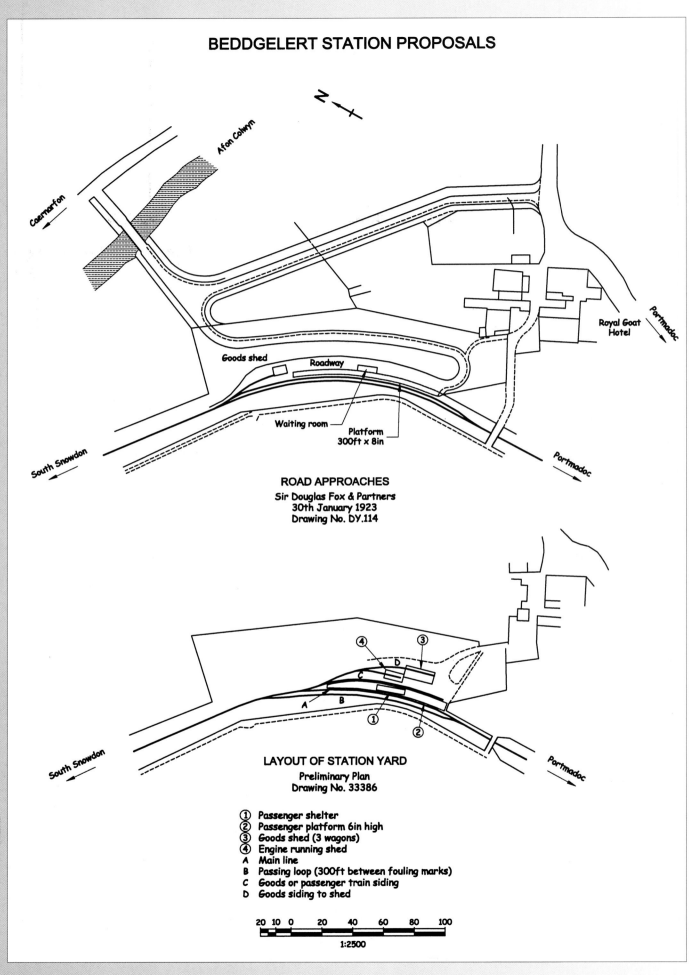

BEDDGELERT STATION PROPOSALS

N

Afon Colwyn

Caernarfon

South Snowdon

Goods shed

Roadway

Waiting room

Platform
300ft x 8in

Royal Goat
Hotel

Portmadoc

Portmadoc

ROAD APPROACHES

Sir Douglas Fox & Partners
30th January 1923
Drawing No. DY.114

South Snowdon

Portmadoc

LAYOUT OF STATION YARD

Preliminary Plan
Drawing No. 33386

① Passenger shelter
② Passenger platform 6in high
③ Goods shed (3 wagons)
④ Engine running shed
A Main line
B Passing loop (300ft between fouling marks)
C Goods or passenger train siding
D Goods siding to shed

20 10 0   20   40   60   80   100

1:2500

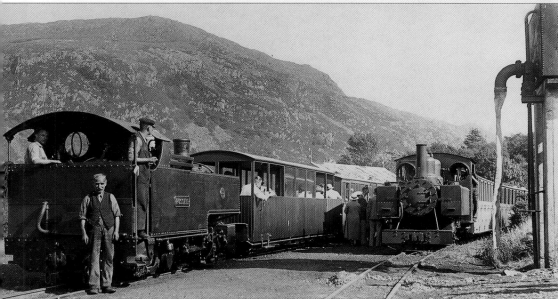

Above:
Moel Tryfan rolls into
Beddgelert from Dinas.
WHR collection

Left:
Crossing trains: *Russell*
and the Baldwin. It is
hardly surprising that
there are no passengers in
the centre, glazed, portion
of the 'Gladstone' car, as it
has no ventilation.
Author's collection

Below:
The buffet car attendant
looks out at the photo-
grapher on a quiet day
during the FR lease period.
A van brings up the rear of
the *Russell*-hauled train.
Ian Allan Library

Top:
Palmerston with a
Pickering brake/3rd
in the 1930s.
William Norman Brown

Above:
The end is near; during the
last summer of operation
the Baldwin takes water
on 9 July 1936. *S. W. Baker*

Left:
The next day, the Baldwin
ran round to return to
Portmadoc and then
Russell arrived from Dinas.
These workings did not
appear in the
contemporary timetable.
S. W. Baker

Above:
Russell runs round a short train at Dinas in 1934; a spare carriage is strategically placed on the right to be added to the train with the minimum of effort if required. On the lower right is perhaps one of the flowerbeds planted by the Snowdon Mountain Railway in 1923. *F.M. Gates/ WHR collection*

Left:
An England locomotive and train await the time to return from Dinas to Portmadoc in earlier days. *Author's collection*

Left:
Slate transhipment at Dinas. Times must have been good, for there are three teams of loaders in evidence. *Author's collection*

Above:
Russell leaving Dinas; the photographer is standing in front of the carriage shed. *Paul Ingham collection*

Right:
Bryngwyn, having a sparse passenger service, was rarely photographed, this view being the only known one of a passenger train there. *Gwynedd Archives*

Below:
Bryngwyn station and incline. Unusually, the incline was part of the railway and was operated by the train crews. Typically 45 minutes was taken for raising and lowering wagons, much of which must have been taken by the time to walk to and from the drumhouse. *R. W. Kidner/Author's collection*

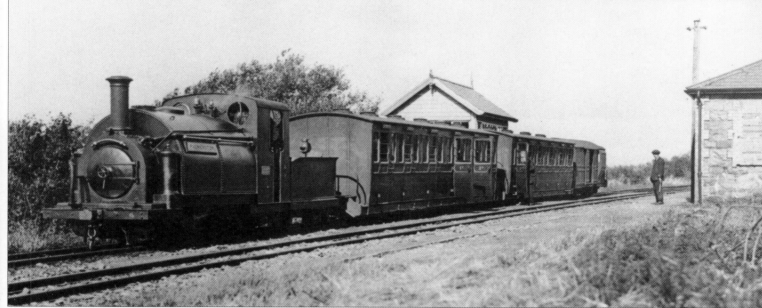

Top:
Top:
Rhostryfan, photographed
during an expedition to view
the WHR demolition in 1941.
The ladies are the wives of the
photographer and his friend,
V. Boyd-Carpenter.
F. Bolton/WHR collection

Above:
Palmerston at Tryfan Junction
during its 1923 publicity run;
the fireman waits with the token
for the photographer to finish.
Author's collection

Left:
Salem Halt, seen from the road
as *Russell* arrives with a short train
from Portmadoc.
Author's collection

Top:
Russell leaves Beddgelert with a long train in the 1930s. *R. W. Kidner/ Author's collection*

Above:
Beddgelert, *c*1934. The coal merchant's stock is still delivered by rail, 'girl stationmistress' Miriam Jones waits for passengers and the guard waits for the photographer to board the train. *WHR collection*

Right:
Some staged ticket inspection going on at Beddgelert during the FR lease period. At this stage the 'Gladstone' car was painted red and No 27, an 1894-built Ashbury, pink. *Gwynedd Archives*

Below:
Croesor Junction was one of those junctions with no road access. Trains could be passed there but its main function was to provide an interchange with the Croesor Tramway. A disused FR carriage body sheltered a token instrument and telephone. *Mowat/WHR collection*

Above:
An FR train approaching Nantmor in 1923.
Francis Frith

Top:
Princess and one of the
Pickerings at Croesor Junction
on 3 April 1926.
LCGB/K. A. C. Nunn collection

Above:
Ynysfor was only a short distance
from Croesor Junction but served
a small scattered community. Milk
bound for Portmadoc was loaded
here, too. *Mowat/WHR collection*

Left:
Ynysfor's posterboard survived
to be photographed in 1950.
WHR collection

Centre right:
Beddgelert Siding 'platform' seen
in 1932 had, clearly, never had
the benefit of official sanction.
The land on the left, Gelert's Farm,
is now occupied by WHR(P).
H. M. Comber/FR Archives

Lower right:
Merddin Emrys running round at
Portmadoc New station in the 1920s.
R. W. Kidner/Author's collection

Left:
At Pont Croesor the railway crossed the River Glaslyn parallel to the road, just visible on the right. Locomotive water could be taken from the tank on the left. *Welsh Pony* is in charge of the train in this 1934 photograph.
*R.W. Kidner/
Author's collection*

Right:
Prince with slate wagons on the FR's junction railway linking with the WHR. This section was in substitution for part of the 1836 railway that had been in the centre of the road.
R. W. Kidner/ Author's collection

Above:
Several photographs exist of locomotives in the centre of trains, as seen here with *Merddin Emrys, c*1935; the reason for these strange workings is unknown but it provided an interesting spectacle none the less. Carriage No 5 remains in the FR's fleet as No 12.
Author's collection

Right:
Merddin Emrys arrives at the FR's Harbour station from the WHR in 1923/4. At this time the station was closed to passengers.
Author's collection

—5—
The Liquidation and Revival Proposals
1937–89

Right:
Rhyd Ddu in 1939. It was later
requisitioned for military purposes.
WHR collection

FOR most companies that would have been it. A few months of legal work, a few meetings, disposal of any assets, a final statement and the whole sorry affair consigned to the history books. However, with the WHR, as has been seen, nothing was straightforward.

The investing authorities asked W. Cradoc Davies to submit the FR's case for being released from the lease in writing. They would not, at this stage, agree to the lease being relinquished but would pass Davies's request on to the Treasury and the Ministry of Transport; if they were agreeable the authorities were prepared to make an application for approval for the receiver not to press for the rent.

Davies's letter was discussed at a meeting of the investing authorities held on 29 April 1937. The authorities had met an officer of the Ministry of Transport's Finance & Statistics Department. It was suggested that the WHR company be wound up, subject to court approval, and the assets realised; the FR should pay a lump sum in addition to the rent due at the time of release. At Caernarvon this course of action was agreed, the sum payable by the FR being set at £500.

The county council, acting for the investing authorities and the debenture holders, formally put the proposal that the FR should be released from the lease in exchange for a payment of £500 and outstanding rent to the company on 22 November 1937. Taking some time to establish its position, the FR responded on 15 February 1938. The letter was signed by company secretary Cynan Evan Davies, a son of Evan R. Davies, secretary from 1924 until 1955, a signatory of the 1934 lease and managing director of the Snowdon Mountain Railway since 1930. He reviewed the situation and said that the rent now due was about £210, which the FR was unable to pay or to borrow. He made a counter-offer of £600 in full discharge of all claims, payable in three annual instalments, recognising that there was no way of telling if the company would be able to fulfil the obligation being offered.

He went on to ask if the FR could keep *Moel Tryfan*, then lying dismantled at Boston Lodge. Davies said it had failed its insurance examination in July 1934 and there was therefore no obligation to return it to working order as otherwise required under the terms of the lease. In closing, Davies laid claim to the railway between 'our Portmadoc station and the GWR main line'. This length was put down at the expense of the FR, he said, asserting the right to remove rails and sleepers along it. The claim, eventually accepted, was wrongly made as the boundary between the FR's 1923 junction railway and the WHR was where the route left Madoc Street. By this time the GWR line had become the most practical boundary due to that company having, apparently without consultation, removed the crossing!

At a meeting held on 1 September 1938 the county council, having previously obtained agreement to terms from the other debenture holders, resolved to accept £600 from the FR in full discharge of all claims 'provided the full amount is paid forthwith, or in the alternative, the sum of £300 is paid forthwith, and the remaining £300 to be paid on 30 September 1939, adequate security being given for the payment of the above terms the Festiniog Railway Company to be allowed to retain the steam engine *Moel Tryfan*'. The FR neither made payment nor gave adequate security for it, so therefore, despite subsequent events, never secured legal title to *Moel Tryfan*.

In further correspondence with the council on 2 February 1939, Davies explained that the FR had 'expended a fair sum of money in advertising by way of posters, handbills and guide books, etc' promoting the combined attractions of the WHR and the FR. He went on 'Our experience, however, has been that the Welsh Highland Railway does not appeal to the public in anything like the same degree as does our own railway. The latter has a length of 13 miles odd and travels an appreciable part of its line through scenery which is not open

Right:
A demolition train on the Glanyrafon bridge in 1941.
J. F. Bolton/WHR collection

Below:
Part of WHR(P)'s rail stack, stored by the Nantmor road bridge and seen on 14 April 1981.
Adrian Gray collection

to the tourist by any other means of transport. In addition its known antiquity and recent centenary are other factors contributing in no small degree to its popularity. The Welsh Highland Railway, on the other hand, with its long length of 22 miles, though passing by or through such well-known beauty spots as the Pass of Aberglaslyn and Beddgelert, has nothing but its novelty to recommend it to the public. The two places last mentioned are equally accessible by road.'

He pointed out that Crosville Motor Services was a strong competitor and whilst the railway took two hours from Portmadoc to Dinas, the bus ran at regular intervals, had greater comfort, ran to the centre of Caernarvon and took half the time.

Iggulden's correspondence with the council, meanwhile, with respect to both Stephens's estate and his own salary of £50, due to him for his six-month tenure as receiver and manager, was as drawn out as anything else to do with the WHR. On 9 March 1939, he threatened to remove rail to the value of the sum outstanding on Stephens's estate. The county council replied on 6 June saying that 'several enquiries have been received in respect of same' and that the authority's London agent was to obtain the instruction of the court concerning the sale of track materials. Iggulden's claim, like that of Stephens's estate, was not settled until 1944.

Some 14 scrap dealers and others were to declare their interest to the council between closure and 1941. The Federation of British Industries, whose assistant secretary V. Boyd-Carpenter was a railway enthusiast, took a particular interest, arranging inspections of the line with Robert Evans for itself (ie Boyd-Carpenter) and for George Cohen, Sons & Co, with Boyd-Carpenter in attendance. On 3 May 1939 the latter had, following a second inspection, offered £3,815, their best price, for 'track, rolling stock, sleepers, buildings, telegraph poles and wire, etc'.

Following his death, Griffith was replaced as receiver by George Gregory Williams, the county council's treasurer, on 8 February 1939.

Some two years after the last train, the LMS Estates Department decided it would be appropriate to establish the boundaries at Dinas, and in July 1939 put down pegs in addition to the existing boundary posts. On 7 December the council noted that 'the boundary appears to run through buildings erected by the WHR and in use by the LMS'! The NWNGR station building was one of those concerned.

Counsel's opinion was sought by the county council on 23 May 1940, W. Gordon Brown QC delivering his opinion on 5 June. It would not be possible to get a Board of Trade winding-up order under Section 7 of the Light Railways Act 1912, he said, because inability to carry on the undertaking arose from financial difficulties, not from the sale of the undertaking. The undertaking, anyway, could not be sold without the authority of Parliament. The railway company could be wound up under Section 338 of the Companies Act 1929, and provided the FR's lease was determined first, the liquidator could then discontinue working the railway and realise the assets. An abandonment order would not be necessary before presenting a winding-up petition. He was unable to determine who should best petition for a winding-up order. Finally he opined that the receiver could not be held personally responsible for any loss sustained by

Right:
Beddgelert station site in January 1985.
The only remnants of the old station are
concrete, including the water tank's base,
the locomotive pit and the base of the lamp
room. *D. W. Allan/WHR Heritage*

Below:
The remains of Bryngwyn station, looking
towards the quarries on 26 September 2001.
D. W. Allan/WHR Heritage

landowners or tenants in respect of abandoned cuttings, nor could he be compelled to repair fencing.

The council responded by commissioning John Lloyd of Ishelen, Caernarvon, to inspect the railway, a function he performed between 22 July and 9 August 1940, charging 69 hours at 1s 8d (8p), total £5 15s (£5.75) plus travelling expenses of 9s 6d (48p). He found all stations to be in a very bad state, broken into, windows smashed and frames removed. The buildings at Quellyn (Snowdon Ranger) and Rhyd Ddu had been converted to dwellings, although the latter was empty. After the tunnel at Nantmor obstacles had been built across and along the line. The military had built a wall across the line at Plas-y-nant as an obstacle.

Lord Stamp, chairman of the LMS, involved himself in WHR affairs on 27 September 1940, when he sent a memo to the secretary of the Ministry of Transport, Sir Leonard Browett. Starting, 'This is nothing to do with the LMS or Whitehall; it is just a bleat from a private citizen! When I was tramping round Snowdon for a week in August I was impressed by the derelict Welsh Highland Railway and the possibility of lifting it for scrap', he concluded 'I got our district engineer to give me a report on what was involved in the way of recovery and cost and I enclose a copy . . .' Browett passed Stamp's memo and report on, asking: 'Is there any possibility of getting at the scrap or must the court procedure continue to grind along its laborious and tardy way?'

Stamp's district engineer, C. R. Irving, looked at the FR before estimating that it would cost some £2,325 to dismantle the WHR, making no valuation of the materials involved. Obviously, not knowing too much about the WHR's set-up he included all of the Croesor Tramway, but only five of the seven river bridges in his calculations.

In January 1941, the county council's London solicitor wrote reporting on a meeting held with the Chief Clerk at Chancery Chambers. Officials there had been critical, saying that the company should not have abandoned the undertaking without statutory powers. 'On the other hand it was pointed out that if in fact the Ministry of Supply should formally requisition under the Emergency Powers the rails then the Receiver can afterwards come to the Court for the necessary directions on the footing that he is no longer able to carry on the undertaking, the rails having been acquired by the Ministry.' This opinion cleared the way for the track disposal, and had actually been mooted in Whitehall during 1940 after the same device had been used on the Southwold and Edge Hill railways.

The topic of the WHR's future was raised in the January and February 1941 issues of *Modern Tramway*, when Arthur E. Rimmer suggested that if it could not be used in substitution for road transport to aid the war effort it could perhaps be acquired by voluntary organisations and run by railway enthusiasts. Mr Rimmer is considered, in some quarters, to be the father of WHR preservation and maintained his interest in it until he died in 1999.

Further attention was drawn to the WHR's plight by a three-part article published in *The Railway Magazine* during the year. These two publications might have been responsible for the Ramblers' Association's Liverpool & District Federation circulating Caernarvonshire County Council and others later that year, proposing the freehold should be acquired with a view to its dedication as a public footpath. When, on 3 December 1942, the county council supported the Federation's proposal the motion was seconded by William George. Hardly surprisingly, there was no cash on offer, so the federation launched an appeal to raise £2,000 to be handed to the county council as an earnest of 'widespread desire to acquire this unique right of way'. By 16 October 1946 £1,000 had been raised.

Meanwhile, the requisition proposal was formalised by a Ministry of Supply requisition order dated 13 March 1941. The order covered the railway and sidings, except for the Croesor section, all equipment at Dinas, goods wagons, 50 wheel sets, two steam locomotives and various scrap items lying around the permanent way. A supplementary order issued on 1 August 1941 referred to the coaches and other rolling stock.

The requisitioned assets were sold to George Cohen, Sons & Co Ltd for £12,855; it seems that the Ministry of Supply charged an administration fee of £55, for the WHR received only £12,800. Cohen started on site in August 1941 and worked through until the following year. With bases established at Dinas, Rhyd Ddu and Portmadoc, the company advertised 40,000 sleepers and 1,200 tons of rail as well as 'trucks & chassis' and 'spare heavy wheels & axles' for sale. Most of the rail was still in Cohen's yard after the war and was apparently offered to the Talyllyn Railway c1951!

The county council's solicitor prepared a summons releasing the FR from its lease for presentation to the High Court in September 1941. Of the £600, £200 was to become due immediately the lease was surrendered, the remainder one year after the end of the war, or from the date of any armistice, whichever happened first, payable in four annual instalments. The order gave the FR all rights pertaining to the junction railways; Cohen's offer of £180 for 600yd of track at Portmadoc on 10 July 1942 was presumably for this section.

The council's winding-up summons was issued on 7 October 1941. When served on the WHR's solicitor, Ninian Rhys Davies, he found the company had no current directors! Using company law he caused the majority shareholders, including himself and Jack, who was then known, according to Davies's affidavit, as Henry Joseph Macinnes, to call an extraordinary company meeting. Not unnaturally the non-existent directors failed to respond, giving the requisitioning shareholders the right to call a meeting, which they did for 29 May 1942. At the meeting, attended by Davies, one other and five by proxy, Walter Cradoc Davies, Ralph Freeman and Crossley Colley were elected directors but took no further interest in WHR affairs beyond accepting the winding-up summons.

Railway buildings also came under military scrutiny and on 18 November 1941 Rhostryfan and Rhyd Ddu station buildings were requisitioned. On 6 January 1942 the track between Pont Cae'r Gors and Hafod Ruffydd was requisitioned for the War Department to use for mobile target practice by shooting

Above:
The girder bridge across the Afon Nantmor on 11 March 1989.
D. W. Allan/WHR Heritage

Left:
The Afon Dylif bridge with John Keylock and Cedric Lodge to the fore on 20 August 1997. These bridges were never painted and neither were the lower channels drilled for drainage as recommended by Mount in 1923.
D. W. Allan/WHR Heritage

at slate wagons; the Air Ministry had first raised this idea with the FR on 16 November 1939. In 1944, the War Department had a tenancy for accommodation at Beddgelert for £15 rent per annum but the circumstances are not known.

Another hiatus in the WHR's winding up occurred in 1942 when on 16 April, further opinion was received from W. Gordon Brown QC. Generally speaking he thought the wrong approaches were being used to secure both the release of the FR from the lease and a winding-up order for the WHR. However, at a hearing on 3 November, the FR gained approval to agree to surrender the lease — it appeared that there were no powers to force the FR to surrender it. The surrender was formalised by an agreement with the receiver dated 12 August 1943, whereby the FR agreed to pay £550, still by instalments, instead of the original £600!

When Rhostryfan station was surrendered by the military on 6 January 1945 the council had it inspected to see if a claim for damages could be made. It was soon told that the building had been in appalling condition when requisitioned! The War Department paid £2 10s (£2.50) rental per annum in 1944. On 13 December 1945, LAC 1103869 W. J. Hughes wrote to the county council, in Welsh, from RAF Langham, Holt, Norfolk. He said he had been born in the village and wished to convert the station buildings to a bungalow for himself and his wife, as after 5½ years in the RAF he had no other hope of getting a house.

On 26 January 1944, the county council finally petitioned the High Court for a winding-up order for the WHR. The hearing took place on 7 February when Mr Justice Uthwatt made the order. The county council's London solicitor reported that there was some considerable argument as to whether the court had power to make the Order. The petition stated that the only assets were £12,800 received for the requisitioned stock and equipment, and £550 due from the FR.

The total deficiency of the WHR at 4 March 1927, when a receiver was appointed, was given as £175,171, of which £150,877 was in respect of land, buildings, permanent way and (unspecified) equipment, written down to £20,000 in 1944. Amongst the unsecured creditors were the FR, owed £1,036, and the NWNGR, owed £1,081. The Kent & East Sussex Railway and the North Devon & Cornwall Railway, parts of Col Stephens's empire, were owed money, as was the Snowdon Mountain Railway. Caernarvonshire County Council was owed £630 due for repairing the roads over the NWNGR bridges. The Shropshire & Montgomeryshire Railway, another part of Stephens' empire, owed the WHR £4.

Of the £90,000 ordinary share capital, issued to secure the NWNGR and PBSSR undertakings, £26,696 was held by the estate of Evan R. Davies and £52,891 by Jack. The next largest holdings, each of £1,430, were registered to William D. Penrot and others of Finchley and the executors of C. V. T. Hodgson. The executors of Charles Breese and William George held £750 each, Ralph Freeman and Crossley Colley, £300 each, Aitchison's executors, £25, and Mrs Eleanor C. Russell, £965. There were 46 shareholders in all.

Debts	£	Assets	£
Unsecured creditors	6,521	Cash	125
Preferential creditors	1,494	Stock	25
Debentures	84,774	Land, buildings,	
Interest to 4.3.27	13,300	permanent way,	
Shares	90,000	equipment at cost	170,877
Total	196,089	Stamp duties	2,316
		Debts	768
		Estimated to produce	
		(in 1944)	20,918
		Rents (annually)	177

The figures in the table below are taken from the statement of affairs produced by company secretary Ninian R. Davies and certified by him on 11 May 1944. A. A. Thomas of Llandudno was appointed liquidator on 20 March 1944 and took over responsibility for the estate on 29 March; representatives of the investing authorities formed an overseeing committee of inspection.

In his 23 June 1944 observations on the winding up, the Official Receiver commented: 'It is clear that after payment of the receivership costs and expenses there will be a substantial deficiency on the debentures and there is no prospect of any funds becoming available in the liquidation for the unsecured creditors. The share capital of £90,000 has also been irretrievably lost.' In a statement to court of 9 November the causes of the WHR's collapse were given as failure of traffic to expand as expected and the financial structure of the company. Given the nature of the share capital's creation, it had been a long time since it had represented anywhere near its face value.

The proceeds of the requisitions had been invested in 2½% National War Bonds. These were redeemed in 1944 and on 12 December dispersal of £13,185 was approved as follows, in order of priority: G. G. Williams (receiver's expenses); estate of the late Holman Fred Stephens (receiver's expenses); R. T. Griffith (receiver's expenses); J. A. Iggulden (for acting as receiver and manager); Minister of War Transport costs; FR Co costs; WHR costs, some £1,800 in total. The remainder was passed to the liquidator.

On the trackbed the track from the Croesor Junction–Portmadoc section was dismantled in 1948/9, as was some of that at Hafod Ruffydd. The remnant of the Parliamentary Croesor Tramway, parts of the non-statutory tramway and the Porthmadog link line between Madoc Street and the GWR were removed by 1950.

The Ramblers' Association's 1941 footpath proposal was strongly pursued during the late 1940s/early 1950s. Some county councillors had indicated support for the scheme but when the county surveyor costed it out his estimates made it prohibitive for the council to undertake. A WHR sub-committee met on 13 January 1948 and, having undertaken a two-day tour of inspection, said it could not recommend the proposal to the council in view of the heavy cost and presumed liability for the erection and maintenance of fences. When the Association pursued the matter with the Ministry of Town & Country Planning the council responded, *inter alia*, on 18 January 1949 that it had 'decided to inquire whether certain sections . . . can be purchased for road improvements, such as eliminating bad corners, 'S' bends and hump-backed bridges'; not the last time that such a suggestion might be made.

As this period coincided with the promotion of the first National Parks, the Association came to hope that the National Parks Commission would register the trackbed as a long-distance route under Section 51 of the 1949 National Parks and Access to the Countryside Act. The Commission, however, felt that traversing the route did not, on its own, qualify as an 'extensive journey' as defined in Section 51(1) because it would take only a day or two to traverse.

The Ministry of Transport tended to badger Thomas for news of the liquidation in the late 1940s, especially as he was not always quick to reply; on 11 April 1949 he managed a long report. He had sold removeable chattels to the value of about £1,600 and was getting valuations for land at Caernarvon and at Dinas station. He had found it impossible to establish the extent of the WHR's land holdings due to poor record keeping in the past; deeds were incomplete, plans were missing and descriptions were vague and impossible to key to

Left:
Although abandoned, Portmadoc
New station survived until it met
with the attention of arsonists
in 1990. The background and
purpose of the extensions
visible is unknown.
D.W.Allan/WHR Heritage

Below left:
There were physical reminders,
too, of the building's purpose,
like the booking office window.
D.W.Allan/WHR Heritage

Below right:
Inside, Portmadoc New station
the adventurous could find relics
of the past, such as this vandalised
poster from 1925.
D.W.Allan/WHR Heritage

maps. He proposed selling the land at auction with possessory title, saying 'unless we do this the liquidation will drag on indefinitely'. It did anyway, but he obviously did not understand that he actually had no power to sell the trackbed. Most of the Caernarvon land and Rhyd Ddu station site were sold by 1952, the latter becoming a car park.

In 1952 Thomas was reporting progress, separately, to the Ministry and the county council, saying that he had been careful to maintain a right of way in case he was able to make a sale to the Ramblers' Association, yet when he sold the NWNGR shed sites to the Gwynedd River Board in 1955, the trackbed separating them, and under the main road, was included in the sale. Dinas station was sold later, the plot being enlarged when amalgamated with the standard gauge part of the site, becoming a council highways depot. Beddgelert Parish Council had declared an interest in the station site there but apart from Waenfawr and Snowdon Ranger he thought it would be difficult to sell the trackbed if he didn't get a buyer for all of it. In October Thomas was asked to negotiate with DW Investment Holdings Ltd, but the purpose of this company's interest is currently unknown.

The investing authorities received some good news later in 1952 when Thomas made a distribution of 2s (10p) in the £. Further distributions of 1s 3d (6p) and 1s (5p) in the £ were made in 1954 and 1962.

In 1953, Thomas approached the Snowdonia Park Joint Advisory Committee, to see if it would buy the trackbed. The committee had no powers to purchase on its own account so put the matter to the National Parks Commission. On

12 November it resolved that the counties of Denbigh, Caernarvon and Merioneth should work together to submit proposals for the establishment of a long-distance route including both the WHR and the FR, then crossing southern Snowdonia with a view to continuing through mid-Wales to the proposed Brecon Beacons National Park and thence to St David's in the Pembroke National Park, and from Dinas to Conway and St Asaph.

Events moved slowly and in August 1959 the county council was advised that the Commission had no plans for a long-distance route in Snowdonia. However, in saying that there had been no intention to consider a Snowdonia route for two years, the Commission had agreed that the council's request, 'that this particular route should be given priority' would be an item on the agenda for a meeting in September!

The council was also informed that there were adequate rights to create footpaths without resorting to purchase; any purchase made under existing general powers would not attract Exchequer assistance even if ultimately the long-distance route were to use it.

Thomas had actually offered the trackbed to the county council in 1958. He must have begun to tire of the WHR, for in 1960/1 he had been considering handing over the trackbed to the Crown as unsaleable but almost as soon as he had formed the thought he received two distinct declarations of interest that he was dealing with in February 1961. By the end of the year he had received an offer 'subject to certain pre-requisite conditions on the part of the purchasers'. The source of that offer has yet to be established.

However, the first concerted public effort to obtain access to the WHR trackbed for railway purposes had begun, with the establishment of a Welsh Highland Railway Society, but the society was not the only interested party, for on 9 May 1961 an organisation called Minitrains offered £40 per acre to buy the section between Beddgelert station and the Nantmor tunnel mouth for a 15in gauge overhead electric tramway, for which the equipment was already in stock.

On 14 March 1962, the Treasury Solicitor was informing the Ministry of Transport that a sale had been delayed due to the refusal of the planning authority to grant permission. Lacking access to any part of the trackbed, the fledgeling society established a depot at Kinnerley, Shropshire, in 1963. It was incorporated as Welsh Highland Light Railway (1964) Limited (WHR(P)) in January 1964. Negotiations with Thomas, whereby the trackbed would be bought for £850, failed due to his death on 6 July 1964, before contracts could be exchanged.

With Thomas's death, responsibility for the WHR's assets transferred to the office of the Official Receiver (OR), based in London. The OR was required to act in the interests of the debenture holders in securing the best price for the assets, of which the trackbed itself was the most significant. The elected representatives of the investing authorities had difficulty in understanding that as debenture holders their first priority was to obtain the best return on their capital investment, not seeking to obtain odd bits of land for other purposes. The best price was always going to be received for the entire trackbed, rather than for isolated sections.

So far as the trackbed was concerned, the OR's objective was to ensure that it would pass to a body with sufficient resources to take on the liabilities, so that it did not return to him via another bankruptcy. Because the WHR was a statutory undertaking, disposal of the land could only take place with either an Abandonment Order under the Transport Act 1962, or Transfer Order under Section 24 of the Light Railways Act 1896, although this was not always understood. Negotiations became complex and protracted, and progress suffered from a lack of consistent local authority policy with regard to the trackbed, a cautious OR and the fleeting interest of outsiders.

The OR had no funds with which to administer the WHR estate; after Thomas's dispersals there was only about £200 in hand. When it became necessary to obtain legal advice the OR sought funds from the investing authorities.

Whilst WHR(P) established links with the OR and the local authorities to progress its ambition to restore the WHR, outside interest was not diminished. Transit Properties Ltd (incorporating Minirail Ltd) of Frampton Cotterell, Bristol, offered £25 an acre for the land between Rhyd Ddu and Nantmor on 24 August 1965, an offer that was repeated on 12 November 1969. One of Transit Properties' directors was L. M. Anderson, who had made the Minitrains bid in 1961.

A Colin Heard of Yeovil offered £1,250 for the section between Beddgelert and Nantmor on 14 March 1966. WHR(P) offered £2,500 for the entire route, an amount that was doubled by a J. R. Green of Bexhill, Sussex, in May 1967. Green was a retired businessman and reputed millionaire. He offered to let WHR(P) be involved in running the railway rebuilt under his control.

The OR took Green's bid seriously and decided legal advice was called for, so on 28 November 1967 the debenture holders were asked for funds. A meeting was held in Caernarvon on 20 March 1968 to consider the request. Due to the absence of the OR no decision was made. The Ministry of Transport's representative observed that the local authorities did not present a united front, with some concerned about the motives of a prospective purchaser, whilst others welcomed the idea, citing the benefits of the FR. He said that the county council was delaying, in order to inform Green of its anxieties and to explore the possibility of making a joint offer. A proposed but unidentified road scheme, requiring an expensive bridge over the railway, was mentioned.

A further meeting, held on 24 April 1968, was attended by the OR, Mr H. C. Gill. Green was not prepared to contribute to the cost of obtaining Counsel's advice but had increased his bid to £5,500 so the debenture holders would not lose out if he were successful. The county surveyor said any delay in establishing rights of access to the trackbed would cost £250,000, as it 'was obstructing the realignment of a main road in the area and a bridge costing that amount would need to be constructed.' Quite how he achieved that logic is unclear. The meeting's chairman suggested that Green sought to buy the land in order to hold the councils to ransom over those sections they wanted.

Receiving Counsel's opinion that the OR had no power to sell without either an Abandonment Order or a Transfer Order, a draft contract was prepared. Green, however, was served with a Receiving Order in May 1968 although he successfully appealed against it on 22 October. WHR(P) matched the £5,500 offer.

The OR appears to have been frustrated by delays in Green's responses to letters and his failure to instruct solicitors, and in January 1969 he was unofficially dropped in favour of WHR(P). Green visited the OR on 17 February 1969, but to no avail. Nothing was heard from him again.

Thereafter, whenever any enquiries were made about the availability of the trackbed the standard reply was that the OR was dealing with a prospective purchaser. This was the response that Tony Hills, now the proprietor of the Brecon Mountain Railway, received on 24 August 1972, after he had enquired on behalf of Hills & Bailey Ltd of Llanberis, saying that they wished to reopen all or part of the railway for tourists.

Another meeting of the debenture holders was held at Caernarvon on 3 February 1969. Development Securities represented the McAlpine company; as a debenture holder the latter was also investigating the possibility of taking a lead in reconstructing the WHR. The debenture holders were in favour of reopening in principle and it was suggested that WHR(P) purchase the trackbed jointly with the county council.

By 1971, WHR(P) had offered £5,750, recommended for acceptance by OR; however, the county council was not prepared to give its approval until it had reached agreement with WHR(P) on the council's land requirements.

The road schemes that threatened the trackbed's integrity came to the fore in 1971. The county surveyor, T. Lloyd Roberts, writing to WHR(P)'s chairman on 13 March, said that railway land at Waunfawr was needed for road improvement, scheduled to commence that year. The new road would cross the site on an embankment and the old bridge would be filled in. He was proposing to seek permission from the OR for consent to enter the site. In another letter the day before, Roberts told WHR(P) that giving the railway a bridge through the embankment would cost £250,000, which it would have to finance.

On 6 July, Roberts sent details of 18 road schemes to the Department of the Environment. Under these proposals 10 bridges, including the PBSSR structure at Beddgelert, would have been demolished. The road was to be diverted on to the trackbed between Gwyrfai Terrace and Betws Garmon and between Castell Cidwm and Snowdon Ranger. Between Llwyn Bedw and Gwyrfai Terrace and between Rhyd Ddu and Pitt's Head the road would have been widened on to the railway. Getting the road into and out of the Beddgelert station site for the village's western bypass would have been

a major civil engineering task. The village would also have benefited by an eastern bypass, too, perhaps using the PBSSR route to Nant Gwynant. Nantmor level crossing was to be widened and at Porthmadog an indication was given of where that town's proposed bypass might cross the line. Of all these schemes only the last has been the subject of any design work and its construction is still some time into the future as this book is being published.

In Whitehall, the Ministry of Transport had obtained Treasury approval, on 11 June 1971, to have the outstanding WHR debt written off. The stock, effectively the certificates, was sold by tender to R. I. G. West on 14 December 1985.

A matter of ongoing concern throughout this period was the incursions taking place on the trackbed along with claims for adverse possession. On 25 August 1965 Mr G. V. Swann, tenant of Snowdon Ranger station building as a holiday home since 1933, offered to buy the property for £350. He added that if his offer was not accepted he claimed possessory title, saying that he had ceased to pay rent, £10 per annum, in 1948 because he was not certain that the person he was paying it to, Thomas, was entitled to receive it! Resident in Newcastle-under-Lyme, Swann was a solicitor.

Llanwnda Parish Council successfully registered Rhostryfan station site as a village green with the county council. An objection being made, the registration was overturned on 2 January 1973 following an inquiry. The objector was George Morgan, Cae Hen, who had himself incorporated part of the trackbed into his farm near Tryfan Junction and demolished an overbridge to improve his access.

In 1973, an exchange took place with property owners at Ynys Ferlas, near Nantmor, when a claim of adverse possession was made. This was resisted, as all such claims were, by the OR and ended with the owner's husband saying he wanted to ensure she was compensated if approval was given for the railway to be rebuilt! By 1975 some 30 adjacent property owners had been identified as making claims for adverse possession of sections of the trackbed. For many years WHR(P) members reported incursions to the OR, with varying degrees of success.

The WHR(P) moved its equipment from Kinnerley to Porthmadog in 1973, after reaching agreement to buy the former Cambrian Railways siding from British Railways. Later the BR land opposite the Queen's Hotel was purchased, as was adjacent land at Gelert's Farm in 1975. A depot was set up, a three-quarter-mile-long railway built and an LRO obtained in 1980. The first trains ran on 2 August that year, terminating at Pen-y-mount, alongside the trackbed. (The WHR(P)'s railway is located on what is commonly known as Beddgelert Siding, in reference to the partially-constructed standard gauge Beddgelert Railway, of which it might have been a part. However, several old plans, including those deposited with the PBSSR's 1901 bill, refer to the narrow gauge, Croesor Tramway, loop as Beddgelert Siding and the standard gauge line, when it is named at all, as the Cambrian Siding. The WHR called it Gelert Siding.

In 1978, WHR(P) succeeded in obtaining restoration to Pont Croesor, just over 1¾ miles, included in the District Plan. The railway had been omitted from the draft plan so the matter was raised at a public inquiry, with the county council objecting to its inclusion. The inspector found in the railway's

Above:
In 1984, WHR(P) signalled its presence in Porthmadog with this Bagnall 4-4-0T. Across the road is the Queen's Hotel and to the locomotive's right the Gorseddau Railway trackbed, intended terminus of the Portmadoc, Beddgelert & Rhyd Ddu Light Railway and the PBSSR. *Author*

favour though, prompting WHR(P) to produce a feasibility study the following year.

Over the years the focus of WHR(P)'s ambitions regarding the trackbed varied according to the whims of the local authorities. The Ministry of Transport had allegedly made it clear that it would not make a Transfer Order in favour of the company. The county council, meanwhile, was prepared to acquire the trackbed but would obtain an Abandonment Order on doing so, a move that would have severely constrained any future railway reinstatement because it would facilitate the use of railway land for any purpose.

A planning application for the section between Porthmadog and Rhyd Ddu submitted by WHR(P) in May 1981 was later turned down by the county council's planning sub-committee.

Gwynedd County Council, created in 1974, did form a WHR sub-committee, on which WHR(P) was represented, to oversee matters relating to the trackbed. Although it tended to be reactive to events affecting the trackbed, the sub-committee proposed that the council buy the assets from the Official Receiver for £1, an offer that was submitted in October 1981. The council would take on responsibility for the liabilities and leasing parts of the trackbed to WHR(P) as that organisation developed the resources to expand. The council also proposed allocating parts of the trackbed for other recreational uses, to do which it would need an Abandonment Order.

During the 1980s, a split developed within WHR(P), when some members thought alternative means to secure the trackbed for railway use should be investigated. They managed to acquire share and debenture certificates in the 1922 company and formed Trackbed Consolidation Ltd (TCL) to hold them. TCL made an offer of £10,000 to the OR for the trackbed.

Although the share and debenture certificates held by TCL could not be registered to it, TCL used its position of beneficial owner to call a 1922 company creditors' meeting to put forward a scheme of arrangement, whereby the company could be removed from receivership. The meeting, in July 1984, was adjourned when TCL could not get the required 75% majority in favour.

When the meeting was reconvened in January 1986 TCL's effective holding was increased by having access to the rights attaching to the former Ministry of Transport holding. Owing to objections from the county, Dwyfor and Meirionnydd district councils it was still unable to obtain the required majority. Dwyfor had been in favour before the meeting but changed its mind. Had TCL been successful at this stage its intention was to act as landlord for WHR(P) rebuilding the railway.

Progress appeared to be made by WHR(P) when, in January 1988, an LRO application for the Pont Croesor section was made jointly with the county council; with events overtaking the application, the order was not made. Unbeknown to WHR(P) the FR had taken an interest in the trackbed, making a secret bid to the OR to buy it for £16,000 in October 1987. County council officers were told on several occasions during 1988 that the FR was concerned about the effect on revenues if the WHR extended beyond Pont Croesor.

The FR's interest became public, amongst considerable controversy, and great dismay on the part of WHR(P), in 1989. Facing a severe lack of credibility the FR eventually announced its intention to restore the complete railway, including the junction railways and to extend to Caernarfon, fulfilling the ambition of Spooner and others of over 100 years earlier. The justification for FR involvement could have been extracted from Spring's report, quoted earlier. In the event the first construction took place between Dinas and Caernarfon, something that Spring might have commended, too.

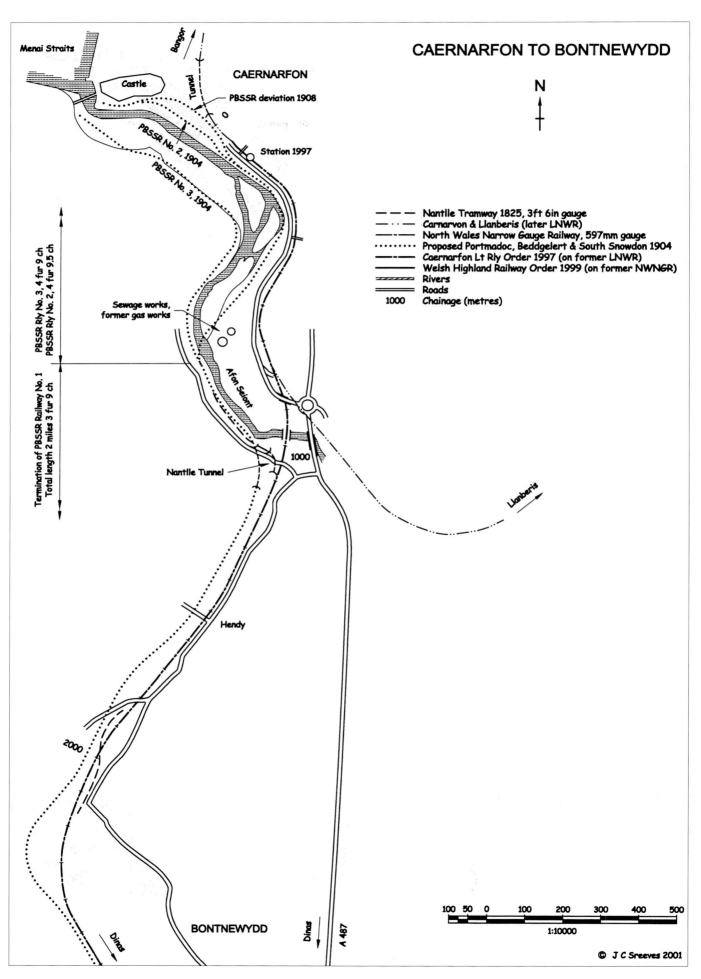

CAERNARFON TO BONTNEWYDD

N

Menai Straits

Castle

Bangor

Tunnel

CAERNARFON

PBSSR deviation 1908

PBSSR No. 2, 1904

Station 1997

PBSSR No. 3, 1904

Nantlle Tramway 1825, 3ft 6in gauge
Carnarvon & Llanberis (later LNWR)
North Wales Narrow Gauge Railway, 597mm gauge
Proposed Portmadoc, Beddgelert & South Snowdon 1904
Caernarfon Lt Rly Order 1997 (on former LNWR)
Welsh Highland Railway Order 1999 (on former NWNGR)
Rivers
Roads
1000   Chainage (metres)

PBSSR Rly No. 3, 4 fur 9 ch
PBSSR Rly No. 2, 4 fur 9.5 ch

Termination of PBSSR Railway No. 1
Total length 2 miles 3 fur 9 ch

Sewage works,
former gas works

Afon Seiont

1000

Nantlle Tunnel

Llanberis

Hendy

2000

BONTNEWYDD

Dinas

Dinas

A 487

100 50 0   100   200   300   400   500
1:10000

© J C Sreeves 2001

92

— 6 —
Rebuilding the WHR
Progress from 1990

IN deciding to start the restored WHR at Caernarfon, the FR saw that the town was recognised as having only one attraction, the castle, then attracting some 400,000 visitors a year, with nothing to entice them to stay longer than the minimum time needed to tour it. As a commercial centre it was in decline. The standard gauge trackbed to Afon Wen was, and remains, part of the Lôn Eifion cycleway; as far as Dinas it could easily accommodate both cycles and trains and at Caernarfon the terminus could be very close to the castle. The rationale was that many of the castle's visitors would easily be tempted to take a train ride if they heard or saw it during their visit.

However, the FR having said that it would rebuild the WHR in its entirety was not the end of the matter. There were considerable hurdles to overcome before work could start on the ground and trains could run again.

The OR made the next move in the saga, announcing that an application was to be made to the High Court for permission to sell the trackbed to the county council for £1. In 1990, TCL was introduced to the FR and concluded that its aims were similar and that the FR had the better chance of success. Therefore, TCL's share and debenture certificates, and those acquired by Mr West from the Ministry of Transport, were donated to the FR Trust, the charitable organisation that owns the majority of the FR's shares.

Ownership of these certificates was deemed to qualify the FR to participate in the court hearing, held in June 1990, applying to have certificate transfers validated, leading the way to a scheme of arrangement by which the WHR's assets could be removed from the OR's control, to prevent the sale of the trackbed to the county council and to allow the OR to sell the trackbed to the FR.

Being made aware that the FR's activities in seeking to take over another railway were probably *ultra vires*, the FR Trust registered FR Holdings Ltd as a device to handle the FR's non-FR activities, the holdings company then being made a party to the application in substitution for the FR company.

The judgment was made on 20 December 1991. It found the application to register share and debenture transfers to be misconceived but that the FR Trust or some other body, but not the FR, should be able to apply for an LRO. It was therefore not for the court to decide between the competing claims but for the Secretary of State (for Transport).

The FR Trust, jointly with FR Holdings, then made an application for a Transfer Order to take over the remaining assets (and liabilities) of the original company from the OR in tandem with an application for a Dinas–Caernarfon LRO in October 1992. In December, the WHR(P)/Gwynedd County Council alliance made similar applications. A public inquiry to resolve the matter was held at Caernarfon in November/December 1993. A new WHR Society was formed to support the FR scheme in 1993; by the time of the public inquiry it had recruited some 800 members.

The inspector's report and recommendation, dated 4 March 1994, and the Secretary of State for Transport's decision were published on 20 July 1994, the package proving to be rather a shock. The inspector found that reinstatement of the WHR would be in the public interest and that either party had the capability of undertaking it. But whilst he found in favour of WHR(P)/Gwynedd, the recommendation was overruled by the Secretary of State. This was undoubtedly a political decision, given that the government of the day had a policy of diverting risk from the public to the private sector wherever possible.

The WHR (Transfer) LRO was made on 4 March 1995. Armed with this the FR could negotiate with the OR for the transfer of WHR's assets, substantially the land. For reasons that are unclear, but perhaps due to caution on the part of the OR, it was 30 June 1999 before the transfer took place, for a price of £1. On 17 August the end came for the WHR (Light Railway) Ltd, when Official Receiver Mark Boyall wrote: 'The winding up is for practical purposes complete. There will be no distribution to creditors.'

Approval of the FR's Caernarfon Railway LRO was given with the Transfer Order decision but it was 1997 before it was made. This section of the WHR has its origins in the Nantlle Railway, a 3ft 6in-gauge horse tramway connecting slate quarries in the Nantlle Valley, a distance of about eight miles,

Left:
The Nantlle Tramway bridge at Bontnewydd on 10 January 1999; it subsequently became a listed structure. *Author*

93

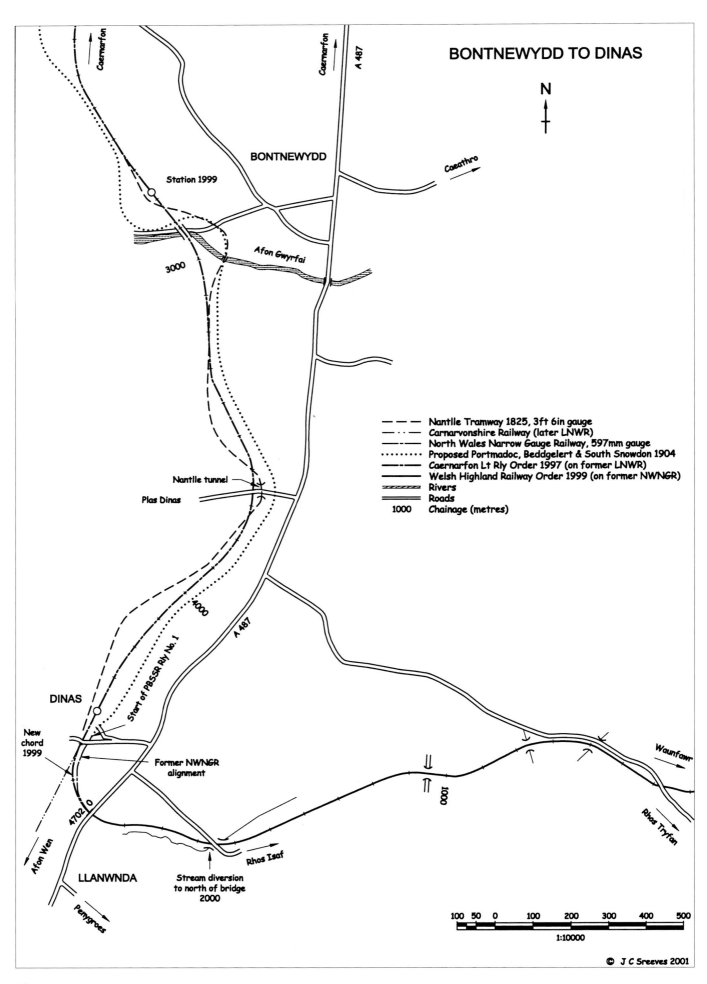

BONTNEWYDD TO DINAS

N

Caernarfon
Caernarfon
A 487

BONTNEWYDD

Caeathro

Station 1999

3000

Afon Gwyrfai

- - - Nantlle Tramway 1825, 3ft 6in gauge
-··-··- Carnarvonshire Railway (later LNWR)
-·-·- North Wales Narrow Gauge Railway, 597mm gauge
········ Proposed Portmadoc, Beddgelert & South Snowdon 1904
-·-·- Caernarfon Lt Rly Order 1997 (on former LNWR)
───── Welsh Highland Railway Order 1999 (on former NWNGR)
▨▨▨ Rivers
═══ Roads
1000 Chainage (metres)

Nantlle tunnel

Plas Dinas

4000

A 487

DINAS

Start of PBSSR Rly No.1

New chord 1999

Former NWNGR alignment

Waunfawr

1000

4702 0

Afon Wen

Rhos Isaf

Rhos Tryfan

LLANWNDA

Stream diversion to north of bridge 2000

Penygroes

100 50 0   100   200   300   400   500

1:10000

© J C Sreeves 2001

Above:
Caernarfon terminus. The Nantlle Railway terminated on the wharves to the left of centre, behind the large shed. The DMUs had brought visitors to the Prince of Wales's Investiture on 1 July 1969, witness the military presence on the left. In the right foreground is the trackbed for the connection to the tramway that served the town's gasworks. The land in the foreground is now owned by the WHR and the station should be extended on to this site some time in the future. *Wyn Hobson*

with the port at Caernarfon. Pre-dating even the FR, it was incorporated by an Act of 1825 and opened in 1828.

Parliamentary approval was given to the Carnarvonshire Railway in 1862. This Caernarvon–Portmadoc standard gauge railway took over the Nantlle from Caernarvon to Pen-y-groes, and joined it to a new line thence to Afon Wen, where it connected with the Cambrian Railways' coast route to Pwllheli.

The Nantlle was absorbed into the Carnarvonshire Railway by an 1867 Act. At that time the standard gauge terminated at a temporary station near Pant Farm, the location now better known as Hendy Crossing, pending construction of the viaduct across the Afon Seiont into Caernarvon. On the former Nantlle section curves were eased or bypassed to accommodate the standard gauge. Despite the long period out of use, some remarkable relics of the original Nantlle route still survive between Caernarvon and Dinas, notably tunnels at Coed Helen and Plas Dinas and the river bridge at Bontnewydd.

The LNWR exercised powers to absorb the Carnarvonshire Railway in 1870, when the line into Caernarvon was completed, paralleled for a short distance by the Carnarvon & Llanberis Railway. To facilitate continued rail access to the harbour a connection was formed between the Carnarvonshire Railway and sidings laid on the wharf by the harbour trustees, the junction being located close to the 1997 WHR terminus. The Carnarvonshire Railway was closed in 1964.

While the high-profile legal work relating to the LROs was ongoing for the new WHR, consideration was given to the operating requirements for the 25-mile long railway. The criteria established to attract the sophisticated traveller of the 21st century were for speeds of up to 25mph to be the norm to give an acceptable journey time, with locomotives capable of good acceleration and power to cope with gradients of up to 1 in 40, trains of 10 or 12 cars hauled by a single locomotive, and high-quality coaches with all conveniences, catering, etc. Throughout, the work was to be to the highest standards attainable, to avoid the need for it to be redone after a short time.

Crucially, it was decided that the project should be fully funded, with no recourse to loans. Whilst the FR and the WHR have some substantial backers prepared to help financially, much of the funding was going to have to come from other sources.

A considerable amount of suitable equipment, in the form of locomotives, wagons and track materials, was found to be available in South Africa. The locomotive requirement would be met by using Manchester-built NGG16 class 2-6-2+2-6-2 Beyer-Garratts from the Alfred County Railway and a South African-built Funkey B-B 350hp diesel locomotive from the Port Elizabeth cement works.

By 1995, the WHR project was priced at around £20 million. In October that year, the Millennium Commission announced it would make a £4.3 million contribution to the WHR from lottery funding. This was 47% of the £9.1 million cost of building from Caernarfon to Rhyd Ddu, a distance of 12 miles, which was anticipated to be achievable by the year 2000. Further grants were obtained from the European Regional Development Fund, the Welsh Development Agency and the Wales Tourist Board, as well as sponsorship from the WHR Society, Historic Houses Hotels and 1st Hydro.

In 1996, the FR established the Welsh Highland Light Railway Co Ltd (WHLR) and gave it the task of building and equipping the new railway. The new company's chairman was Mike Hart, then also FR Company chairman, who had been a teenage volunteer at Boston Lodge in the 1960s. The inaugural board meeting was held in December 1996, when

Right:
BR Class 47 No 1718 on the Carnarvonshire Railway at Bronydd Crossing, near Bontnewydd, on 1 July 1969, when the stub of the line was used to stable Investiture specials. *Wyn Hobson*

Below:
Garratt No 138 at Caernarfon on 12 October 1997, during the unadvertised trial passenger service. *Author*

one of its first actions was to appoint Roland Doyle as general manager.

At the same time, Gwynedd Council, the unitary authority replacing the county council, declared its support for the project by granting a 999-year lease on the Dinas–Caernarfon trackbed for £1 per annum, payable in advance, the railway undertaking to rebuild the cycleway on this section. The former Dinas station site, a council road depot, was sold to the railway and the council donated its WHR debenture certificates, too.

Civil engineering contractor Mowlem received the £¾ million contract to clear the Caernarfon–Dinas route, renovate underbridges and culverts, install drainage and fencing, relocate and rebuild the cycle track, and ballast the formation. The contractor built the platforms at Dinas and

Caernarfon, renewed the prop under the Coed Helen bridge, near Caernarfon, and cleared the route for rail access into the old NWNGR yard at Dinas. Work started on 15 January 1997, when the Funkey and an excavator broke through a paper banner. Track laying, by paid staff and volunteers, started in May and was completed in September.

Whilst this work was in progress the Welsh Highland Heritage Group was formed. Its purpose is to record railway structures that might be removed or altered during construction and to ensure that the railway's heritage is given priority whenever possible.

In late September, Garratt No 138 was delivered to Dinas, as was back-up motive power, the FR's Alco 2-6-2PT *Mountaineer*. The carriages were commissioned on 1/2 October. The scene was then set for the attendance of HM Railway Inspectors. Late on the afternoon of the 2nd, the carriages were taken for their first run to Caernarfon, hauled by the Funkey. On arrival there stood the HMRI inspection team.

The next day they conducted a line inspection and examined the visibility from the locomotives. The certificate to operate arrived on 9 October and the LRO was made on 10 October. Trial running took place the same day, with an unadvertised service operated on the weekend of 11/12 October, attracting 300 passengers a day. The Mayor of Caernarfon performed the official opening on 13 October, followed by public running the next day. During the 22 operating days in 1997, 9,200 passengers were carried, making 18,361 passenger journeys.

Before moving on to the WHR trackbed a Transport & Works Order (TWO) was required. This procedure superseded the LRO for new applications in England and Wales in 1992. It had been made quite clear that any decision taken in respect of the transfer order would not pre-empt any decision on the eventual application to rebuild the railway. An application was submitted in April 1997 for an order to authorise the reconstruction from Dinas to connect with the FR at Porthmadog. The section through that town was defined as a street tramway, permitting the use of marginally cheaper traffic lights to control the road crossings rather than rail-style level crossing installations. A very detailed and complex environmental statement was required to accompany the application, to explain just how the railway was to be built, including environmental protection measures.

The original route was maintained except for deviations at Tryfan Junction to improve sighting on a very minor road, at Rhyd Ddu to bypass the car park located on the former station site and at Porthmadog where a new alignment was devised to connect to the FR. To deal with those claiming adverse possession, compulsory purchase powers were sought, using

Left:
Blanche was used
on off-peak services
during 1999,
and is seen at
Hendy Crossing.
Author

Below:
Caernarfon on the
occasion of the official
opening of the line to
Dinas, 13 October
1997. *Author*

the argument that it would be wrong for an individual, or group of individuals, to be able to overturn the wishes of the Secretary of State. The application also included a request for deemed planning consent, a legal device that avoided a duplicate application under planning laws, although decisions on station buildings and similar were reserved for the local authorities.

When published, the application triggered some remarkable about-turns from organisations previously supportive of the railway, including the Snowdonia National Park Authority, against the advice of its officers, and the National Trust. Perhaps not too remarkably, some of the objections were very reminiscent of those made to PBSSR/NWPT applications 90 years earlier! A public inquiry was held in Caernarfon, starting on 9 December 1997 and ending on 28 January 1998, not continuously but considerably longer than those relating to the railway in 1921, 1922 and 1993.

Great play was made by some objectors on the suitability of the Aberglaslyn Pass for railway use, with claims made that it would be unsafe, this despite the large numbers of walkers who had been unofficially using it as a route. These claims were to have an impact on future events, though, but not as expected.

During the course of the inquiry the FR reached an agreement with several objectors and their objections were withdrawn. Notable amongst them was that reached with WHR(P), by then legally Welsh Highland Railway Ltd and claiming copyright on the name, and objecting to the FR's application. The key point was that in exchange for withdrawing its objection, WHR(P) would build the railway to Pont Croesor, at its own expense, when the Dinas–Waenfawr section was complete. Agreement was also reached concerning the use of the name, vintage train operation and for WHR(P) to develop a WHR heritage centre at its Gelert's Farm site.

The initial train service in 1997/8 was promoted as a Caernarfon-based excursion, with the line marketed as Rheilffordd Eryri/Welsh Highland Railway. In addition to the tourists, there was some local traffic; passengers with children in pushchairs liked having the assistance of a guard to board and disembark, and those with local residents' railcards found the fare a few pence cheaper than the bus, too.

Operation during 1998 continued to attract attention although patronage was not as forecast due to a downturn in Welsh tourism generally; 37,560 bookings produced 59,715 passengers. It was usually found that if Caernarfon Castle was busy then the trains were busy. During the year finishing-off work saw a water tank installed at Caernarfon, replacing temporary facilities at Dinas.

Before the TWO decision was made another relevant public inquiry took place, starting in July 1998, for the Snowdonia National Park Authority had proposed withdrawing support for the WHR from its structure plan. It emerged that the Park Authority had changed its mind about the railway on the basis of a personal objection made by the chairman of the planning committee. One of the key points made was that the Authority's plan was required, by statute, to be in conformity with Gwynedd Council's plan, the latter supporting reinstatement of the WHR.

The Authority maintained that the special qualities of the park could not be appreciated from a railway carriage, but only by moving slowly through the landscape, by walking or cycling. It is not for the Authority, the inspector was to say, to dictate how people should enjoy the park's special qualities, adding that based on his experience of the FR, it is possible to appreciate the landscape in greater comfort and safety from a train. By the time of the inquiry over 5,000 WHR supporters had made their views known to the Authority.

It was on 9 March 1999 that the first of the public inquiry reports was published, ironically from the most recent, the Snowdonia National Park Authority's. Of the WHR the inspector concluded that the 'principle of its reinstatement is in the public interest and does not conflict with national park purposes'.

Shortly afterwards a surprise came from the Department of the Environment, Transport and the Regions, in the form of an interim decision on the TWO application. Published on 7 April, Deputy Prime Minister John Prescott said that he was minded to make the order provided the implications of reconstruction in the Aberglaslyn Pass were understood. This was dependent upon the FR commissioning consultants to examine the pass and proposing a scheme of remedial works, if found necessary, with the Park Authority.

The 'minded' decision in favour of the WHR was, however, contrary to the recommendation of the inspector, just as with the Transfer Order application!

Consulting engineers were appointed by the FR, under terms agreed by the Park Authority, and their report was submitted on 19 May. The FR was anxious to make progress, otherwise the final decision would be devolved to the National Assembly for Wales, then due to come into existence on 1 July, and be subject to further delay. The Authority, though, tried to prevaricate and put off making a decision on its acceptance of the FR's report.

It was to no avail, however, because the final, favourable, decision was announced on 28 June 1999 and the Order was made two days later. Work could be started in the National Park, however, only when the proposed remedial works, including rock stabilisation, shotcreting in two of the three tunnels and raising retaining walls, had been carried out in the Pass, to the Park Authority's satisfaction.

As might be expected in WHR affairs, that was not the end of it. The application procedure allows a 42-day period for an appeal to be made, on very limited grounds, by any aggrieved person affected by an Order. In July, the National Farmers' Union for Wales announced that it was applying to the High Court to have the Order overturned. A ruling in favour of the WHR was made on 24 November. Only then could the reinstatement of the WHR start in earnest.

The new railway's first enthusiast event took place on 19/20 September 1998, introducing Garratt No 143 and the Pullman car to an admiring public, both having performed test trips along the line only the day before! Double-heading of the Garratts provided the spectacle of 164 tons of narrow gauge super-power in action. Locomotives visiting for the event were 0-4-0STT *Palmerston* from the FR, and de Winton 0-4-0VBT *Chaloner* and Hunslet 0-4-0ST *Alice*, both based at the Leighton Buzzard Railway in Bedfordshire. *Palmerston* was used on the 'old' WHR, *Chaloner* was built in Caernarfon, in workshops located opposite the new station, and worked in the Pen-yr-orsedd Quarry in the Nantlle Valley, served by the Nantlle Railway, and *Alice* represented this popular locomotive class, once a regular sight in North Wales slate quarries. During the weekend they performed drive-an-engine sessions at Dinas; on Saturday evening they ran solo light engine trips to Caernarfon, posing for photographs.

Following receipt of a petition from residents, a halt was opened at Bontnewydd in May 1999. An unusual vehicle was seen in action on the line at this time, in the form of an experimental flywheel-

Left:
Garratt No 143 became the first locomotive to steam to Waunfawr on 5 August 2000; on that occasion it is seen crossing on to the WHR trackbed. *Author*

Above right:
A view from the footplate of No 138 as it passes the ruins of Tryfan Junction station on 27 August 2000. *Author*

powered Parry People Mover. The small 20-seat vehicle was promoted as a possible solution to the railway's need for railcars if a demand for commuter or off-peak services were to build up. Following a number of trial trips, the first on 18 March, the vehicle was approved for WHR use on 29 October, entering service three days later. However, it suffered a catastrophic failure on 4 November and was returned to its maker's West Midlands factory.

Following the transfer of assets from the OR on 30 June and whilst awaiting the outcome of the Welsh NFU's application to have the TWO overturned, work started on clearance and fencing. This continued during the 1999/2000 winter, which turned out to be the wettest for years. Contractors' machinery moving on immeasurable years of accumulated silt aggravated the situation severely and caused serious delays to progress.

The trackbed required lowering through five overbridges and two other bridges needed replacing. The Cae Moel bridge, near Dinas, attracted considerable interest as it also had a stream running through it. At the contractors' instigation the stream was diverted to simplify the bridge works. In the Gwyrfai Valley a landslip above the line at some time in the past needed stabilising. Trackbed drainage required considerable attention, having been ignored for over 50 years. Some 80,000 tons of material was removed from the cutting adjacent to the Mount Hotel at Dinas; the land was part of that sold by receiver Thomas to Gwynedd River Board in 1955 and subsequently sold to the hotel.

The WHR featured on a special postage stamp issued by the Royal Mail on 1 February 2000, part of an extensive issue to mark the Millennium. The composite image featured Garratt No 143 on the climb out of Caernarfon with a backdrop near Rhyd Ddu. Appropriately for such a moody image, the launch event at Dinas took place in heavy rain. The FR issued its first WHR railway letter stamp on the same day.

Track laying started from a temporary access at Cae Wernlas Ddu, on the Dinas side of Tryfan Junction, on 1/2 April, the work being carried out by a combination of labourers on short-term contracts and members of the WHR Society led by the North Wales Group of local members.

Elsewhere on the trackbed the river bridges at Bryn-y-felin, Hafod-y-llyn and Hafod Garregog, installed in 1922, were demolished. In the Aberglaslyn Pass two sets of civil engineering consultants' reports and the FR's public liability insurer brought about the closure of the pass to pedestrians.

Opening to Waunfawr was first scheduled to be 27 May 2000 and then 14 July. In the event, the opening took place on 7 August. This followed an inspection on 21 July, when the inspector unexpectedly requested a week's ghost running before opening could take place. This was negotiated down to the equivalent of a week's running, 28 return trips over three days, commencing on 3 August. It was initially operated with a 'Planet' diesel attached to each end of a train of wagons, the two locomotives being needed because Waunfawr loop was incomplete.

Garratt No 143 became the first locomotive to steam to Waunfawr since 1937 during the evening of 5 August, when three runs hauling a short passenger test train, tailed by 'Planet' *Conwy Castle*, took place. During the evening of 6 August the two final runs used the full rake of carriages running from Caernarfon.

Public opening was marred by the threat of an obstruction being placed across the line, causing the second train to be delayed. The first train of the day was double-headed to outstation a diesel locomotive at Waunfawr, to shunt the carriages and release the train locomotive whilst the loop remained incomplete.

Traffic on the first day was very high, despite the short notice, due to a considerable number of local residents seeking 'first day travel'. During the remainder of the summer passenger interest was maintained whilst Waunfawr platform was completed.

The loop was completed in September just in time for the official opening on September 15. On a fine day local MP Dafydd Wigley performed the honours before a large crowd. Amongst them was the FR's president, Alan Pegler, who had travelled from London by train, despite suffering from Parkinson's disease. The speeches were interrupted briefly by a heckler demanding that the money spent on the WHR should have been spent on hospitals. Demonstrators objecting to the railway also waved banners at several level crossings.

To accommodate the opening special train the loop at Dinas was used to cross trains for the first time. The invited guests travelled in the 'normal' train set whilst the 'ordinary' passengers rode in a train of FR vintage stock, most of which had been used on the 'old' WHR.

The WHR's second enthusiast event took place on 16/17 September, immediately after the opening. Despite restrictions on travel caused by a petrol shortage that kept many would-be participants away, the event was a resounding success, with 1,300 passengers travelling.

Without doubt the reason for this was the visit of the WHR(P)'s Hunslet 2-6-2T *Russell*, seen working double-headed with the FR's replica single Fairlie 0-4-4T *Taliesin*. The trains were packed all weekend and on some trains hauled by the Hunslet/Fairlie combination the demand for seats outstripped supply. On the same weekend the FR's England 0-4-0STT *Palmerston* was in action on the WHR(P)'s line at Porthmadog.

The interest and demand for riding on the extended railway were such that the operating season was extended from ending in November until 2 January 2001. The popularity of

the pub next to Waunfawr station was responsible for the 2001 timetable being modified to transfer the lunchtime layover there from Caernarfon.

It was not only the public that paid attention to the extended WHR. In 2000, the restored Dinas station received an Ian Allan Heritage Award. The building's restoration had been a joint effort by the Welsh Highland Light Railway Co and Welsh Highland Heritage supported by Michael Schumann. The following year the British Guild of Travel Writers awarded its 'British Tourism Project of the Year' Silver Unicorn award to the railway. The award is made to a UK tourism project opened within the previous two years. It has to fulfil various criteria, including social and economic benefits to the locality, benefits to the community and be environmentally sound.

Above:
Russell returned to Dinas for the gala that marked the official reopening to Waunfawr on 15 September 2000. Whilst steam is raised on 16 September, a blanket protects the dome cover. *Author*

Below:
Alco 2-6-2PT *Mountaineer* arrives at Waunfawr on 16 April 2001. The train was loaded to six cars, exceeding the Alco's capacity on the gradients out of Caernarfon and Dinas, so double-heading with 'Planet' diesel *Conway Castle* was the order of the day. *Author*

During the autumn of 2000, work started on the remedial rock works in the Aberglaslyn Pass; the scheme was completed the following spring, the contract value being £200,000. Agreement was reached with Gwynedd Council and the National Trust that the WHR would contribute to building a pedestrian footbridge across the Glaslyn near Bryn-y-felin. Proposed for erection at Easter 2001, the installation was delayed by an outbreak of foot-and-mouth disease which swept across much of England and Wales between February and July. This also delayed WHR(P)'s efforts to rebuild the railway to Pont Croesor although clearance work was carried out near Pen-y-mount.

Beyond Waunfawr, contractors started work on the Betws Garmon river bridge in November. The old bridge was removed and new abutments provided, to make the replacement bridge wider than the old, at the request of the Environment Agency. The new structure will have the same outline as the old.

A 'metre of track' appeal was launched in 1997, with track being 'sold' at £60/metre, or £5 per month. Nearly £150,000 had been raised by mid-2002. All subscribers qualify for a reduced fare ticket to inspect both the WHR and the FR. The WHR Society raised £40,000 for Waunfawr station and continued in the same vein by fundraising for Rhyd Ddu station.

Near Betws Garmon village water pipes had been laid under the trackbed, permission having been obtained from the OR, 'provided the works did not impede the reinstatement of the railway'. In consequence the water company had to divert some 200m of water main from the trackbed to the parallel road, the work being carried out during 2001.

North Wales Group members of the WHR Society laid the first track on the Waunfawr-Rhyd Ddu section on 3/4 March 2001. They completed the line to Betws Garmon during the summer, then concentrated on regauging five sets of South African points for use at Plas-y-nant passing loop and Rhyd Ddu, before moving on to the latter location in October.

At its meeting on 4 April, the Park Authority gave formal approval to the safety works carried out on the trackbed in the Aberglaslyn Pass. The Authority also approved the appearance of railway structures between Bryn Gloch caravan park, the Park's boundary, and Rhyd Ddu.

The start of work within the Park's boundaries was delayed, however, due to the foot-and-mouth disease outbreak, although there were no cases near the railway. After an acceptable risk assessment/method statement was agreed,

construction work resumed in mid-May. The railway implemented special working practices, involving disinfectant and disposable suits, at a cost of over £400 a week.

The first work site under this regime was between Rhyd Ddu and the Glan-yr-afon bridge, when fencing and drainage work was carried out. At one location the ground was found to be very soft, requiring excavation to a depth of some 1½m to reach solid ground. Track laying started from Rhyd Ddu in October, to give access to the bridge. The major spans were adjudged fit for reuse although some cross-members will be replaced. An access was made to the trackbed at Fridd Isaf, near Rhyd Ddu.

Three visiting locomotives were turned out for the third enthusiast event, a vintage weekend on 22/23 September. They were England 0-4-0STT *Prince*, single Fairlie 0-4-4T *Taliesin,* and Hunslet 0-4-0ST *Lilla*, all FR-based. A train of five vintage coaches accompanied them. *Prince* and four of the coaches had operated on the old WHR, one of the carriages having been built for and been part of the fleet taken over by the WHR in 1922. *Lilla* had made a single journey between Bryngwyn and Dinas in 1928, when sold from Cilgwyn Quarry to the Penrhyn Slate Quarries.

On 21 September, *Lilla* and *Prince* made a twilight trip over the line for gauging purposes and to test watering arrangements. *Lilla* also hauled a one-coach train from Dinas to Waunfawr on 22 September; intended to be viewed by

Above:
The Funkey, *Castell Caernarfon*, at Tryfan Junction on 8 May 2001. Ten of the 20 signs deemed necessary to protect this extremely minor road can be seen. *Author*

Below:
Garratt No 138 passes the restored award-winning NWNGR station building as it arrives at Dinas from Waunfawr on 26 August 2001. The locomotive is painted in the light green livery that had made its public appearance just a few weeks earlier. *Author*

photographers, the excursion actually ran after dark due to delays caused by shunting. It was apparent that many visitors were from the locality.

In October 2001, Mike Hart stood down as chairman of WHLR, having for some time spent three days a week working on the project. He was replaced by Michael Whitehouse, a solicitor practising in contract law.

Gwynedd Council's contractors moved in to rebuild the Betws Garmon road bridge in November, a 17-tonne weight restriction having been imposed earlier in the year. The council's obligation to deal with the bridge stemmed from the WHR's financial problems in the 1920s. The work on the Bryn Gloch caravan park bridge started in December. The bridges were completed in 2002.

The line's 2002 timetable, announced in December 2001,

saw the introduction of several innovations, the prime of which was two-train working during the peak, the second train being of vintage stock with WHR connections from the FR. Other new features included a named train, the 'Eryri Express', complete with buffet service, and an evening service to Waunfawr.

The construction of 12 miles of 'new' railway to Rhyd Ddu using a mix of contractors, paid staff and volunteers in six years, will be a remarkable achievement in itself, all the more remarkable considering some of the obstacles that have been overcome. However, the railway completed in 2003 will not exactly be the railway proposed in the 1990s. For example, there should have been a fleet of 24 new carriages and enhanced passenger facilities at the stations. That these have not been achieved is naturally due to finance, or the lack of it. One particular aspect that has influenced the outcome has been the workings of the Millennium Commission grant — it was based on 1995 prices, with no allowance made for inflation or contingencies, so when one part of the project cost more than forecast, something else had to be removed.

Achievement of the final 12 miles to Porthmadog will be dependent on many variables, not the least of which, again, is finance. Sources have been under investigation for some time. There will be much pressure to move on from Rhyd Ddu but the SNPA will not permit any intermediate termini before reaching Porthmadog.

The completed Welsh Highland Railway will be like no other. The words 'preservation' and 'heritage', as in preserved railway or heritage railway, will be applied to it only with some difficulty. It could be said that all that is being preserved is the route and some buildings, for the carriages are all new and the locomotives will be workhorses, intended to be master of the job, by some margin. The railway will be a major part of the transport infrastructure in this part of North Wales and the Snowdonia National Park, providing a useful 25-mile off-road link between Caernarfon and Porthmadog.

Above:
The way ahead. Volunteers lay track at Fridd Isaf, Rhyd Ddu, in extremely cold conditions on 30 December 2001. *Author*

Left:
Cae Moel bridge is the location for this view of No 138 taken on 23 September 2001. *Author*

— 7 —
Locomotives, Rolling Stock and Infrastructure

Locomotives

As already mentioned, the NWNGR started with two 0-6-4T single Fairlies named *Moel Tryfan* and *Snowdon Ranger*, ordered by Roberts from the Vulcan Foundry Ltd and delivered in 1875. They were rebuilt/repaired by Davies & Metcalf in 1902/3. The best parts of both were amalgamated into a single locomotive called *Moel Tryfan* in 1917 and the remaining parts scrapped.

Beddgelert was a Hunslet 0-6-4ST of traditional form delivered in 1878. It was more powerful than the Fairlies and most likely spent most of its time working the Bryngwyn branch. It was probably worn out when scrapped in 1906.

The PBSSR, effectively NWPT, ordered a Hunslet 2-6-2T that was delivered to the NWNGR in 1906 and named *Russell*. The reasons for the order are conjecture, but the

Left:
A works photograph of single Fairlie 0-6-4T *Snowdon Ranger*. As delivered, the Vulcan Foundry Fairlies had no cab backsheets. *WHR collection*

Below left:
Snowdon Ranger at Rhyd Ddu *c*1902. The air brake cylinder under the cab is prominent. As always, a steam locomotive proves a magnet for small boys — presumably the locomotive crew had retired for a tea break. *Commercial postcard/John Keylock collection*

Above:
The afternoon sun catches *Moel Tryfan* standing on the locomotive dispersal road alongside the Dinas carriage sheds in August 1934. Once again small boys find an attraction. *R. W. Kidner/Author's collection*

Left:
Moel Tryfan at Dinas in the earlier years of the 20th century. *Author's collection*

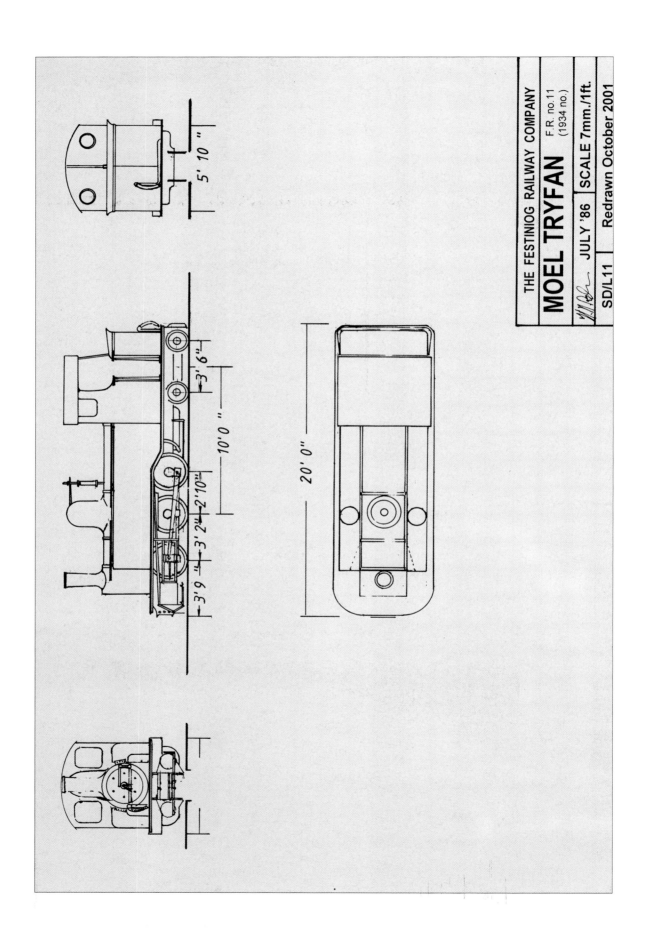

THE FESTINIOG RAILWAY COMPANY

MOEL TRYFAN F.R. no.11 (1934 no.)

JULY '86	SCALE 7mm./1ft.
SD/L11	Redrawn October 2001

5' 10"

3' 6"

10' 0"

2' 10"

3' 2"

3' 9"

20' 0"

0-6-4 TYPE

SADDLE TANK ENGINE

Gauge of Railway	1 ft. 11¼ in.
Size of Cylinders	10 in. dia. × 16 in. stroke
Dia. of Coupled Wheels	2 ft. 6 in.
,, Bogie Wheels	1 ,, 10 ,,
Rigid Wheelbase (Engine)	6 ,, 2 ,,
Total Wheelbase (Engine)	15 ,, 11 ,,
Height from Rail to Top of Chimney	8 ,, 10½ ,,
Extreme Width	6 ,, 4 ,,
Heating Surface—Small Tubes ... ... 377 sq. ft.	
,, ,, Firebox ... ... 39 ,,	
Total ... ... 416 ,, ...	416 sq. ft.
Grate Area	7·5 ,,
Working Pressure	120 lbs. per sq. in.
Tank Capacity	450 gallons
Fuel Space (Coal)	13 cwts.
Weight Empty (Engine)	14 tons 10 cwts.
,, in Working Order (Engine)	17 ,, 0 ,,
Tractive Effort at 75 per cent. of Boiler Pressure	4800 lbs.
Minimum Radius of Curve Engine will traverse with ease	300 ft.
Weight per Yard of Lightest Rail advisable	20 lbs.
Load Engine will haul on Level	250 tons
,, ,, ,, up Incline of 1 in 100	120 ,,
,, ,, ,, ,, ,, 1 in 50	65 ,,

Code Word—**BEDERT**

Above:
Hunslet's sales specification for *Beddgelert*,
the only one of the type built. A NWNGR garter
has been applied to the cabside.
Author's collection

Right:
Beddgelert posed outside Dinas locomotive shed, with the yard signalbox behind. The locomotive was much more powerful than the Fairlies and was used mainly on the Bryngwyn branch; it appears, therefore, not to have been fitted with continuous brakes. An armorial-style crest is on the cabside. The Fairlie behind *Beddgelert* has been identified as *Snowdon Ranger*. The photograph is alleged to have been taken in 1905, a year before *Beddgelert* was scrapped. *Author's collection*

single Fairlies were probably in poor condition, despite having been sent away for overhaul/rebuilding in 1903, and *Beddgelert* was due to be scrapped. It is quite likely that the Fairlies were deemed incapable of handling the Bryngwyn branch traffic, for *Russell* was more than twice as powerful. Keeping the NWNGR going was essential in the PBSSR/NWPT scheme of things, and most of its traffic came from the Bryngwyn branch, not known for light gradients. Whether ownership was formally transferred to the NWNGR has not been determined, but there is a strange entry in the company's 1913 annual report:

Steam locomotives	tank	0-6-4	3
	tender	0-6-2	1

Obviously the report's compiler knew that *Russell* was not a Fairlie but didn't know just what it was!

The PBSSR's electric locomotives would have been 90bhp machines capable of taking 100% overload 'for a short while'. Weighing in at 8½ tons on two axles, their designed 'normal' speed was 18mph. They should have been capable, according to the PBSSR's engineers, of hauling a 20-ton train up short gradients of 1 in 20 or hauling the same load up a gradient of 1 in 43 regardless of its length. A liquid rheostat would have been used to bring the motor on line, and would have been effectively the only means available of adjusting speed. Having a capacity of only 20 tons suggests that the PBSSR intended to run a lot of short trains. Bruce Peebles & Co was

Right:
Russell as modified, unsuccessfully, to fit the FR's loading gauge. The lip on the top of the sidetank provides a useful aid for carrying a wagon coupler.
Author's collection

Below:
The new livery applied to *Russell* by the FR in 1934 looks well worn in this view taken at Dinas on 8 August 1935.
H. F. Wheeller/WHR collection

Left:
Russell as restored, in action on the WHR(P)'s tracks on 2 May 1994. The locomotive is dual fitted to facilitate visits to the FR and the WHR at Dinas. *Author*

Below:
Gowrie was used as a replacement for *Beddgelert*; nominally it was more powerful although its small boiler would have given it a lower continuous capacity. This portrait, taken at Dinas in 1909, shows it coupled to a freight train.
G. M. Perkins/WHR collection

going to supply 10 of these locomotives using designs of the Hungarian Ganz company. A start was made on their manufacture but details of who did it and how far it advanced before PBSSR work ceased are contradictory.

In 1908, Hunslet delivered another 0-6-4T single Fairlie. It was named, not immediately, *Gowrie*, after Aitchison, the line's manager. It was sold to the Ministry of Munitions during World War 1, most likely because the railway was short of funds; being the newest member of the fleet, it would have had more value, and was perhaps not as well liked by the locomotive crews despite being nominally more powerful than the Vulcan Foundry machines. It survived until *c*1928.

The WHR inherited *Moel Tryfan* and *Russell* in 1922. The NWNGR having been a user of air brakes and the FR a user of vacuum, there were initially problems with through working until the NWNGR stock was converted to vacuum. Likewise, there were problems with the couplings, which were similar in appearance but incompatible in practice.

Moel Tryfan was in poor condition and in need of attention. After being repaired, and cut down to fit the FR's loading gauge, it was used regularly on both railways until it entered Boston Lodge for repairs in 1934. As already stated, it nearly passed to FR ownership following C. E. Davies's request to keep it in 1938 but it was still cut up at Harbour station in 1954. During the FR lease period, WHR locomotives were allocated running numbers in the FR fleet, *Moel Tryfan* becoming No 11, although, of course, in this instance it was never carried. The wheel sets from *Moel Tryfan*'s non-

powered bogie survive on the pony trucks of the FR's Hunslet 2-4-0STTs *Linda* and *Blanche*.

Russell became, certainly to postwar eyes, the locomotive most closely associated with the WHR. Before the 1924 season commenced a poor attempt was made to reduce its stature to fit on the FR. Not only was the attempt futile but the locomotive's appearance was also diminished. During the modifications the upper part of the cab backsheet was made removable, to improve crew conditions in hot weather. *Russell* was painted green when the FR took over the WHR in 1934, when its running number was 12. In 1941 it was requisitioned and sold. First it went to the Brymbo Steel Co at Hook Norton in 1942, remaining there until 1948. Then it passed to B. Fayle & Co at Purbeck, where it stayed until withdrawn with a broken axle in 1953.

The Birmingham Locomotive Club (Industrial Locomotive Information Section), now the Industrial Railway Society, acquired *Russell* for preservation in 1953 and moved it to the Talyllyn Railway for restoration to museum display condition in 1955. The locomotive was donated to WHR(P) in 1965 and restoration, including fitting a new boiler and restoring its NWNGR profile, was completed at Gelert's Farm, alongside the WHR trackbed, in 1987.

To expand the WHR locomotive fleet consideration was given to reacquiring *Gowrie*, then resident in a Darlington scrapyard, in April 1923. This opportunity was not taken up so Col Stephens encouraged the purchase of an ex-WD World War 1 Baldwin 4-6-0T. Delivered in July 1923, it was restric-

ted to the WHR except for visits to Boston Lodge for maintenance or overnight lodging, due to its size. At first painted black, the FR painted it red in 1934, when it was allocated the number 13. The Welsh enginemen never got the measure of it and it was never named, although its builder's name was treated as a name. It was requisitioned in 1941 and cut up the following year.

The WHR steam fleet was augmented as required by FR locomotives. It is reported that in 1923 double Fairlies worked through to Dinas but otherwise only the England engines left the FR. McAlpine had hired *Palmerston* for a short time during the construction period.

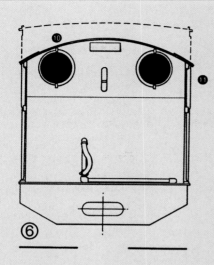
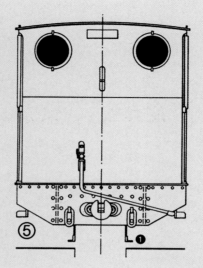
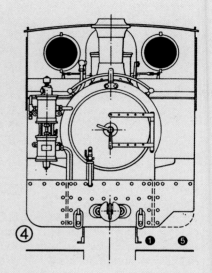

W.H.R. 'RUSSELL'

Built by the Hunslet Engine Company Limited, Leeds. Works Number 901 of 1906.

©1996 W.H.L.R.Ltd
Drawn by Roy C. Link.   Scale 1:43·5

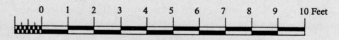

0 1 2 3 4 5 6 7 8 9 10 Feet

NOTES

A variety of material has been referred to while producing these drawings. Makers drawings and photographs were the main sources. The following notes are intended as a guide to the many changes made to 'RUSSELL' over the years. Every attempt has been made to verify these, but ultimately it is strongly advised that reference to period photographs are made, particulary if a model is being built. Only major bolt head detail is drawn, for clarity. Study photographs for rivet placement - which in itself varies depending on period.

① *Side elevation of RUSSELL as built.*
② *Plan view, split along centre line showing RUSSELL as built (lower) and as modified in 1923 (upper).*
③ *Side elevation of RUSSELL as modified in 1923.**
④ *Front elevation of RUSSELL as built.*
⑤ *Rear elevation of RUSSELL as built.*
⑥ *Rear elevation of RUSSELL as modified in 1923.**

* *Original outline shown as dashed line. Only altered details shown.*

● *Plate metal guard irons only visible in earliest of photographs - it is assumed they were removed at an early stage.*

● *Sandbox - removed prior to cutting down.*

❸ *Westinghouse brake piping only shown on plan view.*

❹ *Westinghouse brake hoses omitted - details unknown.*

❺ *Buffer beams modified prior to rebuild - possibly at the same time as the sand dome was removed.*

❻ *Cut-out in lowered cab roof - 1923 rebuild.*

❼ *Vacuum brake gear and piping - 1923 rebuild.*

❽ *Piping revised when vacuum brake gear fitted - 1923 rebuild.*

❾ *Vacuum brake pipe on cab floor - 1923 rebuild.*

● *Cab spectacles lowered front and rear - 1923 rebuild.*

● *Cab rear upper sheet made removeable - post 1923 rebuild. Photos taken during summer months often show RUSSELL running without the top rear sheet.*

● *Wheels, cylinders and motion etc., ommited to show frame outline and cut outs.*

108

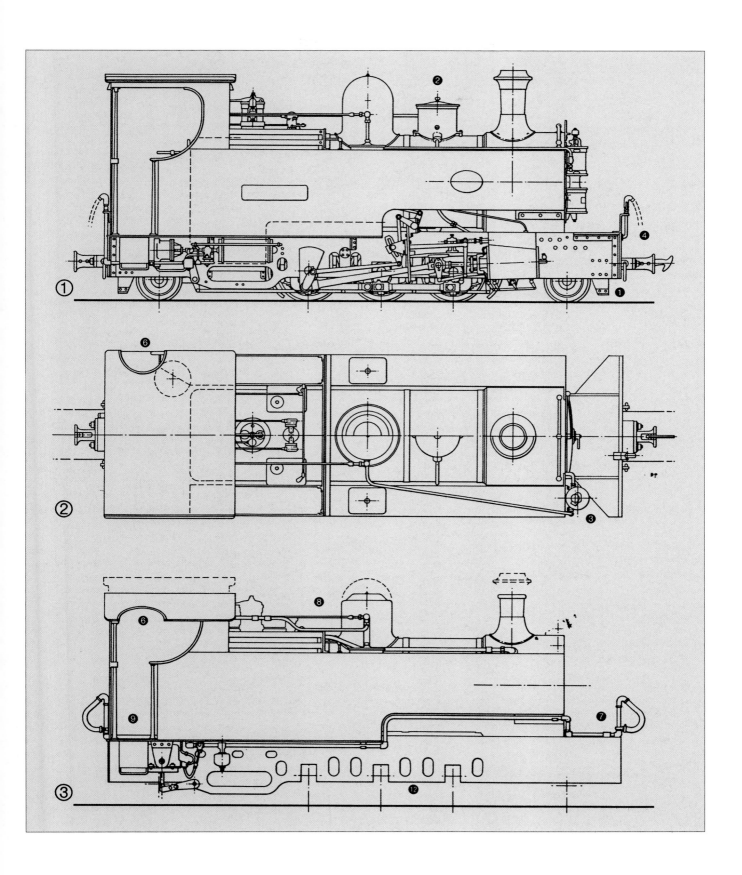

0-6-4 TYPE

ARTICULATED SIDE TANK ENGINE

Gauge of Railway	2 ft. 0 in.
Size of Cylinders	9½ in. dia. × 14 in. stroke
Dia. of Coupled Wheels	2 ft. 4 in.
,, Bogie Wheels	1 ,, 10 ,,
Rigid Wheelbase (Engine)	5 ,, 6 ,,
Total Wheelbase (Engine)	14 ,, 0 ,,
Height from Rail to Top of Chimney	8 ,, 9 ,,
Extreme Width	6 ,, 6 ,,
Heating Surface—Small Tubes ... 252 sq. ft.	
,, ,, Firebox ... 30 ,,	
Total ... 282 ,,	282 sq. ft.
Grate Area	5 ,,
Working Pressure	160 lbs. per sq. in.
Tank Capacity	400 gallons
Fuel Space (Coal)	1 ton 2 cwts.
Weight Empty (Engine)	14 tons 19 ,,
,, in Working Order (Engine)	18 ,, 10 ,,
Total Weight on Coupled Wheels	11 ,, 6 ,,
Maximum Axle Load	4 ,, 5 ,,
Tractive Effort at 75 per cent. of Boiler Pressure	5415 lbs.
Ratio Adhesive Weight ÷ Tractive Effort	4·7
Minimum Radius of Curve Engine will traverse with ease	60 ft.
Weight per Yard of Lightest Rail advisable	25 lbs.
Load Engine will haul on Level	280 tons
,, ,, ,, up Incline of 1 in 100	140 ,,
,, ,, ,, ,, ,, 1 in 50	75 ,,

Code Word—**NORWA**

C P 49/400—6/22

Order 30990

Above:
The specification sheet for *Gowrie*, another single Fairlie,
delivered unnamed in 1908. *Author's collection*

Left:
The Baldwin was pulled out of Dinas locomotive shed for photography when newly acquired in 1923. The FR locomotive performing the duty was *Little Giant*.
Author's collection

Arising from Col Stephens's influence, the WHR saw the use of a former World War 1 armoured Motor Rail 'Simplex' petrol locomotive, from 1923. *Railway Gazette* reported attending a series of tests on the WHR that year, saying that the locomotive 'may be useful for miscellaneous duties or special trips, or for light goods traffic'. The journal noted a lack of familiarity on the driver's part, stating it 'acquitted itself well' during a journey from Dinas Junction to Portmadoc, via Bryngwyn. This locomotive is now the FR's *Mary Ann*.

The FR obtained another former military locomotive in 1925, the 1918-built Baldwin 'tractor', now *Moelwyn*. Following a suggestion that it would be suitable for hauling one-coach winter trains on the WHR it was equipped with vacuum brakes in 1928.

Also in 1928, Kerr, Stuart loaned the WHR that company's first diesel locomotive for trials. This was a six-wheeled machine with a 60hp McLaren-Benz engine. After a period on the FR it was returned to its builders. The locomotive was later exported to the Union Vale sugar estate in Mauritius. It was returned to the FR for preservation in 1997.

The first motive power obtained for the rebuilt WHR was a Funkey B-B diesel locomotive from the Port Elizabeth Cement Co and delivered to the FR in 1993, in company with a second for the FR. These South African-built locomotives have 350hp Cummins engines that have seen very little use. Delivered, they cost £5,000, plus £6,000 carriage, each. The WHR's was overhauled at Boston Lodge and named *Castell Caernarfon* by Dafydd Wigley MP in Caernarfon in 1996, being afterwards stored at Minffordd before being delivered

to Dinas ready for the start of work in 1997. It saw occasional use during the construction phase, serves as back-up to the steam locomotives, and is used for off-peak services.

Two NGG16 2-6-2+2-6-2 Beyer, Peacock Garratts were obtained from the Alfred County Railway at a cost of £90,000 each overhauled. Numbered 138 and 143, the latter was the last Garratt built in Manchester. Their boiler units arrived at the FR's Glan-y-pwll yard on 14 January 1997, their bogies going to Boston Lodge via Minffordd for attention to bearings, bushes and lubrication. Despite work carried out in South Africa both locomotives required additional work to be carried out to bring them up to UK standards.

No 138 was first steamed at Glan-y-pwll in time for display at the FR's 1997 gala and transferred to Dinas just prior to the October opening. Its livery was a rich green. Great interest, from enthusiasts and public alike, was taken in the performance of No 138, used on 19 of the 21 operating days in 1997 and during most of 1998. Crews soon developed finesse with it and competed with each other for lowest fuel consumption. No 138 was repainted in 2001, entering service later in the year; the colour specification supplied by sponsor Edison Mission turned out to be incorrect. The locomotive was repainted during the first weeks of 2002 and named *Millennium* at Waunfawr on 1 March.

No 143's boiler and both its bogies received attention at Ian Riley's works in Bury; it was erected at Dinas and first steamed there on 18 September 1998. No 143 is to retain its SAR black livery in view of its historic significance. Both locomotives have been converted to burn oil.

Left:
As far as it could go from Dinas — the Baldwin outside the FR's Boston Lodge locomotive shed on 9 August 1935. The FR had painted the locomotive red and applied the WHR lettering in 1934.
H. F. Wheeller/WHR collection

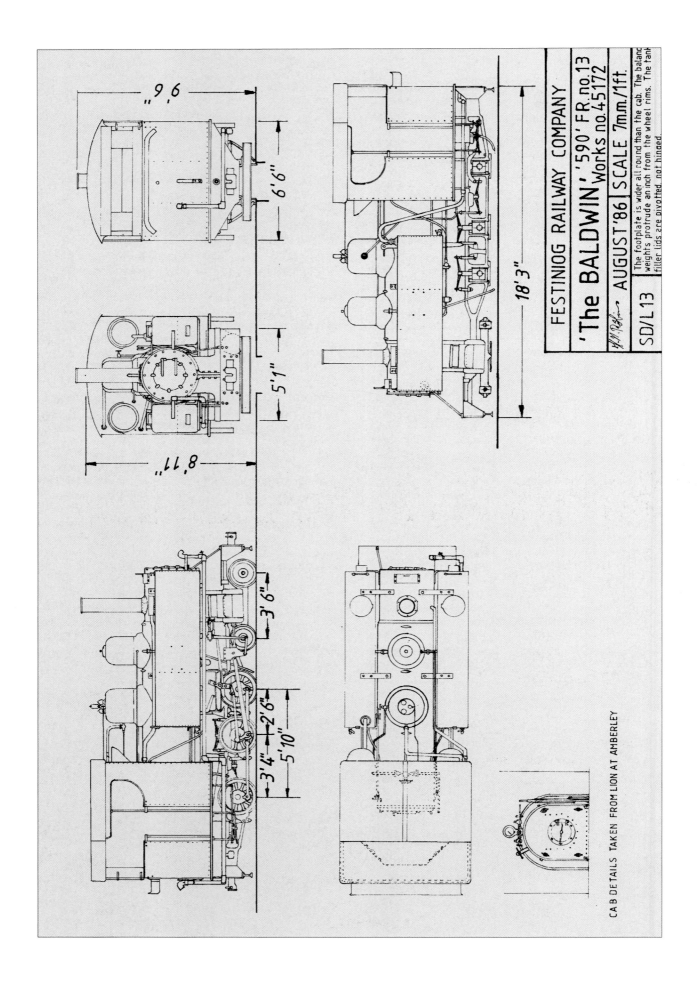

FESTINIOG RAILWAY COMPANY

'The BALDWIN' '590' F.R. no.13
Works no.45172

AUGUST '86 | SCALE 7mm./1ft.

SD/L 13

The footplate is wider all round than the cab. The balance weights protrude an inch from the wheel rims. The tank filler lids are pivotted, not hinged.

9'.6"

6'6"

5'1"

8'11"

18'3"

3'6"

3'4" 2'6"

5'10"

CAB DETAILS TAKEN FROM LION AT AMBERLEY

Left:
Five of the FR's six England locomotives saw action on the WHR; *Mountaineer* had been withdrawn in 1879. Here, at Beddgelert in 1925, *Prince's* lined livery, applied or renewed during a rebuild completed in 1921, still looks fresh except where water has regularly splashed it. The locomotive is running with the only braked tender in the England fleet.
R. R. J. Plummer/ WHR collection

Left:
By 20 July 1934, the braked tender had been transferred to *Welsh Pony*, seen at Beddgelert. At this time the livery was either green faded to sky blue, or sky blue; the main colour was edged in black with reversed corners.
F. M. Gates/Author's collection

Below:
Little Giant, sporting FR symbols on both cabside and tender at Dinas in the 1920s. *F. Moore's Railway Photographs*

113

Left:
Dick, Kerr & Co of Preston developed a petrol-electric locomotive design, intended for delivering supplies to battle fronts in France. In February 1917 one was tried out on the NWNGR, where it failed to impress.
WHR collection

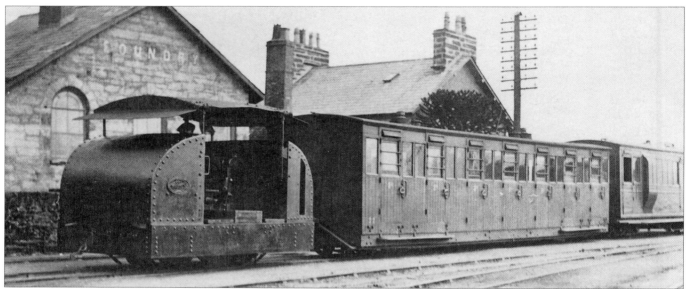

Above:
The Motor Rail 'Simplex' petrol locomotive was acquired by the FR in 1923 and was used on the WHR, mainly substituting for a steam locomotive dealing with Croesor traffic.
The picture shows it on the WHR connection at the FR's Harbour station with FR Ashbury coach No 22 and a WHR Pickering brake/composite.
Author's collection

Left:
The Baldwin 'tractor' shunting wagons opposite Britannia Terrace, Portmadoc.
Paul Ingham collection

Right:
A longer trial was that of a Kerr, Stuart 6-wheel diesel locomotive No 4415 built in 1928, a prototype for the company. It worked on the WHR from July 1928 until March 1929, when it was transferred to the FR. It was later exported to a sugar plantation in Mauritius; in 1997 it was acquired for preservation by the FR Trust and is to be restored to working order by a specialist support group.
Author's collection

A third Garratt, the red-liveried No 140, was offered to the project for a nominal £100 by a group of German enthusiasts; it arrived at Glan-y-pwll in April 1997. Delivered unrestored, it will be put back into working order at a later date. Three more NGG16s have been earmarked for possible future acquisition.

The first Garratt built, No K1, is owned by the Festiniog Railway Trust. Built in 1909, it was reacquired by Beyer, Peacock from its Tasmanian owners in 1947 and bought by the FR in 1966. Too large for the FR's loading gauge, it was displayed at the National Railway Museum from 1979 until 1995. On the WHR, No K1 should be capable of dealing with light trains at line speed. Its restoration, including a new boiler, is being undertaken at Boston Lodge, mainly by a volunteer supporters' group, to be completed during 2002.

The return to service is being funded by donations and covenants.

In 1998, two unrestored South African Franco-Belge NG15 2-8-2s, Nos 133 and 134, were obtained from the proprietor of a proposed tourist railway in Yorkshire that was not built. Some work has been carried out on No 134 at Dinas and it may move to Boston Lodge when No K1 is finished.

A change in the locomotive fleet occurred on 13 May 1999, when the FR shipped Hunslet 2-4-0STT *Blanche* from Boston Lodge to work lighter trains, entering service on 7 June. In March 2000, *Mountaineer* returned, now in black livery, for the same purpose, *Blanche* returning to the FR. *Mountaineer* was returned to the FR late in 2001. *Prince* was supplied to power the Vintage Train at the end of May 2002.

Right:
On the FR, the Funkey is restricted by its size to the line across the Cob. After restoration it ran one passenger train on the FR, and was photographed arriving at Porthmadog on that occasion, 5 May 1996. On 26 July the same year it was named *Castell Caernarfon* at Caernarfon by Dafydd Wigley MP. *Author*

Above:
Garratt No 138 was re-erected at the FR's Glan-y-pwll depot, with its first steaming taking place in May 1997, after which it participated in the FR's spring gala before being transported to Dinas. *Author*

Right:
The second Garratt to enter service, No 143, was re-erected at Dinas. Here it passes before admirers on the adjacent cycle track on 1 May 2000. *Author*

Below:
The strategic reserve: one of the NG15 class 2-8-0s obtained in 1998 being shunted on 3 May 1999, smoke effects courtesy of burning rags in the smokebox. *Author*

Rolling Stock

Spring recorded the existence of 13 passenger coaches and a four-wheeled van at Dinas in 1921. The summer cars had been kept under cover and were in relatively good condition, having, naturally, seen only light summer use. Of the remainder, some required heavy repairs and most repainting. Dark green was the WHR livery. All the carriages had their height reduced to enable them to work on the FR.

Six Hudson open toastrack coaches obtained by the FR in 1923 augmented the fleet. These were cheap and intended for use on both lines. The WHR was expected to pay its share but never did. By 1929, four had had their bodies removed and were in use as flats.

One of the 'corridor' cars was converted for use as a buffet car, first seeing operation in this form in the 1928 season.

The 1934 lease identified the carriage stock thus: three summer open cars, seating capacity 56 each; one corridor coach, seating capacity 38; one corridor coach, seating capacity 20; one inspection saloon coach, capacity 32; two composite carriages, with one van compartment, one 1st class compartment, two 3rd class compartments each, seating capacity: eight 1st class passengers, 16 3rd class passengers each coach.

The inspection saloon was the 'Gladstone' car. The FR painted the carriages different colours — green, blue, pink and red — apparently to make the operation more attractive to the public!

One of the 1894 Ashbury 56-seat tourist cars, No 23, passed to FR ownership in exchange for three ex-WD bogie coal wagons, the remainder of the WHR carriage fleet being sold or scrapped at Dinas in 1942. Ashbury No 26 also survives, having been sold to a farmer in Groeslon for use as a hen house; it was purchased by the FR in 1959 and returned to service the same year. It was rebodied in 1986. The remains of the buffet car and the restored 'Gladstone' car are in the possession of WHR(P); the former was recovered from Waunfawr in 1987, the latter from Llanbedr the following year. WHR(P) are restoring Hudson toastrack No 42, the underframe of which was donated by the FR for the purpose. In 1992, Winson Engineering, then based at Penrhyndeudraeth,

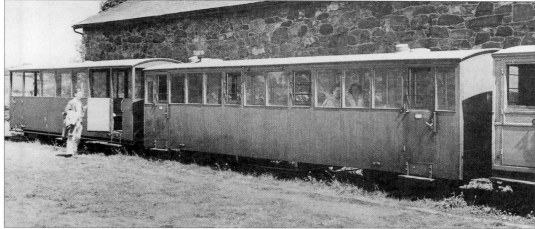

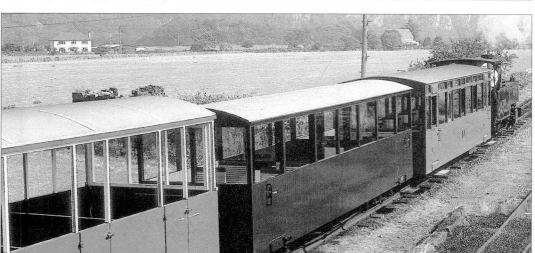

Above:
The Baldwin and *Russell* frame the only known view of a Hudson toastrack in traffic; Beddgelert, 11 August 1934.
T. Middlemass/ WHR collection

Left:
The 'Gladstone' car (left) with an Ashbury corridor coach and Pickering No 8, right, seen at Dinas on 8 August 1935.
H. F. Wheeller/ WHR collection

Left:
The 'Gladstone' car, second from the locomotive, when newly returned to traffic by WHR(P) on 18 August 1996.
Author

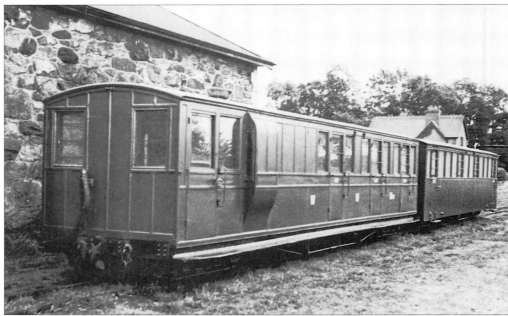

Above:
Pullman car *Bodysgallen* at Dinas in September 1998. *Author*

Right:
A Pickering brake composite of 1907 with an 1894-built Ashbury corridor coach at Dinas. The 'corridor' appellation referred to the internal connection between compartments. *FR Archives*

Below:
Construction details of a Pickering brake.

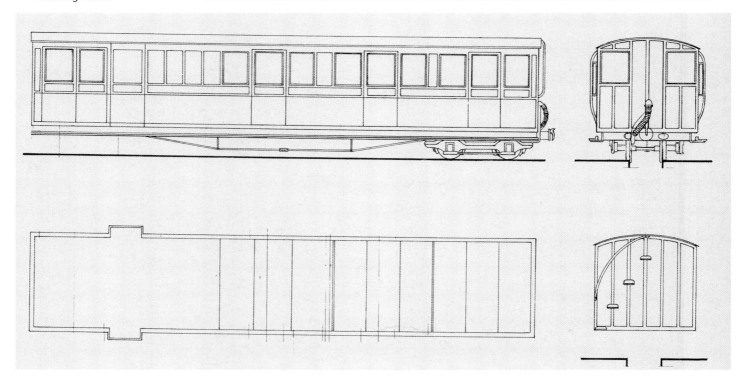

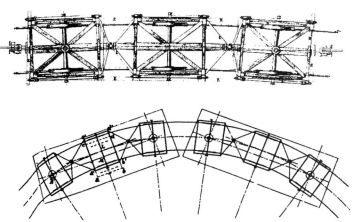

Top:
Contrasting brake vehicles at Rhyd Ddu, c1890;
an Ashbury bogie with a Gloucester Cleminson.
The former was one of two ordered by Roberts
and delivered for the start of passenger services,
the latter being delivered in 1878. The train is not
fitted with continuous brakes.
F. Moore's Railway Photographs

Above:
The Gloucester Wagon Company's photograph
of the NWNGR Cleminson 3rd class carriage.
The railway's name was probably affixed only
for the photograph. *WHR collection*

Left:
Schematics of the Cleminson system
of flexible axles. *Vignes*

built a replica Hudson toastrack, No 39, for the FR by adapting a Hudson wagon chassis.

For the revived railway a fleet of 60 coaches is predicted. Winson Engineering at Daventry received the £400,000 contract for the first six, estimated to be adequate for the Dinas-Caernarfon service. They consist of a brake/saloon (27 seats) composite with wheelchair access, three open saloons (36 seats), a semi-open (36 seats) and a 'Pullman'. Winson also overhauled the South African wagon bogies for the passenger stock, downrating the springing and adding bolsters and shock absorbers.

The coaches were designed by Winson to meet the FR's concept, and the saloons must be the most sophisticated carriages ever put into service on a UK narrow gauge railway. Features include quality timber lining, double-glazing, oil-fired heating, public address, stainless steel body frames and axle-driven alternators. In summer, passengers should appreciate the heating equipment operating as a forced-air ventilation system. The livery is the same as the FR's; internally the seats are covered with hard-wearing moquette woven with an FR/WHR motif.

The semi-open, No 2020, was delivered to the FR for trials in July 1997, the four saloons following directly to Dinas in October the same year. Named *Bodysgallen*, the Pullman was delivered in September 1998. One metre longer than the 12m-long saloons, giving passengers more legroom, it is intended for use on high-quality dining services. The semi-open has proved its popularity; on some of the more lightly loaded trains it was sometimes the only carriage in use, even in the rain! 1st Hydro, operators of Dinorwic power station, sponsored the brake/saloon, and Historic Houses Hotels, operators of the Bodysgallen House Hotel near Llandudno, the Pullman.

No 2020 was returned to the FR in 1998, when it was used in a series of gauging trials. The purpose was to establish the nature of any modifications to the FR's structure gauge that might be needed to accommodate the larger WHR stock when through-running becomes an option. The carriage failed, as expected, to pass through Garnedd Tunnel, and there were other locations where clearances were extremely tight.

An order was placed with Alan Keef Ltd in Gloucestershire in 2001 for two semi-open carriages based on the Winson design. Delivery took place before the 2002 peak season.

Left:
A slate wagon
sandwiched between
a goods brake van
and a braked coal wagon
at Dinas, c1935.
*R. W. Kidner/
Author's collection*

Left:
A covered van and
a coal wagon at Dinas
on 18 July 1941.
*H. C. Casserley/
Author's collection*

Left:
A permanent way
department pump trolley
attached to the rear of a
passenger train leaving
Beddgelert. Regrettably,
especially for those with a
sense of fun, this vehicle
has not survived.
*R. W. Kidner/
Author's collection*

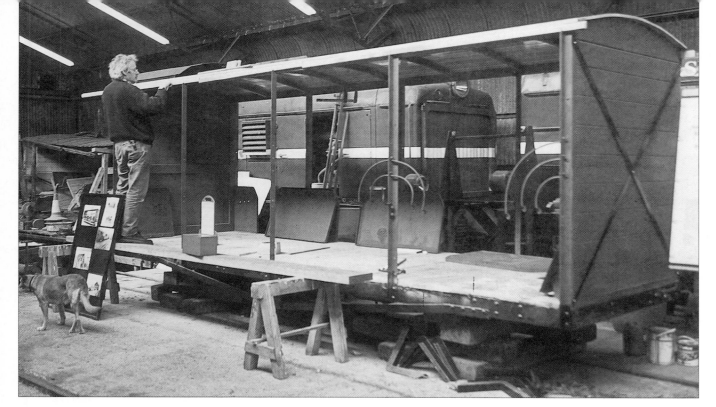

Also ordered in 2001 was a re-creation of NWNGR Ashbury No 24, for use on the vintage train. This vehicle has been built at the FR's Boston Lodge works and has the external dimensions of the original vehicle. A sponsor with an interest in historic narrow gauge railway vehicles has funded this interesting project.

The FR delivered Nos 11, 12 and 23 for the Vintage train service at the end of May 2002. No 23 is an original WHR vehicle.

A fleet of South African bogie wagons, both drop-sides and flats, was obtained for works/construction use. A pair of bogie hopper wagons for ballasting was bought from the same source before track laying to Waunfawr commenced. The former Lodge Hill & Upnor Railway 'combination' car has been converted for use as a mess car on construction trains. D. Wickham & Co of Ware built it in 1957 as a brake coach with separate compartments for officers and 'other ranks'. The Welshpool & Llanfair Light Railway obtained it in 1961, and it was among the first carriages used on reopening in 1963. It was sold on to the South Tynedale Railway in 1988 and arrived at Dinas after a period with a contractor in

November 1998. An arrival at Dinas in 2001 was a four-wheel hand-braked flat wagon, formerly an ammunition truck which was donated by the then WHLR/FR chairman, Mike Hart. Conversion to a flat wagon was undertaken by Mike and his two sons. The wagon is intended for carrying construction equipment on isolated sections of track.

Equipment used during track laying included the Funkey diesel, a 39hp Hunslet *Harold* (on temporary loan from Boston Lodge) and 'Planet' *Upnor Castle*, the latter delivered to Dinas on 15 August 1997, when the former was returned. On 30 May 2002 4w Simplex *Dolgarrog* was moved to Rhyd Ddu, it was loaned by power company Innogy.

A former NCB tamping machine, of minimal proportions for use underground, was obtained from the Yorkshire Engine Company. It was used on the Dinas–Caernarfon section, but was not so useful on the line to Waunfawr. The FR's tamper was also used on the latter but without much success. In 2001, a combined tamper and lining machine was sourced from rail maintenance company GTRM. It is being adapted for WHR use at the FR's Glan-y-pwll depot.

Above:
Ray Ollier at work on the restoration of a Hudson toastrack at WHR(P) on 14 April 2001. *Author*

Right:
The underframes and stainless steel body structures of WHR carriages under construction at Winson Engineering Ltd's Daventry premises on 14 April 1997. *Author*

Above:
Nant Mill, on the Waenfawr side of Salem. The photograph is dated 1909 but the track looks too clean for the period; that to the right appears to be freshly ballasted whilst to the left it is unballasted, suggesting that the picture might have been taken during the line's refurbishment in 1922. The building is the intake house for Carnarvon Corporation's reservoir.
Author's collection

Left:
PBSSR formation, complete with chaired track, just north of Beddgelert in 1920.
Ian Allan Library

Left:
WHR flat-bottom rail near Beddgelert.
Author's collection

Above:
Laying track by machine, Hendy crossing
on 25 August 1997. *Author*

Infrastructure

The NWNGR was originally laid with flat-bottom rail of various sections in 24ft lengths, spiked to sleepers. From 1884 this was replaced with steel rail in 30ft lengths, weighing 41½lb per yard.

The Croesor Tramway mainly used 15ft lengths of 20lb rail laid in cast-iron chairs. At some stage the main line at least was relaid with the 'old' 41lb rail that Mount saw in 1923.

The first supplies of track materials for the reconstructed railway had been previously used on the South African Donnybrook Railway, a 2ft gauge line that had been relaid with new materials just before it was closed due to a landslip; delivery to Dinas began in September 1996. The rail was 30kg/m (60lb) flat-bottom material, laid on termite-proof steel sleepers. New rail of the same section was obtained in 2001, also from South Africa, it having been calculated that the additional cost of new material was offset by the reduced handling required during track-laying.

Rails of approximately 18m lengths are laid on steel sleepers except under the NWNGR bridges, where Jarrah sleepers and check rails are used. For Dinas–Caernarfon 80 lengths were supplied in panels. The remainder of the first order was not shipped in matching pairs as requested, so considerable time and effort was spent on rail sorting, something that was not done when the same rail was used between Dinas and Waunfawr. The fixings can be used in different combinations to allow for gauge widening on curves. These also required considerable sorting, each sleeper needs one of each of four different types of clip; bolts are both metric and imperial and come in two different sizes!

Most track laying has been done by hand. A pair of unpowered rail movers, capable of moving a pair of rails with the minimum of effort, was designed and built at Dinas and successfully employed in 1997; more were built for the extension to Waunfawr. To deal with the track panels a track-laying machine was commissioned from Winson Engineering. Certified as a crane and equipped with an air-powered lifting gantry, it needed a certain amount of 'tweaking' before the gang got the measure of it. When employed between Pant Farm and Coed Helen it probably attracted more interest from local observers than any other activity.

Taking advantage of the South African vacuum-braked bogie wagons, all works trains have continuous brakes, this practice relieving the railway of the need to install trap points.

Train crossing at Dinas had been made possible by the installation of train-operated trailable point operators, brought into use simultaneously with the opening to Waunfawr. One of these devices had been on trial at the Waunfawr end of Dinas loop for about 18 months previously. Similar devices are used on national railways, but Mike Hart devised and built the WHR versions with modifications to suit 2ft gauge use. A weight holds the point shut, whilst a specially designed hydraulic damper allows the blades to shut slowly when a train trails through. An electric switch detects when the blades are shut, lighting a detector lamp visible to drivers of trains approaching in the facing direction.

At Caernarfon, the platform is designed for six-car trains. Portable buildings have been used as a booking office and shop as a temporary measure. A prefabricated timber building of 'traditional railway appearance' is planned to improve retail and booking office facilities and provide public toilets for the first time. The restricted site in St Helen's Road, considered temporary by the railway, will eventually need two 200m-long platforms and an engine release road. The final layout of the station will depend on local authority plans but the railway owns the adjoining car park that could be used to extend the station, taking it closer to the castle. If the final layout has insufficient room for the second platform a passing loop may be built outside the terminal, the formation benefiting from the original need to accommodate both the Llanberis and Afon Wen lines.

The platforms at Dinas are 200m long, to accommodate trains of up to 15-cars, and are located on the site of the former standard gauge station. Two parallel storage sidings alongside the platforms could become bay platform roads if there is demand for a Caernarfon shuttle service after the line is extended. The goods shed has been made weatherproof and is used for locomotive storage, museum displays and stalls during events. A locomotive display shed is proposed for the site. Public facilities to be provided include conveniences, in a style that matches long-vanished buildings previously located on the platform, and further car parking — park-and-ride is likely to be a development here in the future. A grant from the Welsh Development Agency for environmental improvements funded new entrance walling and fencing, car parking, tarmac roadway and lighting standards on this site.

A carriage shed, with capacity for 12 vehicles, was built at the Caernarfon end of the site in 1998; it is also used for locomotive storage and preparation.

The south yard at Dinas, which includes the former NWNGR site, extended whilst owned by the rivers authority, had come into Environment Agency ownership. It became surplus to Agency requirements in time to be reacquired for railway purposes. An existing shed, on the site of the NWNGR carriage shed, has been extended and furnished with a pit and wheel drop. Used as a running shed, it can accommodate two Garratts. Another shed, located on the site of the NWNGR locomotive shed, has been equipped as a workshop. Rail access to this yard, and on to the NWNGR/WHR formation, from Dinas station is via the former standard gauge line, the overbridge on the old narrow gauge route having insufficient clearance for the new equipment.

Waunfawr has a 200m island platform; the contractors who built it also put in the footings for a new station building, to be a larger version of the original, and a footbridge. The latter was a steel structure erected by the railway and was timber clad to give the appearance of a traditional railway structure. It links the platform to a car park and a camp site. WHR Society members took charge of building the locomotive water tower here.

The halt at Snowdon Ranger will have a passenger shelter. The considerable amount of rock to be removed to create Rhyd Ddu station will be used to widen the formation for a passing loop at Plas-y-nant. This was not an original feature, but will increase operating flexibility, the extra land needed being bought in 1997. Rhyd Ddu station will have side platforms and an engineer's siding.

The FR is responsible for running the trains and many of the operating volunteers, engine crew and guards perform the same functions on the FR. The FR Rulebook has a WHR appendix and WHR references appear in the FR's weekly notices. Trains run with a 'one-engine-in-steam' staff for Caernarfon–Dinas and Dinas–Waunfawr, although radio is proposed for use in the future. WHR train control is at Harbour station.

Below:
Track laying by hand, Cae Hen on 16 April 2000. *Author*

Right:
Interior of the long tunnel in the Aberglaslyn Pass on 10 February 2001; the tunnel was lit whilst the remedial works were carried out. *Author*

Below:
Waunfawr, 10 May 2001. A works train propelled by *Upnor Castle* is prepared for action. It consists of two bogie flats, a ballast hopper and a DZ wagon loaded with ballast. *Author*

Parliamentary Powers

The following acts and orders have authorised various stages in, or influenced, the development of the railway route between Porthmadog and Caernarfon:

Nantlle Railway Act 1825
Nantlle Railway Act 1827
Nantlle Railway Act 1828
Carnarvonshire Railway Act 1862
Carnarvon & Llanberis Railway Act 1864
Croesor and Portmadoc Railway Act 1865
Beddgelert Railway Act 1865
Nantlle Railway Act 1865
Carnarvon & Llanberis Railway Extension Act 1865
Beddgelert Railway (Extension and Deviation) Act 1866
Carnarvon & Llanberis Railway Act 1867
Carnarvonshire Railway (Nantlle Railway Transfer) Act 1867
Gorsedda (sic) Junction and Portmadoc Railways Act, 1872
North Wales Narrow Gauge Railways Act 1872
North Wales Narrow Gauge Railways (Lease) Act 1873
North Wales Narrow Gauge Railways Act 1876
Portmadoc, Croesor and Beddgelert Tram Railway Act 1879
North Wales Narrow Gauge Railways (Extensions &c) Act 1885
North Wales Narrow Gauge Railways Act 1890

North Wales Narrow Gauge Railways (Beddgelert Light Railway Extension) Order 1900
Portmadoc, Beddgelert & South Snowdon Railway Act 1901
North Wales Electric Power Act 1904
Portmadoc, Beddgelert & South Snowdon Railway Act 1904
North Wales Narrow Gauge Railways (Light Railway) Order 1905
Portmadoc, Beddgelert & South Snowdon Railway (Beddgelert Light Railway Extension) Order 1906
Portmadoc, Beddgelert & South Snowdon Railway (Light Railway Extension at Carnarvon) Order 1908
Portmadoc, Beddgelert & South Snowdon Railway (Light Railway) Order 1908
Welsh Highland Railway (Light Railway) Order 1922
Welsh Highland Railway (Light Railway) Amendment Order 1923
Festiniog Railway (Light Railway) Order 1923
Beddgelert Siding Light Railway Order 1980
The Welsh Highland Railway (Transfer) Light Railway Order 1995
The Caernarfon Railway Light Railway Order 1997
Welsh Highland Railway Order 1999

Bibliography

Boyd, J. I. C.; *Narrow Gauge Rails to Portmadoc*; Oakwood Press, 1949

Boyd, J. I. C.; *Narrow Gauge Railways in North Caernarvonshire Vol 1 West*; Oakwood Press, 1981

Boyd, J. I. C.; *Narrow Gauge Railways in South Caernarvonshire*; Oakwood Press, 1988/9 (2 vols)

Bradley, V. J.; *Industrial Locomotives of North Wales*; Industrial Railway Society, 1992

Christiansen, Rex; *Forgotten Railways North and Mid Wales*; David & Charles, 2nd edition 1984

David, Trefor; *Tickets of the North Wales Narrow Gauge Railways*; Welsh Highland Heritage, 1999

Grosvenor, David; *Guide Book*; Festiniog Railway Co, 1998

Hopkins, John; *Rheilffordd Eryri The Welsh Highland Railway 1991 to 1999*; Author, 3rd edition 2001

Johnson, Peter; 'The Welsh Highland Railway — a narrow gauge epic'; *Steam Railway*, January 1998

Johnson, Peter; *Portrait of the Welsh Highland Railway*; Ian Allan Publishing, 1999

Johnson, Peter; 'The Welsh Highland Railway: the way ahead'; *Steam Railway*, No 250, October 2000

Johnson, Peter; 'First and Last: Garratt groundbreaker to return'; *Steam Railway*, No 270, April 2002

Jones, Eric and Gwyn David; *Dolgarrog — an industrial history*; Gwynedd Archives, 1989

Knight, Martin; *Rheilffordd Eryri — Welsh Highland Traveller's Guide*, Festiniog Railway Co, 2002

Lee, Charles E.; *Narrow Gauge Railways in North Wales*; Railway Publishing Co, 1945

Millard, Keith and Booth, Peter; *Welsh Highland Railway Rolling Stock Drawings*; 7mm Narrow Gauge Association

Mitchell, Vic and Smith, Keith; *Branch lines around Portmadoc — the Welsh Highland and Festiniog Railways 1923-46*; Middleton Press, 1993

Mitchell, Vic and Smith, Keith; *Branch lines around Porthmadog — the Welsh Highland and Festiniog Railways 1954-94*; Middleton Press, 1994

Moir, Sydney M. and Crittenden, H. T.; *Namib Narrow Gauge*; Janus Publishing, 2nd edition 1982

Official Souvenir to the Snowdon & Welsh Highland Railways; British Publishing Co, no date

Richards, Alun John; *The Slate Railways of Wales*; Gwasg Carreg Gwalch, 2001

Rheilffordd Eryri The Welsh Highland Railway; Festiniog Railway Co, 1994

Snowdon and Welsh Highland Holiday Book; Snowdon Mountain Tramroad & Hotels, 1923

Stretton, John; *The Festiniog and Welsh Highland Railways*; Past & Present Publishing, 1996

Stretton, John; *The Welsh Highland Railway*; Past & Present Publishing, 1999

Thomas, Dewi W.; *Hydro-electricity in North West Wales*; National Power plc, 1997

Vignes, Edouard (English translation by D. A. Boreham); *A Technical Study of the Festiniog & Other Narrow-Gauge Railways (1878)*; P. E. Waters & Associates, 1986

The Welsh Highland Railway — the Ffestiniog Railway's proposals; Festiniog Railway Co, 1992

Index

PORTMADOC BEDDGELERT &
NORTH WALES NARROW GAUGE Ry (LIGHT RAILW
SNOWDON AND BETTWS-Y-COE
NORTH WALES E
SESSION.
Diagram

From Amlwch

From Holyhead

L & N. W. R.

L. & N. W. R.

LLANFAIR

GAERWEN

MENAI BRID

TREBORTH

BA

FEL

PORT DINORWIC

GRIFFITH'S CROSSING

L. &

PONT RHYTHALLT

N.

W.

PONT RUG

CWM-Y-GLO

LLYN PA

CARNARVON

RY No 3

RY No 2

PORTMADOC BEDDGELERT AND SOUTH SNOWDON RY
(2 ft GAUGE)

RY N°1

LLANBER

WALES

TRYFAN JUNC

WAENFAWR

WATERFA

DINAS

NORTH

RAILWAY

RAILWAY

RHOS TRYFAN

BETTWS GARMON

HEA

LLANWNDA

NARROW

RHOS TRYFAN

No 2 1872

BRYNGWYN

GAUGE

QUELL
LAKE

1872

LLYN CWELLYN

GROESLON

RY

CARNARVON
BAY

LLYN
NANTLLE

PEN-Y-GROES

L & N. W. R

NANTLLE

LLYN Y
GADER

SN

AUTHORISED

N.

W.

BY

ORDER

PANT GLAS

NORTH WALES NARROW GAUGE
(LIGHT RAILWAY EXTENSION TO BEDDC
NOVr 1903
(2 ft GAUGE)

&

RAILWAY

GORSEDDAU

BRYNKIR

YNYS

LLANGYBI

RY N°1
1901

PORTMADOC

CHWILOG

RAILWAY

CRICCIETH

PWLLHELI

CAMBRIAN

AFONWEN

1801

ABERERCH